Vladimir Soloviev

Russian Mystic

The Icon of the Divine Sophia, the Divine Wisdom

Vladimir Soloviev

Russian Mystic

PAUL MARSHALL ALLEN

LINDISFARNE BOOKS
2008

Copyright 1978 by Rudolf Steiner Publications.

This edition published 2008 by arrangement with
Rudolf Steiner Publications.

Lindisfarne Books
610 Main Street, Great Barrington, MA 01230
www.lindisfarne.org

ISBN: 978-1-58420-053-6

Library of Congress Cataloging-in-Publication data is available.

To Michael Alexandrovich Chekhov
(1891–1955)

My friend, to whom I owe, among other things, my introduction to Vladimir Soloviev as a mystic of first importance whose ideas—a rich harvest from his past lives—are of a prophetic character, looking toward the future; hence their inestimable value and relevance for humanity today.

Acknowledgment

The author acknowledges with thanks the kind permission of Countess Alexandra Tolstoi and Harper and Brothers to include in this book Tolstoi's statement on Soloviev's *Crisis of Western Philosophy* and Tolstoi's letter to the Tsar dated 1881. Also acknowledged with thanks are the friends who have provided original photographs and other materials, which have been of great help in the preparation of this volume.

Comments on Soloviev's Mysticism

Rudolf Steiner characterizes Anthroposophy as an impulse which unites the essence of the Sophia, the divine Wisdom, with the entire human being in a new way. This union, however, is a marked contrast to the union of the Sophia with the human mind alone, where the true idea of the Sophia becomes an abstract concept of knowledge, as in modern philosophy.

Before our time, the sphere of the divine Sophia was a transcendental one; today the Sophia can illuminate our cultural spiritual life in a quite special way. Hence today our head, heart and hands can become imbued with the divine Wisdom made manifest.

In the teachings of Vladimir Soloviev the Sophia appears as the essence of that self-knowledge which will reunite fragmented knowledge into an harmonious whole. Theology, epistemology and methodology will ultimately unite with mysticism and the creative and technical arts to form what Soloviev calls a free theurgy, embracing the three social principles: the cultural spiritual life, the life of rights, and the economic life. (See Soloviev's *The Philosophical Foundations of Unified Knowledge*, chapter one.)

According to Soloviev, the basis of the new revelation is the knowledge that the divine Sophia is humanity, and that in reality, the Sophia and humanity are a single, individual being. This union of humanity with the Sophia is the union with the divine; in her we are divine thought incarnate. In her, concepts and their reflections (i.e., sense objects) combine to form spiritual thought, that kingdom of the spirit which is the culture of cultures.

The revelation of the divine Sophia as the root of both nature and the human being is a new stage in the development of humanity, its Third Testament.

The cult of this exalted Being, the divine Sophia, and the justification of the human in Godmanhood ... is the new religious idea of Russian culture. It seeps from the level of the unconscious in old Russian iconography. It gives to Lermontov's yearning unusual words about a strange meeting, and pours itself out pantheistically in Fet's poetry. It becomes concentrated in the poetry of Vladimir Soloviev, finally spreading its shining carpet before us in the astounding verses of Alexander Blok.

In the writings of Soloviev the teachings concerning the divine Sophia culminate in an anticipation of a concrete manifestation of her countenance. In the not too distant future she is to unite with humanity and with all cultural life in an entirely new manner.

Today Dante has arisen in a renewed form. But this Dante celebrates in song neither the beloved Beatrice nor philosophy, but the divine Sophia who unites both spiritual image and concrete thought in a quite unprecedented way."

—*Adapted from the article "Vladimir Soloviev and The Divine Sophia" by Andrei Belyi in* Die Drei, *July–August, 1922.*

Soloviev as a mystic, possessed of a rich and unique mystical experience, is more significant, original and interesting than Soloviev the philosopher. Soloviev's teaching regarding the Sophia is the most original feature of his philosophy.

—*Sergius Bulgakov*

Mysticism is needed for philosophy, for without it the latter ultimately becomes absurd.

—*Vladimir Soloviev*

Contents

List of Illustrations

A Dream

Vladimir Soloviev

Wrapped in morning mist, with faltering steps
   I near a mysterious, magic shore;
The starlight wanes before the rising dawn,
   Round me still my dreams are weaving;
In their enchantment I pray to unknown spirits.

In the cold, clear daylight I follow
   A lonely path in this strange land;
The mist has disappeared: now I see
   The steep and rugged mountain trail,
And how far distant is everything I dreamed.

With firm, courageous steps I pursue the way
   Leading to the goal of all my longing;
Until at midnight, shining triumphant
   Upon the mountain summit, crowned with
     new-born stars,
The Temple of the Promise stands before me!

Introduction

VLADIMIR SERGEYEVICH SOLOVIEV, known to most Westerners as a philosopher, was also a mystic whose ideas were the direct fruit of his spiritual experiences, based upon his "Meetings" with the heavenly Sophia, the Divine Wisdom. His entire life-work stemmed from his childhood vision of the Sophia, whom he called his "Eternal Friend," the expression of cosmic, creative impulses, bearing all Nature in her innermost being, as well as the eternal, archetypal idea of humanity itself.

Soloviev's mystical insight was related to his basic conviction that fundamentally *all people* possess powers within themselves which, if properly utilized, can open the way to a direct perception of the "all unity" lying at the core of creation. This conviction he expressed thus: *"Within us an infinite wealth of content and forces lies stored, hidden behind the threshold of our present consciousness, which is only gradually crossed by a definite portion of this content and these forces, never exhausting the whole."*

Soloviev's recognition of what he described as "the ideal human being, no less essential and real, in fact, immeasurably *more* real than the visible manifestations of human beings," was a direct result of his spiritual powers of perception.

These ideas are similar to the thoughts to a number of Russian mystics of the eighteenth and early nineteenth centuries, particularly those who were inspired by the aims and ideals of Freemasonry which had been established in Russia about 1731, and of the Rosicrucian Brotherhood, organized in Moscow and other Russian cities under the leadership of Johann Georg Schwartz and his successors, from 1782. Suppressed ruthlessly by order of Catherine II, these movements nevertheless revived during the brief rule of Paul I and flowered during the reign of Alexander I who, as is well known, was devoted to mystical pursuits, primarily as a result of the influence of the Baroness de Kruedener.

Johann Georg Schwartz (1751-1784), whose writings Soloviev studied in the period before his first journey to England, was a Transylvanian by birth, a professor of philosophy in the recently-founded University of Moscow, and was much appreciated by a circle of students and friends who met regularly in his house to hear his private lectures on the mystical works of Jacob Boehme, Jung-Stilling and Louis Claude de Saint-Martin. His reputation was enhanced for many by the fact that he was the founder of the Rosicrucian Brotherhood in Moscow, St. Petersburg and a number of other cities in Russia, an undertaking which he executed with characteristic fiery enthusiasm and persuasiveness. His preoccupation with the esoteric sciences, including Kabbala, Magic and Alchemy, as well as his enthusiasm for the nature-philosophy of Rosicrucianism which at that time was regarded as an entirely logical outgrowth of natural science, drew a group of highly gifted, idealistic and influential men to his side. Although Schwartz died suddenly at the moment his activities were beginning to attract the attention of the secret police and the censorship, his work was continued by others, among them his pupil, Alexander Feyodorovich Labzin (1769-1825), translator of Jacob Boehme's *The Way to Christ* (1815) and Rosicrucian-inspired works of the Aulic Councilor, Karl von Eckhartshausen (1752-1813)—notably his *Cloud on the Sanctuary* (1791); Nikolai Ivanovich Novikov (1744-1818), a pioneer in promulgating Rosicrucianism as a humanitarian solution of the social problem in the darkest days of Russian serfdom

("O humanity! You are unknown in these villages!"), and Prince Nikolai Vassilyevich Troubetskoi, one of the most able and trusted members of the circle around Schwartz. Troubetskoi succeeded the latter as leader of the Russian Rosicrucian Brotherhood in 1784 when it was reported that the membership included some 6,000 men in various parts of the Empire.

Soloviev's thinking was also influenced by the books of Prince Vladimir Feyodorovich Odoyevski (1803-1869), an ardent student of Schelling and a profound writer on the history, philosophy and practice of mysticism, particularly among the early Fathers of the Eastern Church, as well as by the teachings of Mikhail Mikhailovich Speranski (1772-1834), also a philosopher, devoted to the mysticism of the divine Sophia and to the subject of reincarnation ("There can be no doubt that an all-powerful God can, after all, arrange things so that a person's soul can be reborn on earth a hundred times or more if it is necessary!"). Soloviev was also impressed by the writings of Ivan Viadimirovich Lopukhin (1756-1816), for some years President of the Moscow Criminal Court and an outspoken advocate of humanitarian principles in government and law. With its pronounced Rosicrucian flavor, Lopukhin's *The Nature of the Interior Church* (St. Petersburg, 1798) is a landmark among Russian books on mysticism. We shall return to this work in connection with a certain stage in Soloviev's inner development.

In contrast to his mystical experiences, as a philosopher Soloviev highly valued clarity of thinking. Nevertheless he considered philosophy simply an instrument in the service of something he valued even more highly. He regarded himself as a kind of "voluntary monk" who had taken upon himself not to speak directly about what he really held most dear in life. Hence greatest modesty and resignation became keynotes of his behavior. He wrote and spoke mainly about those things he believed were the greatest dangers and hindrances lying in the path of the constructive development of humanity. For him, philosophy represented a struggle, a struggle for truth. But, as has been said, he possessed a treasure which he valued more highly than philosophy. This was his "mysticism," a term he employed to describe *a direct, personal relationship with the spiritual world.*

From childhood Soloviev had difficulty in clearly observing the physical world around him. For example, he once recalled: "My first impression of the starry sky that I remember refers to *my sixth year*, and even that was due to the special reason that the comet of 1859 was then visible, while the series of clear and connected family memories begins in *my fourth year.*" In contrast, the boy lived from the beginning in rich inner experiences, imaginations, soul-pictures with genuine content, in dreams, in an awareness of and conversations with the dead, who to him were as present as the living. In later life, as these experiences deepened and became even more vivid, he was increasingly loath to speak or write about them. Therefore even as a young man he gave others the impression that there was something reserved about him, something consciously held back, a quality some regarded as an inheritance from his clerical forebearers.

When he had become a university lecturer in St. Petersburg, one of his colleagues, a professor who respected him highly, once said to him laughingly, "Look here, Vladimir Sergeyevich, all those visions of yours are really pathological, you know!" With a half smile and a twinkle in his eye, Soloviev replied, "But *of course* they are!"—refusing to be drawn into further discussion about them.

On the other hand, when it was imperative that he speak or write about his spiritual experiences, Soloviev half-concealed them behind self-criticism, humor and gentle mockery. Hence a first reading of his works—particularly his letters and some of his poems—may puzzle one; but a fuller acquaintance with his writings leads one to find the way step by step beneath their surface, penetrating ever deeper into their rich content until one comes upon the gold-veins of truth, warmth of beauty and all-pervading goodness, the threefold fruit of Soloviev's quest for the all-oneness of creation and for a comprehension of the true biography of the human being as it is reflected in the destiny of humanity as a whole.

Through his spiritual perception Soloviev was convinced that within *every* human being lives a higher self, and that as people learn to order their lives by taking this higher self more and more into account, they will discover their dignity as human beings, and at the same time, the significance of their earthly existence.

This higher self which Soloviev, like Meister Eckhardt long before, likened to a divine spark glowing in the heart of every person, finds its relation to outer existence through the activity of the Sophia, the Wisdom of God. Therefore when Soloviev wrote about universe, earth and humanity, he strove to show how this higher self can lead one to ultimate unity with the Christ as the Body of the Earth. For Soloviev this represented the highest goal attainable on the mystical path.

In this light one can divine the deeper implications behind Soloviev's words: "Those who wish to dedicate themselves to philosophy, must serve it with courage and dignity. They are not to be ashamed of this voluntary service, and they are not to belittle themselves. They must be convinced that to occupy themselves with philosophy is a good and important thing, a thing necessary for the whole world. Philosophy freed the human personality from external compulsion and gave it inner substance. It overthrew all false gods and developed within humankind the inner prerequisite for the revelation of the true divinity. In order to attain true and perfect freedom, human beings must not only control their outer, but also their inner nature. Complete self control can never be achieved with the knowledge confined solely to experience and observation. Human beings must be able to transfer their 'center' from their own inner nature to their higher 'outer' nature, if they wish to become entirely free within themselves."

* * *

Though Soloviev experienced at first hand the cold blight of materialism, the deathly grip of atheism's *"No"* to spirit, the leveling of the uniqueness and worth of each single human individuality at the hands of nineteenth century Western utilitarianism, nevertheless there lived in him an unshakeable conviction that only through the individual's experience of the true *Anthropos*, the archetype of humanity, united with the veritable *Sophia*, the archetype of spiritual wisdom, can succor be found by men and women today, beset as they are by the conflicts, doubts and tragedies of our time.

In his mystical vision of the star crowned, heavenly Wisdom, streaming life giving warmth and Christ-enlightened thoughts upon humankind, the cold moon in subjection beneath her feet, Soloviev caught a glimpse of the ultimate destiny of humanity. From his first childhood "Meeting" with the Sophia, his spiritual perception widened until at last it united present and future humankind in an all-embracing *Anthroposophia*, a genuine "Wisdom of Humanity" in contrast to the menacing power of the "Wisdom of the Beast,"—of *Antichrist*.

The spiritual striving of Soloviev was akin to what Bonaventura described as "the reaching out of the soul to God through the yearning of love." What Soloviev once characterized as "the ideal human being, no less essential and real, in fact, immeasurably *more* real than the visible manifestations of human beings," was a result of his own mystical insight. He was well aware of unseen forces at work, not only within human beings, but also within external nature, for the latter *depends upon humanity* for its very life and existence: "Separated from humanity, the world of nature lies dead; all apparent order dissolves into chaos. The plant has no enjoyment, the flowers cannot experience their beauty. Without human beings, even the diamond lies valueless in the earth. Everything in creation is united in the human being—in whom alone can the wisdom, beauty, order of nature stand revealed, for the human being is the epitome of all creatures."

In his aphoristic description of mysticism in relation to poetry and philosophy, Goethe came close to Soloviev's ideas. "Poetry," said Goethe, "points to the riddles of nature and tries to solve them by means of the *image*. Philosophy directs itself to the riddles of reason, and attempts to solve them by means of the *word*. Mysticism considers the riddles of both nature and reason, and seeks to solve them through both word and image." This dual faculty of *word and image* played a significant role in the creative life of Soloviev.

In relation to his spiritual striving Soloviev recognized the immeasurable worth of earth-experience, and therefore he worked to bring about a balance between his ideas, his feelings and his relationships with others. This quality makes his mysticism, in which his personal experience is always the dominant, the determining factor, so vitally interesting and appealing. His descriptions and observations are always flavored by his own personality; it is this which unites Soloviev as a mystic with the Neoplationists, with Iamblichus, Plotinus and—above all—with the mediaeval mystic, Scotus Erigena.

Pavel Birukov, friend and biographer of Lyov Tolstoi recalled, "Once I heard from Tolstoi that he was certain that just as physiologists divide human life into periods of seven years, so psychological life has the same periods of development, and each seven-year period has its particular moral physiognomy."

The seven-year periods in the life of Soloviev reflect his inner, mystical development, his creative and "moral physiognomy." Therefore in the following pages the story of Soloviev's life and work is described in terms of these seven-year periods of unfoldment.

* * *

The writer wishes to express appreciation and heartfelt thanks to his friend, Andrew Lisovsky for his invaluable technical help in rendering certain difficult, sometimes obscure passages in the writings of Soloviev and other Russian authors quoted in this book. Much rare and otherwise inaccessible material has been made available for study in preparation of this work, thanks to the unfailing assistance of the staffs of the Slavonic Section of the New York Public Library, of the Houghton and Widener Libraries of Flaryard University, of the Library of Columbia University, and of the incomparable Library of Books and Manuscripts in the British Museum. Finally he acknowledges with deep gratitude the encouragement of his wife, as well as the interest of a number of friends which have been indispensable in bringing this book into being.

—*Paul M. Allen*
Botton, Yorkshire, England

Chapter One

BEGINNINGS

1853–1860

VLADIMIR SERGEYEVICH SOLOVIEV was born in Moscow on January 16, 1853, sixteen years after the death of Alexander Pushkin, the father of modern Russian Literature, and a little less than a year after the death of Nikolai Gogol, author of *Dead Souls* and *The Inspector General.*

The Russia into which Soloviev was born was held in the iron grip of the militaristic, ultra-reactionary Tsar Nicholas I. His autocratic rule, characterized by isolation from the life of Western Europe and hatred of anything breathing the spirit of freedom or liberalism as inimical to the well-being of the Russian Empire, was a marked contrast to the reign of his predecessor, Alexander I, the dominant figure at the Congress of Vienna, marking the close of the Napoleonic Era.

Feyodor Dostoyevski, already famous as the author of *Poor Folk*, which the critic Belinski had likened favorably to a novel of the great Gogol, was experiencing the first bitter years of his Siberian exile. Ivan Turgeniev, whose *Sportsman's Sketches* and obituary article on Gogol had focused the baleful eye of the imperial censor upon him, was doing penance for his "liberalism" in exile on his mother's estate in the country, remote from the capital. Count Lyov Tolstoi, whose restless spirit and adventurous longings chafed under the restrictions and formalities of social life in Moscow and St. Petersburg, had escaped to the beautiful Terek River region of South Russia where he was active as a volunteer with the Cossacks.

The theatrical season of 1853 witnessed the premiere of Alexander Ostrovski's first play, *The Poor Bride*, a delight for audiences in Moscow and Petersburg, while international events were fast shaping into the outbreak of the Crimean War, which was to occur when Vladimir Soloviev was less than a year old.

In January, 1854, Charles Greville, Clerk of the British Royal Council, noted in his journal that Nicholas' "warlike preparations are enormous, and it is said that the Church has granted him a loan of four and one-half millions (sterling) to defray them." In July the American Secretary of State, William Marcy, in the name of President Franklin Pierce, offered to arbitrate the struggle between Russia, England and France, but his offer was brushed aside, and the Crimean War went on. Pro-Russian feeling in the United States ran high; a number of American surgeons served with the Russian armies on the battlefields.

The turning-point came early in March, 1855 with the death of Tsar Nicholas: in January of the following year Russia accepted unconditionally the terms of England and France, and the Crimean War was ended.

The gloom of defeat was somewhat lessened, however, on September 7, 1856,—Soloviev was now three years old—when Nicholas' successor, Alexander II was crowned "Tsar of All the Russias." Again Charles Greville commented, "The ceremony of coronation at Moscow appears to have gone off with great *eclat*, and to have been a spectacle of extraordinary magnificence. The event was attended by special ambassadors from all the Great Powers, and Lord and Lady Granville, with a brilliant suite represented Great Britain on this occasion." Greville further noted that the coronation of Alexander II had cost three million sterling, in comparison to that of George IV of England which had cost some two hundred forty thousand, "considered at the time a great sum and a monstrous extravagance," while the coronation expenses of Victoria had totalled a modest fifty thousand. And he concluded somewhat ruefully, "We were probably mistaken, as we were in so many other things, in fancying that the power and resources of Russia were very greatly impaired, but during the war, whatever we wished we were ready to believe."

Arthur Penrhyn Stanley, Dean of Westminster Abbey, described the event in graphic terms: "His coronation was not a mere ceremony, but a historical occasion and solemn consecration. It was preceded by fasting and seclusion, and took place in the most sacred church in Russia; the Emperor, not as in the corresponding forms of European investiture a passive recipient, but himself the principal figure in the whole scene; himself reciting aloud the confession of the Orthodox Faith; himself alone on his knees, amidst the assembled multitude, offering up the prayer of intercession for the Empire; himself placing his own crown with his own hands upon his own head; himself entering through the sacred doors of the innermost sanctuary, and taking from the altar the elements of the bread and wine, of which then and there, by virtue of his consecration, he communicated with bishops, priests and deacons."

Thus in the first years of the childhood of Vladimir Soloviev, Russia underwent profound change as the pendulum of her national destiny swung from the inflexible reign of Nicholas to the reforms of Alexander. On the day of his coronation, speaking to his "God-bearing Russian people" as the divinely anointed head of Church and State alike, in tones more reminiscent of an Old Testament patriarchal ruler than a head of State in the prosaic mid-nineteenth century, Alexander proclaimed: "With the assistance of divine Providence, which has ever blessed Russia ... may supreme Truth and Mercy rule, in order that all may enjoy the fruit of their just labors beneath laws equal for all, affording equal protection for all."

* * *

Vladimir, or Volodia—to use the intimate form of his name—was one of a large family. His father, Sergei Mikhailovich Soloviev, is remembered as a leading historian of Russia, the first of international stature, and a well-known, highly respected professor of history at the University of Moscow.

A quiet, retiring, serious man, Sergei Mikhailovich was devoted to historial research and writing. Recalling his own childhood, he said, "From an early age I was an enthusiastic adherent of Christianity, and in my *Gymnasium* years I said that I would become the founder of a philosophical system that would show quite clearly the divinity of Christianity, and which would put an end to atheism."

However, by the time he reached the University his aspirations toward creating a philosophical justification of Christianity had receded into the background, and he plunged into the life of a historian with complete dedication. Eventually he became a prominent professor whose days were passed between his study, his lecture room, his large family and his church. Outwardly his life was that of the methodical scholar, and his rigid program scarcely altered throughout the whole course of the year. In summer he arose at six o'clock; in winter, at seven. On Sundays and holy days he was invariably present at the early service in the chapel of the University. His relations with his family were somewhat formal, lacking the warmth of personal intimacy. His study was a sacrosanct place, filled with books and manuscripts, and a rule of strict silence was enjoined upon the whole household during the father's working hours there. He willingly left the care and education of the children in the capable hands of his wife, and since his relations with them were based largely upon respect, he had comparatively little influence upon the developing course of their lives.

The mother, Polixena Vladimirovna, was a distinct contrast to the father. Of South Russian and Polish ancestry, highly emotional, of fiery temperament, she was deeply mystical and religious, but at the same time enjoyed humor and liveliness of spirit. The boy Volodia inherited his mother's dark hair and somewhat swarthy complexion, her love of poetry, her creative imagination and her inclination toward mysticism. Devoted to her home and her nine children, she was always at her husband's side at church; together they received guests one evening each week, and on Saturdays during the Moscow season they were invariably present at the Italian opera, which they both enjoyed immensely.

The daily life of the children, passed partly in Moscow, partly at the family countryhouse, Pokrovskoi, was characterized by strict order, and was something of a ritual in itself. The parents loved all their children dearly, but for the boy Volodia, who had been born prematurely, they had a special affection. From the very first, his father and mother were convinced that in him they had a "special child" who was destined to do significant things in his life. Perhaps because of this they gave him the name of Vladimir, the saint so closely identified with the Kiev Period of Russian history and the struggle against the Byzantine and Tartar influences.

The relationship between Volodia and his mother was particularly close. Her gentle piety, the image of her, gliding through the house with silent step, her gaze turned inward as though in meditation much of the time, or bending low and crossing herself fervently before the family icons, their flickering lights reflected upon her beautiful face, absorbed in devotion, the gentle tone of her voice as she read the lives of the Saints, the legends and fairy tales of old Russia, her warmth of heart as it poured itself out in her poetry reading to the children—all this was irradicably fixed in the boy's memory, and accompanied him through his whole life.

Often in the after-years would he recall his mother's beautiful voice as she recited the well-loved lines of Pushkin:

Beside the sea a green oak stands,
A golden chain upon it —
By day and night a learned cat
Walks round the tree, bound by the golden chain.
When he goes to the right, he begins a song,
When he goes to the left, he tells a fairy tale.

The children loved the poems, the *skazki*, the folk stories of Russia, and the unforgettable fairy tales their mother told them. Volodia identified himself with the hero who overcame the forces of evil; he shared in the world of the ancient gods, of nature-spirits, of enchantments by wizards, of hidden stores of treasure, of beautiful princesses, of wise old kings. Particularly dear to him was the tale of *Tsarevich Ivan, the Fire Bird and the Grey Wolf*. With his brothers and sisters he delighted in the charming *Snegouritchka*, the Snow Maiden, shuddered at the tale of the dread *Baba Yaga*, the Witch Grandmother, who rushed through the forest with her dreadful pestle, and was spellbound by the story of the *Tsarevna Legoushka*, the Frog Princess.

Then too they enjoyed the epic tales of the Bogatyri, the ancient heroes of old Russia: of Prince Vladimir, "the Beautiful Sun," who sent ambassadors to Constantinople in search of a new religion, and who eventually Christianized his people at Kiev; of the archetype of all Russian peasants with their close bond and love for the soil of their country, Mikula Selianovich; of the gigantic stature and superhuman strength of the mighty Ilya Muromets; of Sadko, the rich merchant of ancient Novgorod.

Through their father the children met the historical figures of Russia's colorful past: Prince Igor of Novgorod Severiski and his great campaign against the Polovtzes; the adventures of Athanasius Nikitin, who journeyed to India in the fifteenth century; the pathetic Xenia, daughter of Boris Godounov;

Stenka Razin, the bold Volga robber; the tempestuous life and strange death of Ivan the Terrible; the enterprise and the sometimes madly impetuous deeds of Peter the Great, and many others.

But of all the remarkable, unforgettable people the children met in those wonderful, magic hours of storytelling, there was one whom they loved above all the rest—the saintly ancestor of their mother, Grigori Savvich Skovoroda. With shining eyes Volodia and the others listened to the mother's tales concerning Skovoroda's deep religious devotion, his courage, his fiery striving for truth, his utter fearlessness, his profound mystical experiences.

Born of peasant parents in the district of Kiev in 1722, from childhood Skovoroda was intensely religious; his strength of character was evident from his earliest years. At sixteen he entered the Theological Academy at Kiev, one of the oldest in Russia, which had been founded in 1615. His remarkable singing voice caused him to be transferred to the Court at Tsarskoie Selo where Tsarina Elizabeth, daughter of Peter the Great, had assembled the finest church choir in all Russia. Eventually Skovoroda was graduated from the Kiev Academy at the age of twenty-eight. To the surprise of his clerical instructors, however, Skovoroda refused holy orders and instead joined the entourage of a General Vishnevski as a church singer. Vishnevski had recently been given a diplomatic assignment in Hungary, and from there Skovroda later visited Austria, Poland, Germany and Italy. An observant traveler, he took great interest in details of local life everywhere he went, and was an attentive listener in the many universities he visited on his travels. He was at home in German, Latin, Greek and Hebrew; his education was extensive for a man of his time, particularly in Russia. He was intimately acquainted with the works of Plato, Aristotle, Epicureus, Plutarch, Seneca, the Church Fathers and contemporary writers as well.

After his travels in Western Europe, Skovoroda returned to Russia where he was active as a school teacher for a time. Later he visited the Monastery of St. Sergius where he was offered a post as teacher in the famous Theological Academy. This he declined in favor of a position as teacher in the Kharkov Institute which he held until 1765 when he withdrew from a regular occupation and began the wandering that was to characterize the remaining twenty-nine years of his life. Continually journeying from one town to another, from one estate to another, particularly in the Ukraine, he wrote: "What is life? It is a wandering. I choose a road, but I don't know where I go, nor do I know why I go."

This pilgrim quality in the nature of Skovoroda marks him as one of those "homeless souls" whose destiny causes them quickly to outgrow their surroundings, after which their spiritual aspirations cause them simply to go their own way. Spiritual impulses lead them to individual creativeness, to uniqueness in their personal development, to originality in many of the main aspects of their lives.

Therefore when Skovoroda, his Hebrew Bible in a sack slung over his shoulder as his inseparable companion, set out upon his wanderings, this was no mark of personal eccentricity. On the contrary, his years of visiting from place to place, slipping away as quietly and unexpectedly as he arrived, were years of spiritual growth, of meditation and prayer, of the development of the remarkable insights he expressed in his philosophical writings. The latter took the form of dialogues, the rich fruit of his matured observations of life, his original thoughts and conclusions about the spiritual world, and all of them took their start from the ancient admonition: "O Man, Know thou thyself!"

The Soloviev children were frequently reminded of aphorisms their mother quoted from her beloved ancestor, Grigori Skovoroda. Among these were: "If a man has not first assessed *himself*, what profit will he have from judging others?"—"If you want to know something about Truth, look first at the world around you and there in the physical creation you will see the footsteps of God, which will reveal a secret wisdom to you."—"God's spirit enters your heart if your eyes are illumined by the spirit of truth; then you will see things you never knew existed before. You will see the sensible *and* the supersensible as well."—"The most important organ of a person is the heart, not the physical but the spiritual heart. The abyss of the spiritual heart encompasses and includes everything. It is the ruler of everything in the human being; it is the real person."—"Our whole external appearance is but a mask concealing our real faculties which are hidden in the heart as in a seed, for there exists a spiritual body with all its faculties, which are occult, esoteric and eternal."—"In everyone the divine power is hidden, the true self toward which we ascend in spiritual vision, and this real self is complete in everyone. But the serpent of evil creeps along beside one so long as one confines oneself to this world of phenomena alone. However, as soon as one lifts oneself and enters the spiritual world, one lifts the serpent along as well, thus changing its nature, and the serpent then becomes one's divinely-sent helper."— "Humans have plumbed the sea, explored the earth, the skies, the heavens. They have probed the earth's depths in search of metals. And in doing all this they have discovered an infinity of worlds. They have built fantastic machines; every day they invent something extraordinary until it appears that there is nothing they cannot do. But, sad to say, in all this, *greatness*, *stature* is lacking."

Most memorable of all, perhaps is the Platonically inspired epitaph Skovroda wrote for his tombstone, expressing in it what he considered to be the essence of his life on earth:

"The world tried to capture me,
But it did not succeed!"

Chapter Two

THE FIRST MEETING

1860–1867

THE SECOND SEVEN YEARS in the life of Vladimir Soloviev coincided with momentous events both in Russia and in the world at large. In America this was the period of the presidency of Abraham Lincoln, the tragic War between the States, and the beginning of the Reconstruction Era. In Italy Garibaldi achieved victory for the cause of freedom; in Poland an abortive revolution against Czarist oppression was ruthlessly crushed; England held her second International Exposition, and the first permanently successful Atlantic cable went into operation. In the East, Chinese Gordon won a fateful victory at Soochow; Japan sent a foreign mission to the United States—the first she sent to any country in the world—and by the Treaty of Peking, Russia was granted the eastern coast of Siberia, thus extending her possessions to the Pacific at Vladivostok. The Geneva Convention, aimed at working out international agreement on the humane treatment and care of prisoners of war, convened in Switzerland; oil was discovered in Pennsylvania; the city of Vancouver was founded, and a poetic drama by a Norwegian writer, Henrik Ibsen, received its first—and unfavorable—hearing.

In *The Cherry Orchard*, the last play of Anton Chekhov—who was born at the opening of this seven-year period—the octagenarian butler, Firs, says: "That's how it was before the great calamity came." Asked what calamity he referred to, he replied, "Why, the Emancipation, to be sure."

Alexander II's emancipation of twenty-two million serfs was the single greatest event in Russia during this seven-year period. On March 3, 1861, Alexander urged his people to "Gather yourselves under the sign of the Cross, Orthodox nation, and unite with us in praying for divine benediction upon your free work, which is the certain guarantee of your domestic happiness and your social well-being."

All Russia was profoundly affected by the imperial edict. The social, political, economic and cultural life of the country was stirred to new and hopeful activity.

Meanwhile, in 1862 Dostoyevski, returned from his Siberian exile, his health shattered by his experiences, completed his *Memoirs from the House of the Living Dead*, most popular of his books among Russian readers of his generation. In that same year Anton Rubenstein founded the St. Petersburg Conservatory of Music, and one of the students in the first class was a shy young law graduate, Pyotor Ilych Tschaikovski. Three years later, Dimitri Merezhkovski, destined to fame as a historical novelist, possessing "the most encyclopedic mind of his generation," was born on an island near St. Petersburg. This year is also remembered as the time of the violent quarrel between Turgeniev and Tolstoi, which was to estrange them for over seventeen years.

* * *

The time of the change of teeth marks the end of the first period of childhood; the forces employed up to this time for the building of the physical frame of the child can now be "released" for other processes of development. This is the moment when children begin to look about them into the world with new eyes, as it were, viewing the world uncritically at first, seeing its *pictorial* quality primarily. They now long for one thing more than all else: *a guide, an authority* in whom they can confide, in whom they can place fullest, most implicit trust, to whom they can give the complete devotion of their heart and soul.

This period of children's development is frequently interrupted, however, by a moment of crisis, prefiguring the "great" crisis which will come more or less at the end of this time. This "little" crisis appears at around the age of nine or ten, and from then onward the life-tempo tends to accelerate as the children near the end of this span of years, finally reaching the all-important "great" crisis—the entrance into puberty—with all that this involves from the physical, soul and spiritual points of view. In itself the "little" crisis is also of importance, for it recapitulates in certain ways the children's earlier experiences, at the same time pointing toward the new directions their development will follow more and more in the following years.

These crises and trends expressed themselves in the life of Vladimir Soloviev in a remarkable manner.

* * *

In one of his chief philosophical works, published near the end of his life, Soloviev wrote this profoundly significant meditation:

> I alone cannot carry out in practice all that ought to be; I cannot do anything alone. But, thank God, there is no such thing as "I alone." Although in my thoughts and my will I separate myself from everything, it is mere self-deception. For I am not alone. Within me is God Almighty and the world—that is, all that is contained in God. And man is dear to God, not as a passive instrument of His will, but as a voluntary ally and participator in His work in the universe. For this participation of

human beings must of necessity be included in the very purpose of God's activity in the world.

The one in whom the boy Volodia could place his fullest trust, to whom he could look up in almost religious awe, whose very presence he felt to be something sacred was his paternal grandfather, Mikhail Vassilievich Soloviev. From this remarkable, saintly man, for whom the boy felt the most profound respect, he learned that humanity can become of value for the spiritual world as "a voluntary ally," a cooperator in its work.

The grandfather was an Archpriest of the Russian Orthodox Church, a treasured friend of the famous Metropolitan Philaret, a venerated teacher of religion in the Moscow Commercial School, and a man who enjoyed the greatest popularity among the social elite of Moscow. Volodia was convinced that between his grandfather and God a most intimate relationship existed, that his grandfather could converse with the Beings of the spiritual world as naturally and as easily as one person can speak with another. As a result, under his grandfather's teaching and example, Volodia unfolded confidence and trust in the spiritual world and a complete awareness of its constant presence and help. Thus he was ultimately able to say, "Thank God, there is no such thing as 'I alone.'"

This confidence and awareness was deepened by his experience of the Services in the church, so rich in picture-content: the calm, soft light of the candles, the venerable Priests with their long hair and beards, their quietly concentrated, dignified cultic gestures, their rich vestments, the bitter-sweet odor of incense, the reverent silence of the standing congregation, the mysteries of the inner sanctuary, the resounding tones of the deep basso of the Deacon, the mystery-words of the prayers, the melodic responses of the Choir—all these awakened the forces of religious devotion in the boy's soul.

Meanwhile at home the father and mother united with their children and servants in regular family devotions before the house-icons each evening and morning, and the children themselves entered into and returned from the golden house of the world of sleep through the gates of prayer.

From this one can perhaps understand why, near the end of his life, Soloviev wrote these words as dedication of his most mature book, the fruit of a long struggle "to solve the most important problems of existence" which he titled, *The Justification of the Good*:

Dedicated to
my father, the historian
SERGEI MIKHAILOVICH SOLOVIEV
and to my grandfather, the priest
MIKHAIL VASSILIEVICH SOLOVIEV
with a grateful and living recognition
of an eternal bond.

* * *

Volodia's early education, like that of most children of his social class, was in the hands of governesses and tutors at home. His principal governess, Anna Kosminishna Kolerova, was the daughter of a clerical family, and her influence deepened still further the religious feelings of the boy. She was given to frequent dreams, and enjoyed telling the children about them and their "meaning." The children called her "Anna the Prophetess," and her dreams and interpretations greatly impressed young Volodia. Under the influence of her narratives concerning the heroic men of early Christian times, he imagined himself one of the ascetics in the wilderness. One of his brothers related that one winter night Volodia threw off his bedcovers and lay freezing in the darkness "for the glory of God."

The Parents of Vladimir Soloviev

The Rev. Mikhail Vassilyevich Soloviev,
Grandfather of Vladimir Soloviev

Everything Volodia heard in the way of stories from his mother or his governess he transformed into imaginative, personal experience. Likewise, everything around him, particularly his intimate, personal possessions, became animate for him, and he gave them names. For example, his school-bag he called "Grisha," and his lead-pencil he addressed as "Andrusha." As he later recalled in one of his poems,

> I was a strange child there,
> And I dreamed strange dreams.

These "strange dreams" were a most vital part of his childhood, for though he shared fully the life of his brothers and sisters, eventually entering one of the best-known of the Moscow secondary schools, from which he graduated with honors, the world which ever claimed him as its own was the world of fantasy, of visions and dreams, which accompanied him through his childhood, youth and adult life. Only a short time before his death Soloviev at last recognized that these "strange dreams"—these "intimations of immortality," of the immanence of the world of spirit—were really a most fundamental part of the entire fabric of his life-experience. They opened the door to his future destiny, and through them he became the man who one day could write:

> Far and near, not here and not there,
> In the land of mystical dreams,
> In a world invisible for mortal eyes,
> In a world without laughter and tears,
> There, O Goddess, on a misty night,
> For the first time I saw you...
> In strange disguise you came to me,
> Faintly sounded your voice,
> And long I thought you
> But a vague image of a childhood dream.

* * *

It was on Ascension Day in May, 1862 when Volodia was nine years old, that the curtains of the "misty night" drew aside, and the boy had his first direct vision of the spiritual world.

With his German nurse young Volodia is attending Service in the Chapel of the University of Moscow. Standing among the congregation, the boy's thoughts wander. He thinks about a little girl of his own age, for whom he has conceived a childish affection. But there is "another"—a boy whom she seems to favor. Jealousy arises in Volodia's soul.

As in a dream he hears the sublime words of the special *Troparion*, the hymn appointed for Ascension Day:

> In Glory hast thou ascended, O Christ our God!
> Thy disciples thou hast made glad
> By Thy promise of the Holy Spirit;
> Through this blessing Thou hast indeed assured them
> That Thou art the Son of God,
> The Redeemer of the world!

Following the Litany of Peace the Choir responds with a profoundly poignant "Lord, have mercy upon us!" The deep voice of the Deacon proclaims the single, solemn mystery-word: "Wisdom!" He then enters through the north door into the Sanctuary, as the voice of the celebrating Priest is heard petitioning:

> ... that being ever preserved
> Under Thy protection,
> We may give glory to Thee,
> The Father, the Son and the Holy Spirit,
> Now and forever and world without end!

As the Choir intones an ascending "Amen," the doors of the *iconostasis* are opened, and in ecstatic tones the great Cherubical Hymn resounds:

We who mystically image the Cherubim,
Who sing to the life-giving Trinity
The thrice-holy hymn,
Let us now lay aside all earthly cares.

Meanwhile the pungent odor of incense fills the church as the Deacon censes the Holy Table, the Sanctuary, the sacred pictures before the doors of the *iconostasis*, the Priest, the Choir and the standing Congregation. The Priest now responds:

We who mystically image the Cherubim,
Who sing to the life-giving Trinity
The thrice-holy hymn,
Let us now lay aside all earthly cares.

The blue veil of incense ensheaths everything, rising slowly in the quiet air. The Mystery intensifies as the Deacon intones the ancient words:

For now we are to receive the King of all,
Invisibly escorted by the ranks of Angels,
Alleluia, Alleluia, Alleluia!

Together he and the Priest approach the Table of Offerings. Censing the sacred gifts of bread and wine lying upon it, he hands the paten containing the bread, the "Lamb of Sacrifice," to the Deacon, who lifts it above his head. Chalice in hand, the Priest, accompanied by the Deacon, preceded by lighted candles, walks in solemn procession out of the north door of the *iconostasis*. The Great Entrance into the Altar of Sacrifice is about to take place. Once again, Our Lord is going forth to accomplish His Deed of Golgotha and Resurrection, His Passion.

The overwhelming, central moment of the divine Mystery, the reflection of the Mystery of Golgotha, in cultic Imagination, has come.

Young Volodia is enraptured by the beauty and solemnity of the Event taking place before him. A mystical devotion engulfs him like a mighty wave, sweeping away all traces of jealousy. Crossing himself, the boy is absorbed by the divine Drama...

Suddenly it is as if the walls, the ceiling of the church, have vanished; the Priest has disappeared, the Deacon also, and with them the Choir, the congregation... Volodia is alone beneath the vault of heaven; an azure veil surrounds him, streams of golden radiance weaving through and through it. And in the radiance, penetrating into the very center of the boy's soul, stands a Figure, bearing a heavenly flower in her hands. Gently she smiles upon him, her gaze bathing him in an infinitely soothing tenderness. Then, as quietly, as mysteriously as she appeared, she slowly fades from his sight.

Long moments later the boy hears the agitated whisper of his German nurse beside him, feels her tugging impatiently at his sleeve. The Service is over; it is time to leave... He tries to look around him, but it is as though he is blind; darkness hovers over everything... He is weak; he can scarcely stand. "Come, Volodia, stop wobbling about now!" his nurse urges... Gradually he regains his senses; slowly he recognizes his surroundings, his nurse, his father and mother, quietly greeting friends nearby. Slowly, slowly everything becomes familiar once again, but from somewhere deep inside him, Volodia dimly realizes that somehow everything is changed. He has met his Eternal Friend; to her service he will devote himself and all his forces to the end of his earthly existence, and even beyond.

Never again will life be the same.

Some months later his grandfather took Volodia into the Sanctuary of the same Moscow Chapel where he had had his

View of the Chapel of the University of Moscow.
Here Soloviev had his first "meeting."

Sergei Mikhailovich Soloviev, Father of Vladimir Soloviev,
Professor of History in the University of Moscow.

first "Meeting" with his Eternal Friend, and dedicated the boy to the service of the Church. This was a kind of farewell, a summing up of their relationship, for not long after, the elderly Archpriest died.

But to Soloviev, recalling these experiences in the after-years, it was as though his grandfather had helped him, guided him, comforted him, and had brought him to the moment when he was granted his first direct glimpse of the supernal glory of the spiritual world. Having done this, from an earthly standpoint the grandfather's share in Volodia's life was completed. From that time onward, by virtue of "an eternal bond" existing between them, the grandfather could continue to help, but now from the vantage-point of the spiritual world.

* * *

As every seeker of the spirit knows from experience, "the mighty vision of the mountain-top" is not retained indefinitely. Sooner or later destiny requires that one descend into the valley of struggle and darkness, from which slowly, often painfully, one once again emerges into the light.

This happened to the boy Volodia also. The Meeting with his Eternal Friend was a kind of "little" or first crisis, designed to prepare him for the greater struggle he was to experience in his fourteenth year.

The conflict which began to shape itself during the twelfth and thirteenth years of Soloviev's life was at length to reveal itself as a first-hand meeting with the dark dogmas of materialism sweeping like an evil miasma over the mid-nineteenth century, leaving spiritual havoc in their train. For the social, economic, political and cultural changes brought about by the Emancipation reforms of Alexander II in the early sixties underwent a profound metamorphosis following the introduction into Russia of Western, particularly German materialistic, scientific teaching.

For Soloviev this experiencing of the dark impact of materialism was like a kind of counter-meeting to that with his Eternal Friend of some years before. And to this second meeting he also surrendered with all the powers of devotion of his child-soul, for—as he later recalled—"Then it was that Philaret's *Catechism* (the basic text of religious instruction for all Russian Orthodox children) was rudely displaced by the catechism of Ludwig Buechner (the German teacher of materialism)."

This new "gospel" was taken up widely by outstanding members of the Russian intelligensia who, out of their hunger for anything "progressive," avidly studied the ideas of German writers like Buechner and Moleschott. They called themselves "thinking realists," but were denounced by their opponents as "Nihilists," a term invented by Turgeniev. Their leader in Russia was the brilliant journalist, Dimitri Pisarev; soon articles and books by him and other writers of the "thinking realist" persuasion were eagerly studied by young Vladimir Soloviev.

At this distance one wonders what these highly idealistic men and women who so eagerly embraced this imported by-product of Western culture would have said had they realized that some fifty years later a political leader, representative of this same godless materialism in a far more intensified, sinister form, would be smuggled out of Western Europe into Russia in a sealed railway carriage, thus precipitating events which would shatter their country from one end to the other, would bring a catastrophic conclusion to the "thousand year rule" of the Russian Tsars, and would attack their Church, making adherence to its teachings and even the practice of personal religion a crime.

Indeed, the course of history is strange, but strangest of all, perhaps, is the blindness of that idealism which can so easily be duped by the power of evil which, in response to the children's cry for bread, offers them a stone.

Chapter Three

SCHOOL AND UNIVERSITY

1867–1874

LIKE MANY YOUNG PEOPLE, Vladimir Soloviev passed through a time of great inner tension and turmoil at about the age of fourteen. With the approach of puberty he experienced many doubts and questions about himself, his parents, their ideas, their convictions, his home life, the religious training he had had, and so on. Again and again he reviewed his childhood years—the first time he had done anything of the sort—and brooding introspection and fears concerning his past and future began to torment him day and night. The religious fervor which had culminated in his profound spiritual experience at the age of nine gradually faded into the background, and with it his faith in Orthodoxy, Christianity and God. From the summit of his "Meeting" with his Eternal Friend, he had descended into the valley of the shadow. The golden light of her presence was replaced by darkness and doubt. *He was alone.*

Into this loneliness of spirit came the teachings of the new gospel of nineteenth century scientific materialism. Immediately it was as though the boy was set afire with enthusiasm. The same heart-forces which had responded so ardently to the profound mysteries, the spiritual-artistic beauty of the Orthodox ritual and tradition, surrendered readily to the new catechism of the materialistic teachings from the West.

After months of study of the new "creed," Vladimir decided the moment had come to share the "glad tidings" of this gospel with his family. He wished his grandfather were alive that he might acquaint him with these wonderful ideas! But there were his parents; he would begin with them.

The consternation and horror of Polixena Vladimirovna when her talented son confronted her with his new disbelief in the family religion, proclaiming the gospel of materialism with the fervor of the newly-converted, can be imagined. Firmly he denied his former tie with the spiritual world, oblivious of the impact his words were making on his mother. Shaken to the core, she clung to the slender hope that this "godless Westernism" which had infected her favorite son would play itself out at last, hoping that before long he would free himself from these monstrous ideas that had taken hold of him.

Vladimir found it more difficult to reach his father, for Sergei Mikhailovich was hardly visible to the family except at mealtimes. His university duties occupied some hours of each day, but his thought and energy were almost entirely devoted to the completion of the twenty-nine volumes of his monumental *History of Russia* which had been appearing volume by volume since 1863. Therefore it was hard for Vladimir to find opportunity to tell his father about his new-found interest, and had he done so, probably the latter would scarcely have heard him, so preoccupied was he with his research and writing. Finally, the only outward sign of his "conversion" to the new gospel Vladimir could give his father was that he ceased to accompany him to church. From his side, the father silently allowed his son to go his own way, perhaps realizing this was best in the long run. This turned out to be the case, for, as Soloviev later recalled, "With his attitude in this instance, my father gave me the possibility of feeling religion as a moral force, and that was stronger than any denunciations or admonitions."

* * *

Polixena Vladimirovna Soloviova, mother of Vladimir Soloviev,
from a portrait in later life

Grigori Savvich Skovoroda (1722-1794),
maternal ancestor of Vladimir Soloviev

The climax came one evening, shortly after Vladimir's fifteenth birthday. He had invited a number of his school friends to his house, and in their presence made a speech in which he solemnly repudiated his former belief in the Church, in Christ, in God, proclaiming his adherence to the new creed of materialism. As a sign of his irrevocable determination to follow this new path, he asked his friends to his room and, taking down his personal icons from the wall, he destroyed them.

Startled by this deed and the passionate zeal of this convert to the "new religion," one of the boys later recalled, "Nothing could shake his conviction in the slightest. His father and mother were in despair, but this changed nothing for him. Never in my life have I known anyone so completely convinced that social revolution alone could bring about the immediate salvation of humanity as was Vladimir Sergeyevich on that occasion."

Inspired by the article by Pisarev on "Our Science of the Universities," graduated from a Moscow secondary school with a gold medal (the highest honor attainable), filled with the desire to help humankind by means of materialistic science, Soloviev entered the University of Moscow at the age of seventeen.

During his second year at the University, however, Soloviev's enthusiasm for the gospel of scientific materialism slowly paled. No longer did Pisarev's writings, the Darwinian conception or his own scientific studies grip his imagination or fire his will. Finally Soloviev failed his examinations between his second and third years, quite largely because of disinterest and inattention to the questions put to him.

* * *

The young man's decisive break with materialistic philosophy came as the result of a quite unusual experience which, as he recalled years later, "though it had a quite insignificant beginning, its conclusion left a deep impression upon my inner life."

Enroute to Kharkov to visit his cousin, with whom he was in love, Soloviev met a girl on the train. They changed trains in the city of Kursk, and later, as they were passing from one carriage to the next, Soloviev suddenly fainted. Only the quick, energetic action of the girl saved him from being dragged beneath the swiftly moving wheels. As he regained consciousness, Soloviev recalled,

"I saw only clear, sunny light, a strip of blue sky, and in this light was bending over me the image of a beautiful Woman who looked at me with wonderful, familiar eyes as she whispered softly and tenderly to me."

Again, in place of the young girl who undoubtedly had saved his life, Soloviev saw the Figure of his Eternal Friend he had met long ago in the Chapel of the University. The effect of this vision he described:

"Everything had changed. Inside me something had happened, something miraculous, as if all my being had been melted into something infinitely sweet, filled with light. Motionless, as though in a clear mirror, one wonderful Image was reflected, and I knew and felt that in this One was included everything. I loved with a new, all-embracing, infinite love. In this love I experienced for the first time the fullness and meaning of life."

The conclusion is highly significant:

"*Only now* did I understand that there is God in humanity, that goodness exists, along with true joy in life, and that the goal of life is not to be found in the cold, deathly negation."

With his usual reticence in speaking of his most intimate spiritual experiences, Soloviev clothed this event—all-important as it was for his entire future development—in fictional guise many years later when he included it in a short story titled *The Misty Dawn of Youth*. But this title is significant in itself, recalling accounts of similar spiritual, initiation-experiences, many of them referring to the dawn in various ways, some of the most notable originating in the stream of true Rosicrucianism.

Doubtless as a result of this crucial experience, Soloviev became an auditor in the Historical-Philosophical Faculty of the University in 1872, and in June 1873 he passed his candidate's examination with the highest grade in his class.

While preparing for his degree during the academic year 1873-74, Soloview enrolled as a student in the Theological Academy of the Monastery of the Holy Trinity—the Sergeyevskaya-Troitsa Lavra—about fifty miles north of Moscow. This was the same institution which some decades before had invited Soloviev's ancestor, Grigory Skovoroda, to join its faculty.

His decision to study at the Theological Academy of the Troitsa was a significant step in Soloviev's spiritual development, for here the best in Russian theological and philological teaching was to be found at that time.

In the time of Soloviev the monastery was still surrounded by a wild forest. The Troitsa included a large monastery proper, an academy, a palace, a cathedral, ten churches, many chapels, refectories and a great library. All was enclosed within a wall twenty feet thick, thirty to fifty feet high, nearly a mile in circumference, surmounted by nine towers, and pierced by two gates. Outside the wall ran a deep moat, giving the impression of a curious combination of ecclesiastical institution and military fortress. Within the enclosure, the great tower near the Church of the Assumption of the Virgin was two hundred ninety feet high and contained forty bells, one of them weighing some sixty-five tons.

* * *

From the time of its foundation in 1338 and particularly after the Black Death visited Russia in 1351, the monastery rapidly increased in size and fame as a shrine to which thousands upon thousands of pilgrims streamed from all parts of Russia. In addition to the immense throngs which visited this place throughout the year, the Tsar and the royal family from 1712 to the end of the Monarchy in 1917 never passed between Petersburg and Moscow without pausing to pray at the Troitsa. Fully half the buildings were constructed at the direction of Ivan the Terrible; later Peter the Great twice took refuge there from his enemies.

Foreign visitors were warmly welcomed at the Troitsa as the future American President, James Buchanan discovered in June, 1833: "When we arrived we were first presented to Father Antonius, the Archmandrite or Abbot of the monastery. In all my life I have never beheld a more heavenly expression of countenance. It spoke that he was at peace with heaven and with his fellow men, and possessed a heart overflowing with Christian benevolence and charity. I shall never forget the impression this man made upon me."

After Buchanan and his friends were shown various other parts of the monastery, "Father Antonius accompanied us to that portion of the buildings for the students of divinity, of which there are one hundred at the Troitsa, and the same number of monks. There we were presented to the Archmandrites: Polycarpe, Rector of the Ecclesiastical Academy, a fat, jolly looking monk, who laced his tea strong with cherry brandy and took his wine kindly; to Peter, ancient Archmandrite of the Russian Mission at Peking, who has a long white beard and a venerable appearance, and who read Chinese aloud for our amusement; to Neophyte, formerly substitute for Peter at Peking; and to the monk Isidore, librarian of the Academy. Their wine and their tea were

Vladimir Soloviev as a young student

Vladimir Soloviev as a student at the Theological Academy

both excellent, and we spent an hour or two very pleasantly with them."

During the boyhood of Soloviev the direction of the Troitsa was in the hands of his grandfather's friend, the Metropolitan of Moscow, the saintly, highly-respected Philaret, who had been entrusted with the important State Secret of the Will of Tsar Alexander I, and who officiated at the coronations of both Nicholas I and Alexander II. This scholarly man, whom Soloviev once described as "the only really outstanding character produced by the Russian Church in the nineteenth century," was one of the most famous preachers in Russia. His administration of the Troitsa earned it the name, "the Oxford of Russia" during his lifetime.

* * *

On a beautiful summer day only a few years before Soloviev began his studies there, another party of Americans, led by Secretary Gustavas Vasa Fox, on a peace mission to Russia, visited the Troitsa, coming there by train from Moscow. Having lunched at the hotel opposite the monastery, the party was greeted by a great ringing of bells, and the same Archmandrite Antonius who had welcomed Buchanan thirty-three years before, greeted them at the main gate and took them to meet Philaret himself. The latter, then seventy-four years of age, received them warmly and accompanied them through the great Church of the Assumption, explaining to them everything of note in it.

One of the features of the Troitsa which most impressed the American travelers were the subterranean cells where monks were living who had taken vows of seclusion from all light of day forever, devoting themselves entirely to a life of strictest seclusion and prayer. The guests were shown two churches which connected with these cells, one of them built above ground, the other entirely beneath it. They were also told of some thirty other monks who lived some distance from the monastery in a place called the "Paraclete," each man living a totally secluded life, shut off in every way from direct contact with any other human being.

As the visitors left the monastery, taking the mid-afternoon train back to Moscow, it is not difficult to imagine the feelings with which they recalled what was probably their first and well may have been their only glimpse of the life of Russian ascetics of the mid-nineteenth century.

The enormous wealth and splendor of the Troitsa, with its manifold buildings and activities once caused Nicholas I to ask the Prior, "Where do you find all the money necessary to maintain this work and these buildings?" In reply, the Prior silently pointed to a large open chest standing nearby which at that moment and at all hours of the day and half the night was receiving the gifts of the long line of pilgrims from all parts of the Empire, who were streaming into the main entrance of the monastery.

There was, however, a great contrast between the wealth and prestige of the Troitsa as it existed in the nineteenth century, the result of the veneration and lavish gifts of nearly half a millenium of Tsarist favor, and its humble beginnings when the first Sacrament was celebrated there centuries before by Sergius of Radonegl, beloved by every Christian heart in Russia. As a boy Soloviev had heard from his grandfather wonderful stories about this remarkable saint. He was told how the holy man had lived as a hermit here in the depths of the forest with bears as his only companions, how his saintliness was so great that angels came to serve him when he celebrated the divine Liturgy, using a simple wooden cup as a chalice.

* * *

In the 1840s a young Russian prince applied to the famous member of the Berlin Academy, the German philosopher, Friedrich Wilhelm Schelling, for permission to attend the latter's lectures at the University of Berlin. Schelling inquired, "Why do you wish to do this?" The young man replied, "Because I wish to learn all I can about modern German philosophy. Schelling asked, "Have you then never heard of your countryman, Feyodor Alexandrovich Golubinski?" "Never," replied the Russian prince. Drawing himself up sharply, his clear blue eyes opened wide in surprise, the philosopher exclaimed sternly, "Young man, you ought to be ashamed of yourself for coming to seek instruction in other countries, when you do not know what is to be found in your own! Of all men now living, no one better understands and explains the very philosophy you have come here to study!"

The Russian returned home and sought out the man whose name he had heard for the first time from Schelling. He discovered him serving as parish priest in the village of Troitsa, at the same time acting as professor of philosophy in the Troitsa Theological Academy.

Feyodor Alexandrovich Golubinski was born in 1797, the son of a sacristan, later a priest in the city of Kostromah. The boy made a name for himself as an outstanding student in the Kostromah Seminary; upon graduation at seventeen he was sent to the Troitsa to study in the Academy. Thanks to the instruction of V.E. Kutnevitch he became interested in the ideas of Kant, Schelling and Jacoby. He learned several foreign languages and soon translated into Russian a number of textbooks on the history of philosophy. Upon his graduation in 1827, Golubinski was appointed lecturer on philosophy in the Academy, was married, and the following year was ordained a priest. Soon after this he was offered the chair of philosophy in the University of Moscow, a signal honor, but since he did not wish to leave the Academy and his village parish at Troitsa, he declined. He remained active in these two positions to the end of his life in 1853, the year of Soloviev's birth.

When Soloviev studied at the Troitsa, the son of Golubinski, Dimitri Feyodorovich, was there and the two became good friends. From this son Soloviev learned how the father had carried deep within him a most cherished treasure: the living idea of the Sophia as a part of the universal power of life, "an eternal Being, existing as a cosmic fact."

Two professors at the Troitsa Academy who greatly influenced Soloviev at this time were Father Ivantsov-Platonov and Father Alexander Vasilievich Gorski. The latter's contention that the reason for the exaltation of the Holy Virgin above all the angels of Heaven was the one-sided nature of the angels, later became a favorite among Soloviev's mystical-philosophical expressions.

Upon his arrival at the Troitsa Soloviev took a room in the guest-house outside the walls of the monastery proper. There he surrounded himself with a large collection of books on Greek philosophy and the Eastern Church Fathers.

His decision to study at the Theological Academy when he was enrolled as a candidate for a degree in philosophy at the University caused a small sensation among his fellow-students and professors. The latter had scant regard for the instruction given in seminaries in general, considering them centers of reactionary ideas, and the priests as collaborators in the politics of an arch-conservative, bureaucratic government. Therefore neither Soloviev's professors nor fellow-students could understand what he could possibly gain from clerical teachers that he could not find in a far more "progressive" form at the University.

Though they doubtless admitted him out of respect for his historian-father and the memory of his grandfather, the authorities at the Troitsa also regarded him with a certain reserve at first. Soloviev noted this in a letter to a friend:

"My arrival here made the same impression as the arrival of the false Inspector General in that famous town from which 'If you were to gallop at top speed in any direction from here for three years you won't get anywhere.' They imagine that I came with the sole aim of disturbing their peace with my criticisms. They are extremely polite to me, like the Mayor to Khlestakov. Thankful for this, I have left them in peace as far as possible, although the lectures I have attended so far are rather good ones. By the way, they estimate themselves and their work very modestly, and they can't believe that a man from the outside, a gentleman and a candidate from the University could get into his head the fantastic idea to study the theological sciences here. And actually I am the first such instance of this kind. Therefore they suppose that I have some ulterior motive in coming here. But the Academy looks by no means like such an absolute desert as does the University. The students, despite all their coarseness, seem to be quite serious. They are also good natured and merry, and are great masters of the art of drinking. In general they are quite healthy people."

Eventually Soloviev was to discover that, surprisingly enough, the teaching by the priests in the Academy was actually of a far higher order and much less dogmatic than that he had experienced in the Faculty of Science at the University of Moscow.

From their side, the priests and instructors at the Troitsa found Soloviev a curious figure. In his memoirs Archbishop Nikolai Zeorov described Soloviev when the latter attended a lecture on the history of philosophy by Professor Potapov: "Soloviev came to the lecture wearing a great-coat, felt boots, a beaver hat and a muffler wound about his neck. He spoke to nobody. He merely walked to the window, stood there for a while, drummed with his fingers on the glass, turned round and went away."

Soloviev did not attend many lectures during his residence at the Troitsa. Instead, he immersed himself in the history of philosophy and theology, working alone in his room for long hours at a time. He delved deeply into the writings of the German philosophers—Kant, Fichte, Schopenhauer, Hegel— into the works of the Englishmen, Bacon and Mill—and many others. He read the classic Greek philosophers with great care, Plato in particular. But of all the philosophers, it was Schelling who enabled Soloviev to find rational, philosophical grounds for Christian belief. Through his study of Schelling, whom Prince Troubetskoi, one of Soloviev's later friends and followers described as "the teacher of Russian religious philosophy," Soloviev found positive orientation for his life-activity.

Thanks to Schelling, Soloviev once more stood upon the mountain-top of the spirit; never again was he to lose his way entirely, despite the severe trials, disappointments and struggles he was to experience in the years ahead. In the light of the "fire of Truth and Knowledge" that lived in Schelling's works, Soloviev acquired a new awareness of the implications of the Johannine aspect of Christian revelation and mystical experience. With the great German philosopher he came to recognize that "the true Church which has its basic foundation in Peter, goes *through* Paul, finally to become the Church of St. John."

One of Schelling's statements impressed Soloviev particularly: "The true content of Christianity is altogether the *Person* of Christ. Christ is not the teacher whom one should obey; Christ is not the founder: He is the *Content* of Christianity."

This thought of Schelling's was reflected in Soloviev's statement that "Christianity has its own content, and this content is singularly and exclusively Christ. In Christianity we find Christ, and Christ alone." Soloviev also characterized the Christ as "the unconditionally-individual center" of the world-process, "the spiritual center of a universal organism," the Being who "from the center of Eternity became the center of history 'when the fullness of time was come.'"

Through Schelling's teaching Soloviev became aware that his own task was to help humankind to find once again the true unity of things, to awaken men from what he described as "this heavy, tortuous dream of a separate, egotistic existence." Soloviev was convinced that this loss of community among humanity can only be overcome as men find the way to the essence of Christianity, which he was convinced "...is not dogma, nor hierarchy, nor liturgy, nor morality, but the life-giving spirit of Christ, actually though invisibly present in humanity and acting through the processes of spiritual growth and development."

As preparation for this task Soloviev studied the early Church Fathers and mystics, with emphasis upon the writings of the shoemaker of Goerlitz, Jacob Boehme (1575-1624) and three of Boehme's followers who had made a particular impression upon him. These were John Pordage (1607-1681), an English clergyman, with Jane Lead (1623-1704), a co-founder of the mystical group known as the Philadelphians, Johann Georg Gichtel (1638-1710), the lawyer from Speir and Regensburg, editor of the first edition of the writings of Jacob Boehme, published at Amsterdam (1681-1682), a mystic whom Helena P. Blavatsky identified as "a Rosicrucian of importance" whose plan for the reunion of all Christians, described in his *Theosophia Practica*, interested Soloviev deeply, and Gottfried Arnold (1666-1714), German theologian and historian whose work was especially valued by Lyov Tolstoi, particularly his *Unparteiische Kirchen- und Ketzerhistorie* (An Unbiased History of the Church and Heretics), Frankfort a/M, 1729, a monumental source-book, his *Geheimniss der goettlichen Sophia* (Secrets of the Divine Sophia), Leipzig, 1700, and his *Historie und Beschreibung der mystischen Theologie* (History and Description of Mystical Theology), Frankfort a/M. 1703.

The key to Soloviev's interest in Boehme, Pordage, Gichtel and Arnold is the fact that in various ways each of them concerned himself with the subject of the Sophia, the Divine Wisdom. He felt a common bond with them, as he expressed it, because "all three have had a personal experience almost identical with my own, which is the most interesting thing about them."

* * *

Soloviev was aware of the terrible destiny of the first apostle of Jacob Boehme's teachings in Russia. This was Quirinius Kuhlmann, born in Breslau on February 25, 1651. In 1670 he entered the University of Jena to study law; in 1673 he went to Holland where he continued his studies leading to a doctorate from the University of Leyden. At this time he was introduced to the mystical teachings of Jacob Boehme, and in 1674 he wrote a book proclaiming Jacob Boehme the "prophet of the age," announcing the immanent "fall of Babylon"—meaning the church and clergy of the time—and the ushering in of a new age of peace and happiness—which he called "the Enochian period in the history of humankind." Soon Kuhlmann's extravagant expression of his ideas made him a somewhat controversial figure, even in the liberal atmosphere of seventeenth-century Holland. He therefore went to England where he made the acquaintance of the Rosicrucian scholar-mystic, Franciscus Mercurius Van Helmont. Later he visited Paris, Constantinople, Prussia and Liefland where he actively proclaimed his interpretation of the mystical teaching of Boehme.

In the early summer of 1689 when Kuhlmann arrived in Moscow, almost immediately a circle of followers assembled in the house of a German merchant, Konrad Nordermann to hear his discussions of Boehme's ideas. Despite a growing concern among his friends for his safety in view of his outspokenness, including even a public warning by Magister Johann

Meinecke from the pulpit of the little Lutheran church in Moscow, Kuhlmann prepared a manuscript on Boehme's teachings supplemented by a sharp attack on prevailing conditions in the Russian Orthodox Church, and prophesying the rapidly approaching destruction of the latter. He then had this manuscript translated into Russian and gave it to a Moscow publisher who, in conformity with the law, turned it over to the censor for approval. Almost at once Kuhlmann and Nordermann were seized by the authorities and thrown into prison. After some days of horrible torture the two were confined in a tar-smeared wickerwork cage, their bodies so broken from the excruciation that they could no longer support their own weight, and were burnt alive as "false prophets." This ghastly example of mediaeval barbarism took place before a huge crowd of onlookers on one of the great squares of Moscow at eleven o'clock on the morning of October 4, 1689.

As well may be imagined, this ended any efforts at public promulgation of the mystical teachings of Jacob Boehme in Russia until about a century and a quarter later. At that time Alexander Feyodorovich Labzin produced his translation of Boehme's *The Way to Christ* from the German, including four copper plate illustrations taken from the Amsterdam edition edited by Gichtel in 1682. This was titled *Christosophia ili Put' ko Christu, v devjati knigach; tvorenie Jakova Bema, prozvannago Teu ton ikeskim filosofom*, St. Petersburg, 1815. However, even this modest effort to make one of Boehme's shorter works available to Russian readers did not pass unchallenged, though by no means was Labzin punished as Kuhlmann had been. *The Catalogue of the Imperial Library of the Tsar* published by the University of St. Petersburg in 1897 lists the book, remarking that the copy in the Tsar's collection bears a censor's notation dated 1815, recommending that circulation of the book be forbidden "lest it spread the dark teachings of the Rosicrucians." As a result, few books by Jacob Boehme appeared in Russian translation, though his

works were read in German by a wide circle of people in nine-
teenth- and early twentieth-century Russia, Vladimir Soloviev
among them.

* * *

In the year 1600 Jacob Boehme underwent a spiritual
experience which radically changed his life. It occurred on
an afternoon not long after his twenty-fifth birthday when
he happened to notice a beam of sunlight reflected upon
the surface of a pewter dish. Suddenly he apparently found
himself able to penetrate into the most secret depths of the
wisdom of the universe. It was as though a spiritual "eye"
had opened within him—and doubtless it had—for his enraptured gaze could probe the esoteric secrets of the workings of
the forces of nature—of earth, water, air, fire—in the depths
of the earth, in minerals, plants, animals, humans, and even in
the movements of the planets in the heavens. In that moment
of time he recognized that the work of Creation had by no
means ceased at the conclusion of "the sixth day" described
in Genesis, for he beheld the forces of Creation in continual,
endless activity, eternally bringing into being minerals, plants,
animals, men—even worlds upon worlds—out of the "deep
Abyssal Womb" of "Eternal Nature." Thus he realized that,
far from God having created all that is out of "Nothing" as
customarily taught in his time, this "Nothing" is in reality a
profoundly pregnant, spiritual substance within the Divine,
out of which Creation is continually being brought forth.

Some years later Boehme described this spiritual experience
or "illumination" in the introduction to his famous book for
which his Rosicrucian friend, Dr. Baithasar Walter, physician
of Goerlitz, suggested the title: *Aurora, the Day-Spring or
Dawning of the Day in the Orient, or the Morning Redness
in the Rising of the Sun:*

"In a quarter of an hour I observed and knew more than if I had attended a university for many years. I recognized the Being of Beings... the eternal generation of the Trinity, the origin and creation of this world and of all creatures through the Divine Wisdom, the Sophia."

Later Boehme described the Sophia as "the outpoured Word of divine power, virtue, knowledge, holiness, a resemblance of the infinite and unsearchable Unity, a substance in which the Holy Spirit works, forms and shapes." For Boehme the Sophia stood revealed as the means by which "the powers, colors and virtues of God are expressed... the mirror in which the Spirit of God has seen all objects from all Eternity. She is the Divine Chaos, that is, the divine Imagination, in which the idea of angels and souls has been existent from all Eternity, resembling the divine; not yet as creatures but as resemblances only, as when a man sees his own face in a mirror; therefore the angelic and human idea flowed out from Wisdom, and was then changed into an Image, as Moses said, God created him in His Image, that is, He breathed into him the divine breath of knowledge, pouring out from the three divine principles." Soloviev parallels Boehme's description thus:

"The Sophia occupies the mediating position between the multiplicity of living beings, forming the actual content of her life, and the absolute unity of Divinity, the ideal beginning and norm of that life... Through her, God is manifested in all creation as the living, acting Power."

Boehme's imagination of the Sophia acting in presence of the Christ and the individual human being at one and the same moment, is reminiscent of Fra Angelico's representation of the joyfulness of the divine world expressed in the form of the sacred dance he depicts in the Paradise section of his painting of the *Last Judgment*. Of this joy of the divine Sophia, Soloviev wrote: "The rejoicing of the Divine Wisdom, Sophia, shows God that all that is positive belongs to Him in fact and by right, that He possesses eternally in Himself an infinite treasure of all real powers, all true ideas, all gifts, all graces." Boehme had amplified this thought in a picture of unforgettable beauty:

"When Christ, the Corner-Stone (the divine principle latent in humanity) stirs himself, then the Virgin Sophia appears before the soul. Then the Reader may be desirous to enter into the Inner Choir, where the soul joins hands and dances with the Sophia, the Divine Wisdom."

The student and editor of Boehme, Johann Georg Gichtel, whose writings on the Sophia were studied by Soloviev, as noted above, wrote: "Without Christ we cannot understand or approach the heavenly Sophia or Wisdom. She is not God, but is His mirror; she is not Jesus, but his heavenly flesh and blood, and when we put on Christ we put on Wisdom... This Sophia is a pure, burning Love which changes everything and which nothing can change. One who is clothed with her in time can stand in the fire of Eternity. She is the tincture and body of our inward, spiritual human, and without this priestly ornament we may not enter into the Holiest of Holies nor stand in the strife with the dragon-devil in flesh and blood."

One of the most important esoteric revelations made by Gichtel concerns the help the Sophia brings to the task set by the Apostle: "To 'pray without ceasing' is not to utter many words with the lips, but ever to raise up the thoughts to God. The devil cannot easily bewitch the senses of the man who does this, because the latter's senses are immediately chastened by the light of the heavenly Sophia, the Divine Wisdom. Our office is spiritual, we ourselves are the temple, the soul is our sacrifice, Divine Wisdom, Sophia, is our fire. Our mouth eats the spiritual food, and in this our worship and our spiritual activity consists."

* * *

On a lovely spring day in 1670 an Englishwoman named Jane Lead was walking in the country and, as she so quaintly described it, "was contemplating the happy state of the angelical world, much exercised upon Solomon's choice, which was to find the Noble Stone of Wisdom." In her beautiful diary, bearing the charming title, *A Fountain of Gardens*, she describes what followed:

"There came upon me an overshadowing bright cloud, and in the midst of it a Figure of a Woman, most richly adorned with transparent gold, her hair hanging down, and her face as terrible as crystal for brightness, but her countenance was sweet and mild. At this sight I was somewhat amazed, but immediately a Voice came saying, 'Behold, I am God's eternal Virgin, Wisdom, whom thou hast been enquiring after. I am to unseal the Treasures of God's deep Wisdom unto thee.'"

Three days later, when Jane Lead again stood in the shade of a flowering tree in the same country lane, "The same Figure in greater glory did appear, with a crown upon her head, full of Majesty, saying, 'Behold me as thy Mother and know thou art to enter into covenant with me.'"

The heavenly Sophia appeared for the third and last time to this remarkable woman a few days later: "Then the Virgin proceeded, saying, 'I shall now cease to appear in a Visible Figure unto thee, but I will not fail to transfigure myself within thee, and there will open in thee the spring of Wisdom and Understanding.'"

From this time to the end of her long life in 1704 at the age of eighty-one, Jane Lead enjoyed remarkable gifts of esoteric insight, as evidenced by her spiritual diary, a large portion of which she dictated to her devoted student, the highly accomplished Oxford physician and learned Orientalist, Dr. Francis Lee (1661-1719) during her last years when physical blindness had come upon her. But no earthly darkness could dim the light from "the spring of Wisdom and Understanding" constantly welling up within her from the time of her Sophia visions of thirty years before. Out of her own experiences with the Sophia and the inspiration she found in the writings of Jacob Boehme, together with John Pordage, Francis Lee, Richard Roach and other Boehme students, she established in London the group of mystics known as the Philadelphians.

In 1697 Dr. Francis Lee undertook to edit a monthly journal for the Philadelphians under the title, *Theosophical Transactions by the Philadelphian Society*. In one of the first issues appeared a description of a certain secret Temple, hidden from the world, reminiscent of the "House of the Holy Spirit" described in the *Fama Fraternitatis* of the Rosiciucians which had appeared in an English translation in 1652. This description interested Soloviev deeply:

"The fabric of the Temple is circular, supported by seven pillars, as of massy gold. In the midst of the Temple is a throne ascended by six steps; it is continually filled with the glory of a great king and priest. Around this priestly throne are twenty-four arch-priests or royal presbyters, bearing the sacred *Mishpat* on their breasts and called the Sovereign Order of the Hierophantae, of the line of Meichizedek; also a numerous company of subordinate priests, perpetually ministering in their courses, clothed in white and crowned with gold crowns, who cease not to worship Him Who lives in their midst. Daily some priests are admitted to the Temple, but there are also certain solemn seasons and convocations when there are particular invitations to those who are to be initiated and anointed into this priesthood. There are also priestesses as well as priests, the disparity between male and female ceasing as they come to bathe themselves in a certain miraculous fountain which runs from under the threshold of the Temple."

* * *

Dr. John Pordage's diary entry for June 25, 1675, published with other diary entries for the same period under the title, *Sophia, the Blessed Eternal Virgin of the Divine World*, Amsterdam, 1699, an account written five years after Jane Lead first experienced the presence of the Divine Widsom, opens with the words:

"As I turn my gaze inward to my new earth..."

And in the pages that follow one can trace his struggle to separate himself step by step from the things of earth until the climactic moment arrived when he experienced first-hand the meeting for which he so longed. When Vladimir Soloviev read Dr. Pordage's account, he recognized in it strong affinities with his own experiences and desires.

* * *

Turning over the pages of the apocryphal *Wisdom of Solomon*, Soloviev's attention was caught by such lines as these: "What Wisdom is, I will tell you ... Wisdom, worker of all things, taught me, for in her is an understanding spirit ... kind to humanity, having all power, overseeing all things ... For Wisdom is more moving than any motion: she passes through all things by reason of her purity. For she is the breath of the presence of God, the brightness of the everlasting light, the unspotted mirror of the power of God ... Sophia makes all things new, *in all ages* entering into holy souls, making them friends of

God. For she knows the mysteries of the knowledge of God and great pleasure it is to have her friendship."

Meditation upon such passages, together with his reading of Gnostic literature and other Wisdom books at this time undoubtedly resulted in Soloviev's writing a certain prayer during his stay at the Troitsa. The text, discovered in one of his notebooks after his death, was included among the addenda to the sixth edition of Soloviev's works published in 1915. A more complete version, from which the following translation was made, is included in Album No. 1 of Soloviev's writings for 1874.

Though it is titled a prayer, it is really a meditation of extraordinary scope and depth. It is believed that Soloviev carried a copy of this text with him in his pocket notebook for years; obviously it occupied his thinking for decades.

A Prayer for the Revelation of the Supreme Mystery
In the Name of the Father, the Son, the Holy Spirit

Ain-Soph   Yah   Soph-Yah

In the unutterable, awe-inspiring, all-powerful Name, I call upon the divine beings, demons, humans, and all living creatures! Gather into a oneness the rays of your power. Put aside your own will, and share my prayer with me, that we may capture the pure Dove of Zion, that we may find the priceless Pearl of Ophir, that the Roses may unite with the Lilies in the Valley of Sharon.

O most holy, divine Sophia, essential Image of Beauty and Sweetness of the all-existent God, glorious body of Eternity, Soul of the universes, only Queen of all souls!

By the immeasurable profundity and grace of your first Son and beloved, Jesus Christ, I implore you: Enter the dungeon of the soul, fill with your radiance our darkness; melt with the fire of love the fetters of our spirit; bestow upon us light and freedom; embody yourself in us and in the Universe, restoring the Fullness of the Ages, so the Deep may be covered with a limit, and God be All in All.

* * *

In Soloviev's mystical terminology the *Ain Soph* (Hebrew, "the Infinite") is identified with the Father, the Yah with the Son, and the *Soph-Yah* (Sophia) with the Holy Spirit. The figures of the Dove of Zion, the Pearl of Ophir and the Valley of Sharon are reminiscent of the Old Testament and of Hebrew mysticism in general. The image of the uniting of Roses with Lilies is a theme to which Soloviev will return in his later poetry.

His longing for the all-oneness is reflected in Soloviev's poem, *Prometheus*, written in August 1874, about the same time as the *Prayer for the Revelation*, given above:

When your soul in single light will see
Falsehood and truth, goodness and evil,
And will embrace all the world in one greeting of love,
What is, and what has been,

Then will you know the joy of reconciliation,
Your thought will understand
That only in phantoms of childish notions
Live falsehood and evil.

Then will come the hour—last hour of creation—
When your light with single ray
 A whole world of nebulous visions will disperse
Along with the heavy, earthly dream.

Barriers are falling, fetters melting
In the fire divine;

And the eternal morning of new life is dawning
In All, and All in One.

* * *

Soloviev was well aware that hand in hand with knowledge of the Sophia—as with all spiritual knowledge—go
certain possibilities of error, even of moral perversions. In
the preface to his collected poems he indicates these dangers,
beginning with the question, "Is not the feminine principle
thus introduced into the Deity as such? Without entering into
this theosophical problem itself, I must state the following
in order to protect my readers from temptation and myself
from blame: (1) the introduction of carnal, animalistically
human relations into the realm of the supersensible is the
greatest abomination and the cause of total destruction: the
Flood, Sodom and Gomorrah, the 'satanic depths', and so
on; (2) the worship of the feminine nature as such, that is, of
the principle of ambiguity and indifference, sensitiveness to
falsehood and evil not less than to truth and good—this is a
terrible madness, the main cause of the current slovenliness
and weakness; (3) the true adoration of the Eternal Feminine as having accepted from all eternity the power of the
Godhead, and as having truly embodied the fullness of good
and truth and—through this—the deathless glory of beauty,
has nothing at all to do with this foolishness or that abomination. On the other hand, the more perfect and intimate
the revelation of true beauty which clothes the Godhead
and by His power frees us from suffering and death, the
narrower is the boundary separating it from its false image,
from that illusory, powerless beauty which merely continues
the kingdom of suffering and death. But all this has been
predicted, and the end has been foretold: at last the Eternal
Beauty will bear fruit, and from her will come the salvation
of the world, when her unreal images will have disappeared

as did that sea-foam out of which Aphrodite was born. No single word of my poems is intended to serve *this one*; in this lies the only, indisputable merit I can and must recognize in them."

* * *

During Soloviev's studies at the Troitsa in October, 1874 occurred the death of his beloved teacher, Pamfil Danilovich Yurkevich, from 1863 professor of philosophy at the University of Moscow. The son of a country priest in the Poltava region, Yurkevich was born in 1827 and later attracted attention as a student gifted for philosophical thought and teaching. The Holy Synod cited him for his "exceedingly diligent and most useful works," and in 1861 gave him further recognition, appointing him professor in ordinary "for his exemplary service, vast knowledge and excellent teaching." Soon he was invited to the chair of philosophy in the University of Moscow, where from 1869 to his death he was Dean of the Faculty of History and Philology.

Yurkevich's writings—particularly those on philosophical subjects—were little known to most of his contemporaries at the time of his death, for they had been published in obscure provincial and clerical journals. In order that this situation might be corrected, Soloviev undertook to embody their leading ideas in a long essay published in the Annals of the Imperial Ministry of Education in St. Petersburg for the year 1874. Most important for an appreciation of Soloviev's interest in certain mystical teachings he had originally received from his teacher is the former's lengthy consideration of Yurkevich's article, "The Heart and its Significance in the Spiritual Life of Humanity."

This was probably the first of Yurkevich's writings to be published, and it appeared in the *Writings of the Theological Academy of Kiev*, Vol. I, 1860. This article, until now not published in English translation, Soloviev set out "to discuss in considerable detail and for the most part in the words of the author himself."

Yurkevich contrasts "two principal, basic components of humanity's spiritual being: the 'heart' and the 'head,' elements of the spiritual being which have their closest expression or incarnation in certain parts of the physical body. The moral or practical element of the spirit, i.e., the will-principal and the soul's life, is centered mainly in the heart as the central organ of the blood-bearing system, while the theoretical principal of the spirit—the intellect—has its external expression in the head, the seat of the most important part of the nervous system." He then describes the heart as the core and essence of the human being rather than merely the seat of the emotions, as non-Hebraic thought tends to interpret it. As illustration of his point of view he turns to the Bible "as the most ancient memorial that expresses not a personal but a general popular consciousness."

He goes on to say that "according to the Bible the heart is the keeper and bearer of all body-forces and *is the center of the whole soul and spirit life of humanity*. In it are rooted not only the many-sided feelings of the soul—the emotions, passions and moral conditions—but also *all cognitive actions* of the soul are deeply based not only in the head as such, but *in the heart*. Contemplation, *meditation*, is the consultation of the heart; to comprehend with the heart means to understand; to perceive with the whole heart means to understand completely. As the center of the entire corporeal and many-sided spiritual life of humanity, the heart is the source of life, a circle or wheel, in the rotating of which is included all our life. The soul's condition expresses itself through the condition of the heart, and the latter's revelation *through thought, word and action* never exhausts this source."

"Regarding the heart as the center of humanity's spiritual life, the writers of the Bible saw in the head something like

The Monastery of the Holy Trinity as it looked in 1874 when Soloviev studied there. From a contemporary sketch.

The Main Hall of the University of Moscow, erected 1786-93, designed by Matevy Kazakov (1738-1812), architect

a visible summit of that life which originally and directly is rooted in the heart. However, many places in the Bible express the quite definite thought that the head has its importance as an organ playing an intermediary role between the whole being of the soul and the influences it experiences from outside and from above. It is fitting that a governing dignity is assigned to the head where the entire system of the actions of the soul are concerned, *but these* actions of the soul in the head *by no means* exhaust the activity of the whole being of the soul. By necessity of thinking we have to admit that there exists some original spiritual substance that needs the intermediary governing actions of the head. *But*, according to the Bible, *this original spiritual substance possesses its most closely related, most intimate organ in the heart.* In this way the heart is seen not merely as the incarnation-point of one side of our spirit, but at the same time as *the expression of the deepest basis of all our spiritual being."*

Yurkevich next discusses "the meaning attributed to the head and heart... and scientific philosophy." He does not deny the value of physiology and psychology in investigating these areas of the human being, but takes issue with the conclusion that "the very essence of the soul is thinking, or that thinking represents the whole spiritual person," with willing and feeling as merely "phenomena, aspects and occasional conditions of thinking." Finally he concludes that "with these definitions is quite incompatable the thought that there is in the soul something *intimate*, something so deeply substantial that *it can never be exhausted by the phenomena of thinking.*"

That the forces of the heart to which Yurkevich points are not the heart-forces we experience in ordinary life, but imply *a further development*, a "mystery" not penetrable by ordinary thinking, is explained by him thus: "Whoever thinks that in the human soul, as well as in everything which exists, there are sides which are inaccessible for a relative cognition, such a person can see in advance the great significance of the

Biblical teaching about *the deep heart*, the mysteries of which only the divine Mind is able to know."

Turning to the materialist-philosophers, particularly of the mid-nineteenth century, whose views played such a great role at the time, and to an extent continue to do so in our own day, Yurkevich declared, "It is evident that a philosophy based on the assumption that the substance of soul is nothing more than thinking, *must deny everything basically moral in humanity*. It replaces the commandment of love—which is deeply significant for the heart—with an abstract sense of duty... This philosophy comes to an abstract understanding of God's being, defining all the richness of Divine Life as an idea... But thinking undoubtedly does not exhaust all the amplitude of human spiritual life, just as the perfection of thinking does not mean the perfection of the human spirit in its entirety. Whoever hopes to explain all the diversity of soul-life out of thinking will succeed no better than a physiologist who would explain the phenomena of hearing—sounds, tones and words—out of the phenomena of seeing—space, shape, color, and so on.

"The essence of the soul, as well as its link with the body must be *much richer and more manifold* than is usually thought. The corporeal instrument of the soul has to be nothing other than the human body. Therefore, since the heart unites in itself all the forces of this body, it serves as the most intimate organ of the soul's life.

"Contemporary physiology knows that *the heart is not merely a muscle, nor is it an unfeeling mechanism*, regulating the flow of blood in the body by means of mechanical pressure. In the heart are united the two most remarkable systems of nerves: the so-called sympathetic nerves, dealing with all vegetative functions of the body, and the nerves which serve as necessary organs of sensation or ideas and arbitrary motions. It is possible to say that in the heart, which is a well of blood, the heart, which is *the real body* of all beings possessing a soul, both nerve systems come together and touch each other in such closeness and interaction as in no other organ of the human body. Can we not say, without contradicting the physiological facts, that all the most important systems of the human body have in the heart their representative, which out of this center cares for their safety and life?

"Our thoughts, words and actions are *originally* not images of external things, but images or expressions of the soul, the offsprings of our heart-moods. Of course, in daily life, filled with worries, we pay little attention to this *intimate* side of our thoughts and actions. Nevertheless the fact remains that everything that enters from outside into the soul through the sense-organs is worked over, changed, and receives its final and constant quality by the specific, privately defined heart-mood of the soul. The human heart is the basis where a person's thoughts, feelings and actions acquire that particular quality that they are not the expression of a general spiritual being, but of an individual, living, truly existing person.

"If one were to manifest oneself merely through thinking only, then the manifold universe, rich with life and beauty, would reveal itself to the consciousness as an accurate but lifeless mathematical value. One would be able to see this value completely, to the core, but nowhere would one meet true existence, filled with life, which surprises one by the beauty of forms, the mystery of attractions, the endless fullness of its contents. In the real soul there does not exist such onesidedness of thinking in which thought is as definite as mathematical values, but such knowledge of things can be expanded only in width and not in depth. The best philosophers and the great poets are conscious that their heart is the place where those deep ideas which they transmit to humanity are born, while the consciousness connected with the activity of the sense organs and the brain gives these ideas only clarity and the definiteness that belong to thinking."

Here Yurkevich's thought reflects the conviction expressed by Pushkin in his well-known lines:

"We were born for inspiration,
Sweet melodies and prayers."

* * *

It was doubtless due to his teacher, Yurkevich, as well as to his own insight that Soloviev was convinced of *the reality of eternal development*, of endless possibilities of growth for the soul and spirit-life of the human being. In his article on Yurkevich, Soloviev quoted his former teacher with approbation: "The being of the soul, boundless to the external eye, is destined to undergo a development not only in time *but in eternity as well*, for the spirit cannot be limited by the conditions of soul evoked in the latter by impressions of the external world ... But the Tree of Knowledge is not the Tree of Life, and the life of the spirit is something more precious than knowledge. For this particular original life of spirit, which is not subject to mathematical reckoning, maintains the closest relationship *to the human heart*."

Every creative person knows how impossible it is to translate into exact knowledge what Yurkevich calls "those fine, imponderable motions and conditions of our soul," in other words, our experiences of joy and sorrow, of goodness and love, of fear and hope. In presence of beauty, whether in Nature or in art, when we are touched by the sounds of a Beethoven sonata, or when a deed of courage evokes our wonder—"all these conditions of greater or lesser *enthusiasm* are instantly reflected in our heart."

Yurkevich goes on: "In their writings the early Christian mystics often condemned the human mind for its slowness in acknowledging what is immediately and directly known to the heart. But this does not deny that the slow motion of the mind, like a slow walk, has a quality of exactness and correctness that are wanting to the too energetic movements of the heart. Nevertheless *if the light of knowledge is to change into warmth and life of the spirit, it must penetrate the heart in order that it enter into the whole mood of the soul.* So if truth descends upon our heart, it becomes our blessing, our inner treasure. Only for this treasure and not for an abstract thought can a person enter into the struggle with conditions and other people; *only to the heart is a heroic deed and self-sacrifice possible.*"

From these beginnings Yurkevich proceeds to discuss the more esoteric, mystical, occult aspects of the subject: "There exists in the human soul something original and elementary, as it were, a 'person' hidden in the heart; there exists a 'depth' of heart, the movements of which cannot be calculated in advance on the basis of general conditions and laws of the soul's life. For this *most particular* side of the human spirit, science is unable to discover any general and permanently definite forms. When Mysticism tries to find forms that will entirely correspond to the spiritual content of the human heart it can only deny all forms and expressions available to us through the finite world and finite thinking. To Mysticism the qualities of the 'lower' soul do not correspond to the dignity of the heart's life, while the intellect, since it thinks in particular forms, generating *one thought after another in time*, is no more than a weak, inaccurate expression of this life. Mysticism is based on the true conviction that the fullness of spiritual life we experience in the heart is not exhausted by those soul-forms which are shaped out of the conditions of this finite sense-world, and that our development cannot be limited to those definite phenomena of intellect which come into being under temporal conditions.

"Contrary to the point of view of true Mysticism is that psychological theory which hopes to classify and define all the phenomena of the life of the soul as final and unchanging. This theory cannot reach the deepest foundations of the individuality and the embryo of its future life on the one hand, while on the other, many phenomena of the soul's life are and will ever remain unsolved and unexplained by the intellect. Among these phenomena are *the significance of dreams, instances of clairvoyance, and particularly the various mysterious forms of spiritual consciousness itself.*

"We find the truth expressed in the Biblical teaching regarding the heart as the center of the life of the human soul. However, the heart cannot transpose all of its spiritual content into expression directly; in its depths, inaccessible to intellectual analysis, forever remains the source of new life, new activities, new strivings, *which go beyond the limits of the ordinary life of the soul and make it capable for eternity.*"

* * *

Professor Mikhail Danielovich Muretov, who knew Soloviev at this time, described the latter as he appeared at the *Troitsa*: "A small, somewhat round face, pale, almost bluish... large, dark eyes without life or expression, constantly gazing into the far distance, black eyebrows, clearly defined; long, thin hands with pale, nerveless fingers; long legs, covered by tight, threadbare trousers; a tall, thin, dark, self-centered, enigmatic creature."

This enigmatic, self-centered quality was characteristic of Soloviev throughout his life. Though he had a wealth of devoted friends and admirers, few of his contemporaries really knew or fully understood him. Though he enjoyed social events and spent much time in company of others, his real self was shut away from his fellow-creatures; at heart he remained the loneliest of men.

In the spring of 1874 Soloviev presented his thesis to the Faculty of History and Philosophy at the University of Moscow. This work, titled, *The Crisis of Western Philosophy — Opposition to the Positivists*, attracted considerable attention upon publication. Based on the work of the Slavophils generally, and upon the writings of Ivan Kireyevski (1805-

1856) in particular, Soloviev's study was a courageous, forthright attack upon the dominant materialistic thinking of the time. His principal point was that the positivist, rationalist thinking of Western Europe had weakened the latter's creative faculties, and that only through the forces of the faith and reason of Eastern Europe—of Russia in particular—could a new future arise for European culture and humanity. Only the inherent spirituality of the Russian people and their Church could strengthen and restore the weakened and dying culture of the West.

The book created considerable interest and controversy in Russian intellectual circles. The Slavophils were delighted, for they saw in the young Soloviev a champion of their cause. On the other hand, the Westerners—who were in the majority in university circles—frowned upon certain of Soloviev's ideas, criticizing him personally for what appeared to them as his claim to be able to prophesy the future course of events.

Soloviev's oral defense of his thesis, which took place in the University of St. Petersburg, was brilliant. Afterward a colleague of his father, the historian, Dr. Bestuzhev-Ryumin, congratulated him heartily, exclaiming, "Russia is indeed fortunate in having a new genius!" Soloviev was made a Fellow of the University of Moscow; the path to a full professorship opened before him.

Lyov Tolstoi read *The Crisis of Western Philosophy* and later commented: "My acquaintance with Soloviev, the philosopher has added very little that is new to my knowledge, but it is a great stimulus; it has caused a philosophic ferment in me and has confirmed many things in clarifying thoughts of paramount necessity for the remainder of my life and for my death—thoughts that are of such comfort to me that, had I the ability and time, I would try to pass them on to others."

Tolstoi's friend, the philosopher, Nikolai Strakhov, however, sensed another aspect of Soloviev's thinking. In a letter to Tolstoi dated January 1, 1895, Strakhov wrote: "Soloviev obviously separates himself from Hegel, but secretly follows him all the same. His entire criticism of Schopenhauer is based upon this, but the matter seems to me even worse, for Soloviev is of the opinion that everywhere *a metaphysical substance* is to be found. He sees it on all sides, even face to face, and is inclined to believe in Spiritualism. He also tends to illness, is very thin, so that one fears that eventually all will not be well with him."

Undoubtedly these words were prophetic in that they indicated the direction Soloviev's thinking and interests were to follow in the next seven years. Meanwhile, however, after receiving his degree, he accepted an invitation to lecture on philosophy at the University of Moscow, at the same time acting as instructor in the Women's University College which had recently been founded.

In his pedagogical tasks Soloviev displayed the same devotion to duty, conscientiousness, appreciation of scientific methodology and, above all, the enormous capacity for work which had characterized his father's activities. Sergei Mikhailovich had chosen as his life-motto: "Always at work, from youth onward!" and the son also carried this out in life-practice.

The publication of *The Crisis in Western Philosophy*, completed the preparation for Soloviev's professional work which in reality had begun with the writing of his thesis, *The Mythological Process in Ancient Paganism*, published in the well-known "Orthodox Review," 1873. In addition to the months he spent at the Theological Academy of the Troitsa (autumn 1873 to early summer 1874) and his studies at the University, Soloviev experienced a further intensification of his sense of social responsibility, though, as he wrote in a letter to Yeltsova V. Romanova, "From the time I began to understand anything, I was aware that the existing order—primarily the social and civic order—is not what it should be ... The present condition of humanity ... must be changed, reformed." Hence with his attainment of academic honor and professional standing, he now turned to a search for those solutions he felt were imperative for the social well-being of humanity. Here Soloviev struck a theme to which he was to return ever and again: "What is needed above all is that we should treat our social and cosmic environment *as an actual living being*, with which we are in the most intimate reciprocal action, though without becoming merged into uniformity with it."

At this time Soloviev sketched an outline of his thoughts about the social question which takes this *actual living being* into consideration in a remarkable way. He observed three spheres at work interrelatedly in human life: the spheres of living, of knowing, of doing. Within each sphere we can discriminate between the subjective foundation and the objective principle, thus: the subjective foundation expresses itself in Feeling, Thinking, Willing, while the objective principle manifests itself in Beauty, Truth, and what Soloviev calls "the general Good, the Good of all humanity," similar to what was expressed by the phrase, "the general welfare," used by the Founding Fathers in America.

Subjective foundation: Feeling, Thinking, Willing
Objective principle: Beauty, Truth, The
General Good, the Good of all Humanity

From this Soloviev indicates that history develops in three stages or steps: an absolute stage, a formal stage, a real, or factual stage. These stages each unfold themselves in a three-fold, living way:

Absolute Stage: Mysticism — Theology — Church
Formal Stage: Art — Philosophy — State
Real, Factual Stage: Technology — Natural Science —
  Community

For Soloviev, "Church" is *the spiritual Community of humankind*, born out of a oneness and cooperation with spiritual Beings, and not primarily an institution as such on earth.

It is notable how for Soloviev, out of the chaotic unity or oneness of "Mysticism" in the absolute stage a threefold organism develops, which in turn expresses itself as Art and finally as Technology. Thus Soloviev sees in Mysticism something of a beneficial magic, theurgic, element working in the affairs of humanity. All creativity, then, is the fruit of the working of spiritual or, in other words, archetypal elements; Mysticism is the root of all creativity, whether at the level of Art as such or of Technology. In similar fashion, Theology at another stage becomes Philosophy, and at still another, is the parent of Natural Science. *The spiritual community of humankind*, which Soloviev calls "Church," becomes the foundation for the State, and is the foundation for social community among people on earth, for the economic community.

Soloviev traces this overall development one step further, so that out of a threefoldness *a fourfoldness* appears:

Absolute (Archetypal) Stage: Mysticism—Theology— Church
Formal Stage: Art — Philosophy — State
Real (Factual) Stage: Technology — Natural Science — Community
Fourth Stage: *Theurgy — Theosophy — Theocracy*

This fourth stage comes about, however, only as a result of the cooperative action of humanity with the Christ *and the Sophia*, working *together* toward the goal that not only humanity, but humanity *and the world of Nature* become permeated with the Impulse of the Christ. Thus Mysticism, the archetype of artistic and technological creativity, results in a manifestation of theurgic, magical power. Similarly, Theology as the archctypal divine "speech" expresses itself in a love of wisdom (philosophy) and in a science of nature, eventuating in a *Wisdom of God*, a *Theo-Sophia*. Finally, the spiritual community of humankind (the "Church") reveals itself in a body of humankind bearing the Impulse of Christ, and in turn a Community of humankind which unites itself in a *Theocracy*.

The foundational reality for Soloviev is the oneness of the world-soul, the Sophia, and the soul of humanity. Out of this he sees evolving a community of Christians in the broadest sense, in whom the will of the Christ works in a most living, most real way. Thus he lifts the social life of humankind into the Heights.

Chapter Four

SECOND AND THIRD MEETINGS

1874–1881

IN REPLY TO THE QUESTION, "Whom would you like to be? Soloviev wrote in a friend's album: "I would like to be myself—turned inside out!" This desire to communicate to others his most intimate, most cherished ideas, was one of the strongest impulses in Soloviev's life. He longed to share with others "the things that really matter, after all."

During the year he was preparing his thesis, Soloviev occasionally attended meetings of the Moscow Association of Lovers of Religious Education. There one evening he was introduced to a visitor from St. Petersburg, a man of medium height, with broad, somewhat stooped shoulders, thinning hair and beard, curious pinched temples, his face strangely pallid, suffering etched deeply upon it, his eyes aglow with a dark, inner fire. Almost before a mutual friend mentioned the stranger's name, Soloviev knew: this is the author of *Crime and Punishment*, the portrayer of Raskolnikov; these eyes have probed the depths of the soul of the saintly Prince Myshkin, *The Idiot*; these broad hands, with their sensitive, long fingers have sketched the terrible path of degeneration of the lost soul, Stavrogin, in *The Possessed*, which Soloviev had just read.

When he shook hands with the young Soloviev, Dostoyevski was immediately reminded of the representations of the face of the Christ by the talented sixteenth century Italian painter,

Annibale Caracci, whose work he had seen on his travels abroad. On the other hand, Soloviev was instantly attracted to this writer who knew the heights and depths of human beings as few people have. Perhaps this man who had experienced first-hand so much suffering, so much of the good and evil in humanity, might be able to help him find the way to reach others.

They soon became friends. In reply to Soloviev's questions, Dostoyevski suggested that perhaps the young man should consider further study, but somewhere abroad—perhaps Paris, or Berlin—or London. His own travels abroad had meant a great deal to him, Dostoyevski explained. And of all countries, perhaps England was the place where Soloviev would learn most. Of course the English were obsessed with ideas of "progress," of commerce and industry, ideas Dostoyevski considered utterly inhuman. Take their Crystal Palace, for example, that monument to their notions of human achievement: he thought he was in the Babylon of the Apocalypse when he first saw it! Fourteen acres of ground covered with glass, crammed with all the manufactured ugliness that could be imagined! Was this glorified hothouse what humanity had suffered and struggled for through the ages? What a commentary on modern achievement was this epitome of soulless materialism, this apocalyptic monster of iron and glass, after all! And the slums, the cess-pools of human degradation, the gin-palaces of London, these would open the eyes of this gentle, soft-spoken, shy young philosopher to the hard facts of life! On the other hand Dostoyevski knew that a scholar of Soloviev's capability and breadth of interests could profit greatly from England's museums, libraries, universities. And despite their shortcomings and preoccupation with their peculiar brand of materialistic culture, the English were extremely kind and considerate, particularly to foreigners. Once one grew accustomed to their reserved, quiet ways—and particularly their food—one could live in London quite happily.

At Dostoyevski's suggestion, therefore, Soloviev applied to the University of Moscow for a travelling fellowship for a year abroad, principally in England, "in order to study the Gnostic, Indian and Medieval philosophies," as he wrote in his letter of application.

Soloviev left Moscow in June 1875, arriving in Warsaw without incident. From there he went to Berlin where he had intended to visit the philosopher, Edouard von Hartmann. However, at the last moment, Soloviev changed his plans and passed through Berlin without stopping in the grey city of the north. From there his train took him via Hanover and Cologne; just two days and nights after leaving Moscow he arrived in London. The first night he spent in an inexpensive hotel near the railway station but the following day, with the assistance of some Russian friends living in London to whom he had letters of introduction, he found lodging in a rooming house run by a Mrs. Siggers, located in Great Russell Street, just across from the British Museum.

London attracted Soloviev, as Dostoyevski had been sure it would. He felt certain he would spend a happy, productive year there. With characteristic energy and thoroughness he set to work to master the English language; soon he could read it without difficulty. Conversation he practised on every possible occasion, particularly with street urchins and boot-blacks, with whom he did not feel shy; in turn they were attracted to this young foreigner, whose kind eyes and gentle ways won their confidence.

Two features of British life gave Soloviev some difficulty. The first was the matter of the tall black silk hat, a part of the customary dress of scholars and gentlemen. He felt extremely awkward wearing it at first, soon discovering that consider-able care was necessary before he could manage to keep it securely on his head despite sudden gusts of wind. The other problem concerned British food, not because of the manner of cooking, but because as a vegetarian from childhood he could not accustom himself to the fact that meat occupied so prominent a place on Victorian menus.

Soloviev made friends with a number of Russians then resident in London, including several among the congregation of the Russian Orthodox Church. He frequently passed evenings with the brilliant young sociologist, Professor Maxim Kovalevski, later to be editor of the well-known *Viestnik Evropi*, the Messenger of Europe, the student Igoi Kapoustin, and the university lecturer, Evgenyi E. Yanzhul. The latter was very kind to him; soon Soloviev became a frequent and welcome visitor in the Yanzhul home. Mrs. Yanzhul took pity on this young fellow-countryman who, as she recalled, "usually forgot to have his dinner, and went about most of the time in a half-starved condition." Her motherly heart was touched by his "gloomy, ascetic expression," and she extended the hospitality of their table to Soloviev on every possible occasion. After a few weeks she wrote her parents: "A strange man is this Soloviev. He is very weak, sickly, with a mind unusually prematurely developed. Devoured by scepticism and searching for salvation in mystical belief in spirits, he makes me very sorry for him. There are those here who think that one day he may become insane."

* * *

When Vladimir Soloviev was a boy, Daniel Dunglas Home, a native of Scotland, world-renowned as a medium and exponent of the principles of spiritualism, visited Russia. He was accompanied by the French novelist, Alexander Dumas, who was combining the function of acting as Home's "best man" at his forthcoming wedding to a Russian noblewoman, with collecting material for a travel book he intended writing.

Home's fame had preceded him, and he was not long in Petersburg before Alexander II summoned him to give a seance at Peterhof, the summer residence of the Tsar. The

Emperor is reported to have declared the results of the seance "marvelous," and the further seances Home conducted by royal command made him one of the best-known foreigners in Russia.

In July 1865 Home again visited Russia, spending some time as a guest of the well-known poet-dramatist, Alexei Konstantinovich Tolstoi (1817-1875) at Pustynka, the latter's beautiful country estate outside St. Petersburg, where in later years Soloviev was to be a frequent guest. During the following winter Home gave a number of seances in the presence of the Tsar and the royal family, among whom the Grand Duke Konstantin was particularly impressed by him.

In the winter of 1871-72 Home once again returned to St. Petersburg, this time as the guest of Baron Meyendorff, a leading member of the Court. Meanwhile, the Orthodox Church had forbidden spiritualistic seances, but this of course applied neither to the Imperial Court nor to the nobility. Moreover, in his many years' activity, Home never exhibited his mediumship before public audiences in any case. Hence it was always by royal command that an imperial carriage appeared before Home's lodgings, and shortly afterward the great medium, accompanied by an honor-guard of cavalry was to be seen whirling up the Nevski Prospekt to the Winter Palace. After one of these seances, the Tsar, greatly pleased by the results, asked Home to name a wish, which the Emperor promised in advance would be granted. With characteristic selflessness, somewhat to the surprise of the Tsar, Home asked that a certain criminal under heavy sentence, whose relatives had approached him only that morning asking his help, be pardoned and released. True to his word, the Tsar granted Home's desire.

On February 24, 1871 Home gave a lecture in a great hall in St. Petersburg. The room was filled to suffocation as representatives of the nobility and leading members of the Faculty of the University vied for seats or standing-room. After Home had concluded his address, Professor von Bouteriow, a highly respected member of the Academy of Science, arose and testified to the scientific correctness of Home's remarks. This caused a great sensation, as did the fact that when in March of that same year, Home saw Alexander for the last time, the Tsar presented him with a ring containing a magnificent sapphire surrounded with diamonds as a token of the Emperor's gratitude and favor.

* * *

For Soloviev, the phenomena of mediumism were not something alien or strange in themselves, for from childhood he had had full awareness of the presence of the dead. At times he "spoke" with the dead as naturally and directly as one speaks with one's friend, and he often had difficulty in distinguishing clearly between incarnated and excarnated souls, so alike were they to him. However, Soloviev was well aware that there was considerable difference between his own inner perception and relationship with the dead and those manifestations current in his lifetime under the name of spiritualism. Nevertheless the latter interested him to the point that he attended a number of seances during his stay in London, then the world-capital of spiritualism.

On one of these occasions Soloviev had the unique experience of meeting and witnessing a seance conducted by none other than the famous Kate Fox, one of the American sisters whose discovery in a farmhouse in western New York State on the evening of March 31, 1848 had opened the way to a new perception of life after death for hundreds of thousands of people. It is not difficult to imagine the interest with which Soloviev witnessed the mediumship of one of the celebrated sisters who, as a little girl had given new hope of human immortality and for many had bridged the chasm of the grave.

Among the many important figures associated with the spiritualist movement at that time Soloviev met the well-known British naturalist, distinguished friend of Darwin and Layell, Alfred Russell Wallace, then at work on *His Miracles of Modern Spiritualism*, published in 1881. Soloviev heard lectures on spiritualism by Professor (later Sir William) Crookes, celebrated Oxford scholar, one of Britain's leading chemists, whose papers on his mediumistic investigations in the conservative *Quarterly Journal of Science* he had read with considerable interest.

Meanwhile Daniel Dunglas Home had recently returned from one of his Russian visits, and Soloviev attended one of his seances. Though greatly impressed by Home's personality and reputation, as well he might have been, Soloviev was not entirely convinced by his mediumship, despite the testimony of Viscount Adare, Lord Lindsay and Captain Charles Wynne who swore they had seen Home levitate himself while in a mediumistic trance and float out of one window and in at another in a London apartment. In the literary world were many who avowed total belief in Home's powers, among them Elizabeth Barrett Browning, though her husband was not so enthusiastic, portraying Home in a poem titled *Mr. Sludge, the Medium*. Thomas Carlyle also did not share the current enthusiasm for the powers of his fellow-Scotsman, as John Ruskin reported in a letter to his own spiritualist friend, Mrs. Cowper-Temple: "I had a long talk with Carlyle yesterday. He says spiritualism is real witchcraft and quite wicked. I have a great notion he's right, for he knows a thing or two." However, Carlyle's skepticism did not wholly persuade Ruskin against spritualism, for after attending a seance Home conducted at Broadlands, the home of the Cowper-Temples, he wrote his American friend, Charles Eliot Norton of Harvard: "I have heard wonderful things this very afternoon. I am as giddy as if I had been thrown off Strassbourg steeple and stopped in the air; but thing after thing of this kind is being brought to me. *All spiritualism, however mistaken is not cold.*" (Italics Ruskin's.)

Nevertheless Soloviev' s initial interest soon turned to doubt and finally to disbelief in the phenomena he witnessed. In a letter addressed to his friend Tsertelev in Moscow, Soloviev writes: "I was at the seance of the famous Williams, and found that he was a kind of cheap magician, more insolent than clever. He produced the Egyptian darkness, but performed no other miracles. When a bell, flying through the darkness lighted upon my head, along with it I grasped a muscular hand, the owner of which was certainly no spirit. John King appeared, who looked about as much like a spirit as I resemble an elephant. Yesterday I attended the meeting of the local spiritualists and met the well-known Crookes and his medium, the former Miss Cook. In another week a test will be held in the Spiritualist Society, a seance in light, but with the same Mr. V. who was confused by my expose the last time."

* * *

One can understand the transformation of Soloviev's attitude toward mediumism if one takes into account his spiritual sensitivity which enabled him to detect in the seances he witnessed a materialistic trend—refined though it perhaps was—but which nevertheless tended to drag the spirit down into matter. For the birth of spiritualism in modern times coincided with a kind of climax of materialism in the West, and though beneficent spiritual powers undertook by means of mediumistic manifestations to renew humankind's awareness of the reality and immanence of the spiritual world—an awareness which had been drowned in the flood of materialism of the time—the result was a failure, inasmuch as people erroneously interpreted the manifestations as having their origin *in the world of the dead.* The ultimate effect was that humanity's vision of life beyond the grave became even *more* materialistic than it had been before, and it is an interesting fact that for the first time in our modern era, embalming of corpses began at about the same moment as the Fox Sisters' discovery was made known to the world. It was as though the "voices" sounding out of the heights of spirit were heard only as "voices from the dust," and the cult of the dead of ancient Egypt once again appeared among the living.

In this light it is not surprising that many sensitive, spiritually acute persons like Soloviev ultimately reached conclusions regarding mediumism which coincided with what he wrote to his father: "On one side charlatanry, on the other, blind faith, together with a tiny seed of real magic, which in such a setting it is impossible to get to the bottom of... The spiritualism locally—and all spiritualism generally, since London is its center—*is something very pathetic.*"

* * *

On the other hand, his disappointments in mediumism by no means affected Soloviev's keen interest in other aspects of the esoteric sciences, for he continued his studies in Gnosticism and Kaballa in particular. Examples of automatic writing which he did at this time have been preserved, and he also spoke with enthusiasm of "table-turning" which then enjoyed a great vogue in intellectual and cultured circles.

Soloviev studied with great absorption the alchemistic manuscripts in the British Museum, particularly the most beautiful Splendor Solis, ostensibly written by one Solomon Trismosin, 1582. In this remarkable work, whether he was aware of it or not, Soloviev was faced with a true Rosicrucian document of most extraordinary depth and importance.

Another work which Soloviev studied during August and September, 1875 was the celebrated compilation by the two scholars, Baron Christian Knorr von Rosenroth (1636-1689) and Franciscus Mercurius van Helmont (1614-1699), the *Kabbala Denudata*. The first part of the book, in two volumes, was published at Sulzbach, 1677; the second part, likewise in two volumes, was published in Frankfort a/M in 1684. Incorporating earlier writings and commentary on the esoteric wisdom, the occult "traditions" of the Jewish sages, this work is centered around the *Zohar* which was first published in three volumes, Mantua, 1558-1560, and included some two thousand four hundred closely printed folio pages.

For Soloviev the most important sections of the *Kabbala Denudata* were certainly the extensive discussion and quotation concerning the *Sephir ha Zohar* (which at that time had not yet been published in any modern language), for in the latter work are found reflections of the esoteric reality underlying all exoteric phenomena. There all external creation is represented as the result of a series of "emanations" which have come, stage by stage, out of the *En Soph*, the Infinite One, the primal Cause. Therefore, since in reality humanity's greatest desire is to find the way back to the Divine whence we came, it is necessary first to trace the path of our descent, for the ascent is but the reverse of the latter.

Because of its remarkable content, and because in essence it is a unique esoteric-artistic achievement, born out of the profound spiritual striving of a people, so recorded that the reading of the book can be in itself a personal, spiritual adventure of the most rewarding, exalted kind, the *Zohar* is one of the most important works in the world-treasury of mystical literature.

As the summer wore on, Soloviev became ever more absorbed in his study of the esoteric books and manuscripts he found in abundance in the British Museum Library. His friend Yanzhul recalled seeing him day after day sitting over his studies in the Reading Room, "a concentrated, sad gaze, and the marks of some sort of inner struggle constantly on his face." This "inner struggle" is reflected in a letter Soloviev wrote to his friend, Father Pyotor Preobrazhenski in Russia: "I am busy with something very great, and—if I am not wrong—a very important work which requires my whole strength, and does not allow me to turn my attention to anything else."

* * *

However much he was absorbed in his studies of esoteric subjects, Soloviev nevertheless was also keenly interested in practical social ideas and modern efforts at social reform. He was by no means solely a theoretical scholar; the urge to discover a means of transforming the world by some sort of social miracle arising out of Christian esotericism was strong in him. He was not satisfied with the writings of the contemporary economists and socialists *per se*; he felt their ideas lacked the living warmth and vital power he was convinced a renewed Christian impulse could bring to the solution of the social question.

One of the most remarkable things about Soloviev is that no matter how apparently remote from contemporary life-needs were his areas of research and concern, he never lost his longing to discover practical steps by which he could help others. Though a mystic of extraordinary range and depth, he never alienated himself from the world, nor did his concern for the well-being of humanity, particularly in the social sphere, ever slacken.

Soloviev recognized that although one side of his being is united with the world of spirit, humanity has tasks on earth and a relationship with the earth which also claim his efforts; this he expressed in a poem he wrote in London at this time:

Although to distant shores beyond
By chains unseen we all are bound,
Even in fetters we must fulfill
The round the gods for us have drawn.

Within themselves, as by a higher Will,
All things create yet other wills;
Beneath the mask of matter's calm
The fire divine burns on and on.

* * *

Shortly before Soloviev's arrival in England, the well-known London publisher, John Murray brought out the first British edition of a book which was already making a name for itself in America. Written by Charles Nordhoff, a Californian, it was titled *The Communistic Societies of the United States, from Personal Visit and Observation, including detailed accounts of the Economists, Zoarites, Shakers, the Amana, Oneida, Bethel, Aurora, Icarian and other existing Societies, their Religious Creeds, Social Practices, Numbers, Industries, and Present Condition.*

With the help of his friend Yanzhul, Soloviev studied this book with intense interest, particularly the sections dealing with the life and practice of the members of "The Millennial Church, or United Society of Believers in the Second Appearance of Christ, commonly called Shakers." In the latters' social-religious Christian principles Soloviev found much that was congenial to his own way of thinking. In the Shakers' devotion to Mother Ann Lee, their Foundress, "the embodiment of the Spirit of the Christ in His Second Advent, this time in Female Form," Soloviev believed he found an affinity with his own experience of the divine Sophia. In the Shaker description of "the Archetypal Duality in God," he recognized an element not far removed from his own thoughts and deductions:

"In the Almighty Being we call God, there existed, before humanity was created, and before the worlds were formed, an Eternal Two in One Spirit, who are termed Almighty Power and Infinite Wisdom... the first holds the Seat or Throne of the Eternal Father, and the second, that of the Eternal Mother, and by the co-activity of these Eternal Two the heavens and earth were created, were set in order and are sustained."

* * *

In August, 1871 a leading English-American exponent of Shakerism, Elder Frederick W. Evans had visited London and there delivered a lecture in St. George's Hall on the principles and teachings of Mother Ann Lee, under the title, *Religious Communism*. The well-known English traveler and author, William Hepworth Dixon was in the chair, and the entire text of Evans' address was printed in the newspapers. Soloviev read with interest the report of Evans' lecture and also his *Autobiography of a Shaker*.

In Nordhoff's book Soloviev read Evans' statement to the effect that the Millennial Church of the Shakers included among its fundamental tenets, "revelation, spiritualism, celebacy, oral confession, community, non-resistance, peace, the gift of healing, miracles, physical health, and separation from the world." Nordhoff also reported a conversation with Elder Evans when the former visited the large Shaker Community at Mount Lebanon, on the border between New York and Massachusetts: "Elder Frederick told me that 'spiritual' manifestations were known among the Shakers many years before Kate Fox was born; that they had all manner of manifestations, but chiefly visions and communications through mediums." Nordhoff recorded that one form of "manifestation" was the writing of "inspired books," among them *The Divine Book of Holy and Eternal Mother Wisdom*, in the preface of which it is stated that:

"This work is called 'Holy Mother Wisdom's Book' because Holy and Eternal Wisdom is the Mother or the

Bearing Spirit of all the works of God; and because it was especially revealed through the line of the female, being Wisdom's likeness; and she lays special claim to this work and places her seal upon it."

These words about "Holy Mother Wisdom" touched a responsive chord in Soloviev, for they were, he felt, akin to his "Meetings" with his Eternal Friend, whom he described as the personification of the Divine Wisdom, the Sophia.

Here, however, it should be emphasized that Soloviev's Sophia-mysticism was not primarily the result of tradition or study, but was the fruit of his personal vision, his own spiritual insight. This is borne out by his statement: "I have found in the mystics many confirmations of my own ideas, but no new light."

In the teachings of others Soloviev found no accounts of esoteric experiences surpassing his own spiritual illumination and personal experience, because in him had been unlocked that faculty Goethe called "the Eternal Feminine," which ever "leads humanity upward and on."

Rudolf Steiner once pointed out that the Eternal Feminine is really a power in the human soul which permits itself to be transformed by the world of spirit and hence unites with and progresses in that world. He further indicated that this soul-faculty of the Eternal Feminine exists potentially *in every human being*, capable of lifting that person into the eternal worlds.

Soloviev noted with interest Nordhoff's report of the Shakers' conviction that with the founding of their spiritual community the Day of judgment, the beginning of Christ's millennial kingdom, had come to the earth. They were certain that the "last things" were being accomplished, that the new heaven and the renewed earth were "now in process of formation," that they were living in "the last dispensation." Hence their conviction that their communal activities were completing the course of creation and preparing for immortality, was highly eschatological in essence. When they established their communities, set up their farming and industrial activities, developed their remarkable inventions and crafts, as well as their carefully regulated manner of living according to "Order," each single detail, down to the smallest, carefully prescribed according to rule, this was done because they saw in the community they were establishing on earth the ultimate fulfillment of God's intentions, *in the light of the Divine Wisdom, the Holy Sophia.*

In Mother Ann Lee's advice to the pioneer Shakers to "live as though you had a thousand years before you, and as though you were going to die tomorrow," Soloviev recognized a clear expression of Christian eschatology. Her words reflected an attitude characteristic of the Christians of the first centuries, when Christ's *Parousia*, His Second Advent, was expected momentarily, thus bringing about the fulfillment of prophecy, the "last days" of earth-existence. In the ideas of Universal Christianity and Free Theocracy which Soloviev was to develop in his later years, one can see how much he owed his brief "meeting" with the Shakers during his London visit, and what an indispensable element in Christian life and practice he considered their esoteric and eschatological viewpoints to be.

* * *

As summer turned to early autumn, Soloviev found himself more or less alone in London, for a number of his closest Russian friends returned home in early September. From his letters one can discover his increasing preoccupation with the immanence of the end of the world, of the divine consummation of all things, and there arose in him the strong desire to serve as an instrument in preparing for that event. On the other hand, he longed to be back in Russia, as he wrote his parents: "I feel homesick indeed, and I shall try to return to Russia next July."

Nevertheless, his studies in the British Museum continued to occupy him fully, and there one afternoon of a cloudy September day he had the second great spiritual experience of his life.

Blessed months, could I ever forget you?
Though not because of beauty's phantoms fading,
Nor human passions, nor Nature's grandeur,
But because my soul was filled with you alone, Beloved!

Most of the time I was alone in the Library,
And, believe it or not, but God is my witness:
Mysterious powers led me to choose for reading
Everything possible concerning Her.

And if by chance my erring whims suggested
That from the shelves I take down other books,
Such strange things happened then
That, quite confused, I left for home.

Eventually, simply reading about the Sophia, his Eternal Friend, was not enough. Recalling his childhood experience, his first "Meeting" with her, he determined to call upon her once again.

Once in days of Autumn
I said to her, O flower divine,
I feel your presence here! But why
Have you not appeared to me since childhood?

Hardly had I thought these words
When suddenly all was filled with golden azure,
And you were there in heavenly radiance;
There I saw your face, your face alone!

That single moment brought me years of happiness,
No worldly matters could distract my soul;
But were I to mention more of this,
My words would empty seem, and meaningless.

But now the appearance becomes clearer; he is in the very presence of his Eternal Friend:

I said to her, you once let me see your face,
But your noble image I yet long to see;
The gift you granted to a child
To a grown-up man you'll surely not refuse!

Within me then I heard the message: "Be in Egypt!"
To France then and to Southern countries lies my road;
My feelings struggled not at all with reason,
And reason—like one dumb—said not a word.

As quickly as he could, Soloviev terminated his work in London and booked passage for Cairo. In as casual a manner as possible, giving no hint of the intensity of the spiritual direction he was about to follow, Soloviev wrote a brief note to his mother:

London, October 14, 1875

Dear Mother:

It will be quite unnecessary to send me an overcoat because inside the houses here it is colder than it is outside. The winter has not yet begun, but already I have quite a cold. Fortunately, my studies require several months' stay in Egypt, and I depart thence day after tomorrow. I shall go via Italy and Greece, and shall write you enroute.

Vladimir Soloviev as he looked at the time of his
London and Egyptian journeys

Soloviev's signature in the Readers' Register at the British Museum

Friedrich Wilhelm Joseph von Schelling (1775-1854),
German philosopher

His travel southward took Soloviev through Paris (where in a letter to his father he characterized the French as "A more ordinary people I don't know!") to Turin, Piacenza, Ancona, Brindisi by train. Then by British steamer he crossed the Mediterranean to Cairo. He took lodging at the Hotel Abbat where he met a retired Russian General Faddeyev, with whom he had many conversations "on philosophic subjects and on many other themes as well." In Cairo he renewed his friendship with Prince Zertelev, nephew of the poet-dramatist, Alexei Tolstoi. The former was distinguished as the first authority on Schopenhauer in Russia, author of a book titled *Schopenhauer's Philosophy*, and of a volume of poems with a strong Buddhistic flavor.

Soloviev passed the weeks in studying Coptic, but always he awaited "the moment," which at last came:

There I awaited the promised meeting,
Till finally in stillness of the silent night
Like a cool breeze I heard the whisper,
"I'm in the desert; you'll surely find me there!"

Soloviev hurried to the desert, despite the stifling heat, dressed as he was in his London clothes, his thin form hidden beneath the heavy folds of his long coat, tall silk hat on his head, his hands encased in black gloves. Suddenly a band of wandering Bedouins appeared and took him prisoner, uncertain whether to kill him outright or hold him for ransom. But the moment they had a good look at his long black hair and beard, his pale, almost bloodless face, his unusual costume, they were convinced they had captured the Prince of Darkness himself. Tremblingly they released him, and he wandered off alone as the setting sun cast long rays across the desert sands.

Meanwhile, silent night descends to earth,
All at once, without twilight;

Around me, only silent darkness,
Above me, night and shining stars.

Lying on the sand I look and listen,
Somewhere, far away, a jackal howls;
Probably he would devour me,
For quite unarmed I'm lying here.

Yet worse than jackal is the piercing cold;
The day was hot, but now the air is chill;
The cold glitter of the stars above,
The bitter frost below, conspire to banish sleep.

Long I lay there, until at last
A gentle whisper: "Sleep, my poor friend!"
I fell asleep, and upon awaking,
Celestial vault and earth with roses breathed.

In radiance of heavenly glory,
Your eyes aflood with azure fire,
Shine forth like ethereal dawning
Of cosmic creation's primal day!

Everything that was, is, and ever will be,
One moment's fleeting glance encompassed;
Distant forests, seas and rivers far below me,
Snowy mountain-heights, enwrapped in shimmering blue.

I gazed upon it all, and all was fair,
In form of Womanhood, embracing all in one;
The infinite encircled there, yet limitless,
Before me and within me—You alone!

O radiant Countenance, you have not deceived me!
Your fullest glory I beheld amid the desert waste;

Ever will your heavenly roses bloom within me
Where'er my stream of life may flow.

It lingered but a moment, ere the vision faded;
The sun rose glorious in the eastern sky;
The silent desert spread around me; my soul was praying
To the blessed sound of chiming bells within.

Exalted by this supernal atmosphere of transcendent beauty,
having met his Eternal Friend in "the holy land of Shem," the
land of Isis, whose veil was lifted for him, even if but for a
moment, Soloviev knew beyond a shadow of a doubt that
the blessing of the Holy Sophia, the Divine Wisdom of God
rested upon his life's course.

* * *

During his stay in Cairo, Soloviev wrote two short poems
in which he speaks further about his Eternal Friend, the
Sophia. The first is reminiscent of his meeting with her in the
desert:

Today my Queen appeared to me in azure,
My heart was beating in sweet ecstasy;
In the rays of dawn my soul
Began to shine with silent light —
As far away, the fading embers
Of evil flames of earthly fire
Were dying, vanishing in empty vapor.

The other poem, somewhat more pictorial in quality,
employing images drawn from Soloviev's esoteric experiences,
also reflects his study of mystical writings. Although this poem
was written in Egypt, he already imagines himself in Russia,
hoping that his Friend's love and care will accompany him in

that far country, despite the distractions that may cloud his
vision of her meanwhile:

A lofty palace with seven golden pillars
Has my Queen —
A crown of seven faces, with countless jewels
Has my Queen.

A garden filled with roses and with lilies
Has my Queen —
The ripples of the silver stream reflect the tresses
Of my Queen.

But my Queen hears not the plashing waters,
She gazes not upon the smiling roses;
The light within her eye is veiled in sadness,
Her dream is heavy now with mourning.

Far away, in a clouded, midnight land,
Amid cold mists and winter storms,
In lonely struggle with dark, evil powers
She sees her friend,—alone, forsaken.

Casting aside her diamond crown,
Leaving behind her golden palace,
To her friend, all unexpected,
She beckons with her blessed hand.

As tender spring o'ershadows winter's gloom,
Radiant with joy, o'er him she bends,
Enwrapping him in silent tenderness
Within her shining mantle's folds.

Powers of darkness collapse in dust,
The lonely one now flames with pure fire;

Eternal love is shining in her azure eyes
As thus she softly whispers to her friend:

"Like ocean waves, unstable is your will, I know,
To me not long ago you pledged your faith;
Though your word you've broken, think you
That by this you could change my heart?"

* * *

Soloviev's "Meetings" with his Eternal Friend whom he identified with the divine Isis, the Sophia, "the universal substance,
the absolute unity of the whole, the essential Wisdom of God,"
are central to his entire life. His visions of the Sophia have
been described as his "Damascus-experience," a reference to
St. Paul's supersensible meeting with the Risen Christ.

In his attempts to convey something of his Sophia-ex-
perience, particularly in his poems on this theme, Soloviev
employs figures which are used by others to describe their
own spiritual encounters: the roses, the azure, the golden
radiance, and so on. Nevertheless, his description is essentially his own, and one can sense his difficulties, his hesitancy
in attempting to convey the profound realities which stood
before his vision. This is somewhat similar to the experience
of Goethe when the latter struggled to embody his own spiritual vision in the concluding scenes of his mighty *Faust* Part II:
"I found this part," he wrote, "extremely difficult to render,
and treating of such supersensible, such almost inconceivable
things, I might easily have lost myself in the void, had I not
used clearly-defined conceptions borrowed from Christianity
and the Church."

Soloviev described the Sophia in various ways; once he
characterized her as "the guardian angel of the world, overshadowing all creatures with its wings as a bird her little
ones, *in order to raise them gently to true being*." But in order

that such a principle could become active in the world, Something had to enter into earthly evolution. This Something is described by Soloviev in his work on Plato:

> "By his noble death Socrates finally consumed the power of purely human wisdom ... In order to advance further and higher than did Socrates, not only in theory and desire, but in actual, heroic accomplishment, more than the human was necessary. After Socrates, who by word and example taught people how to die in a manner worthy of humankind, no one was able to go further nor higher, with the exception of Him who has the power of resurrection to everlasting life. The weakness and decline of the great Plato are significant because they strongly indicate and explain humanity's inability to achieve its destiny by the strength of intellect, genius and moral will alone—because they explain the necessity for the actual existence of the Divine Human."

The role of the Sophia and the Christ is clearly and wonderfully explained by Soloviev: "In the creative sphere of the Word and the Holy Spirit, the divine substance, the Sophia appears in its true nature as a radiant, heavenly Being, free from the darkness of earth. The sphere of the Father is absolute, self-contained Light, having no relationship with darkness. The Son, or the Word, is the light revealed, the shining ray, illumining external objects by reflection. Finally, the Holy Spirit is the ray reflected by the earthly element, refracting and creating in this element the heavenly spectrum of the seven archetypal Spirits, like the colors of the Rainbow."

* * *

The French author, de Vogue, who met Soloviev in Cairo wrote: "To have beheld his countenance once was to remember him forever; pale, thin, framed by his long, some-what curling hair, his face with its well-defined features was completely dominated by his large eyes—wonderful, pene-trating, visionary eyes. Such faces must have been the inspi-ration of the monastic icon-painters of earlier times as they searched for a model for the countenance of Christ. Here was the face of Christ as he was beheld by the Slavic peoples—the long-visaged, introspective, meditating, sorrowful Christ."

In March, 1876 as he prepared to leave Cairo for his journey home, Soloviev wrote his mother in a half-humorous vein: "In Italy I shall pass a month at Sorrento where in the quietness I hope to write a mystical-theosophical-philosoph-ical-theurgical-political work in dialogue form." However, this work seems never to have been written, perhaps because of an injury Soloviev sustained as the result of a fall from a horse while climbing Mount Vesuvius, necessitating some weeks in bed.

From Sorrento Soloviev went to Nice where he wrote his poem, *The Song of the Ophites*. The latter were an early Gnostic sect, described by Iranaeus, Origen and others. They honored the serpent as a part of their cosmological ideas, related to beliefs and traditions of Babylonia, Egypt and the East. According to their picture of Creation, as the Christ ascended into the heavens with his Mother, the Holy Spirit, a spark of light fell from them upon the primeval waters, as the Sophia. The Ophites taught that the Serpent was sent as a blessing to Adam and Eve by the Sophia, but brought about their Fall and Expulsion instead. In the figure of the Christ himself the Ophites saw the Serpent returned to earth to bless humanity.

Soloviev's *Song of the Ophites* pictures the mystical marriage of the lily and the rose, reminding one of the Annunciation paintings of the old masters, where the heavenly visitor, Gabriel, is frequently represented carrying a lily in his hand, while the listening soul in the figure of the woman, of Mary, sits in the shelter of the house, often surrounded by a garden of roses, deep in silent, inward meditation.

In the *Canticles of Solomon* "the lily of the valley and the rose of Sharon" are spoken of. There the lily and rose are more than two members of the plant kingdom, for they are images of deep forces working in and through the human being, the lily connected with the Past, with heredity, with the laws of necessity, the rose identified with the Future, with the infinite possibilities which can arise out of the fact of the freedom of humanity.

Thus the lily is frequently identified with the forces of Gabriel, the announcer of the divine birth out of the world of heavenly necessity, out of the sphere of the Father God. It is related to the *head* forces, pictured in the three petals of the Fleur de Lys, the "flower of light," bearer of heavenly *wisdom* from the world of the stars to the earth. In the three rays, the three petals, are prefigured the Three Kings, described in the Gospel of Matthew.

On the other hand, the rose has long been identified with the forces of the *heart* which grow up in earthly men, working in perfect balance between what is above and what is below, evidenced in the quality of *faith* which starts in poverty and simplicity, and from that tiny seed, leads on to freedom. Thus Luther's characterisation of faith as "*a new sense* beyond the other senses," points to the quality of *future* involved in the heart-forces pictured in the rose, prefiguring the Shepherds of the Fields, described in the Gospel of Luke.

Thus the Christ comes to the listening, awakened soul in the darkness of Nature, in the cold of winter, and unites the lily of knowledge and the rose of faith. Shepherds and Kings are joined in a mystical marriage of the forces of knowledge and faith, the lily and the rose. Thus is portrayed the task confronting every human being on the journey toward the spirit.

In his *Song of the Ophites* Soloviev makes use of other images as well, for example, the pearls—bringing to mind "the pearl of great price"—which are cast into the cup, the chalice, in which the deed of a transformation, a divine Alchemy, takes place. The dove figures the Holy Spirit, which in the "coils of the Serpent," the embrace of Christ, is at peace.

The Song of the Ophites

White lily with red rose
We marry,
And with secret, prophetic dream
We attain eternal Truth.

Speak the prophetic word!
Quickly cast your pearls into the cup;
Now bind our Dove
With new coils of the old Serpent.

The free heart hurts not!
Should the Dove fear Prometheus' fire?
The pure Dove is calm
In the flaming coils of the mighty Serpent.

Sing about violent tempests!
In violent tempests we find repose;
For white lily with red rose
We marry.

The working of the Rosicrucian divine Alchemy, the marriage of the lily and the rose, the uniting of the forces of head and heart, of necessity and freedom within the human being, is pictured in these verses. The working of the Promethean fire, cutting away the fetters of the past, the chains of ancient necessity, which comes about as human beings take the first steps in the direction of true freedom, cannot frighten the heart which has found its relationship with the Christ-imbued forces of Divine Wisdom, of the Sophia. The last verse pictures the mystical union; inasmuch as this brings new possibilities to birth, it creates a "violent tempest," reminiscent of the tempest described in the opening scene of *The Chymical Wedding of Christian Rosenkreutz*. However, under the guidance of Divine Wisdom, secure and certain of the working of a divine purpose acting in human destiny, the human being finds "rest" and calm. Thus Soloviev's poem is not mere imagery nor empty fantasy; it is an artistic achievement pointing to profound mysteries in the spiritual life of humanity and nature.

* * *

In May, 1876 Soloviev's sojourn in Western Europe drew to a close, and he wrote in a half-humorous vein to his father: "Since it appears you have been longing for me, I shall travel no more, either in the Eastern graveyards or the Western, and since many persons gifted with the ability to foretell the future prophesy many wanderings for me, I therefore shall wander in the vicinity of Moscow!"

One of the students who attended Soloviev's lectures in the University of Moscow, wrote this impression of them: "He experienced at that time days of veritable triumph. His eloquence evoked approval from all the students. With breathless excitement we followed his daring expositions as one follows the deeds of an acrobat on a tightrope. Which misstep will hurl him into the depths? But with Soloviev this was not to be thought of! Equipped with great learning he led the thought again and again to the religious ideal, and thereby pacified even the strictest conservatives. Nevertheless, his thought balanced itself just at the brink of deep abysses with such flexibility that sometimes we were amazed and confused, for one had to traverse areas where one could say nothing and everything at the same time!"

Often the way grew dark, however, and he had to wait for the return of those forces of life and renewal which came to his consciousness like the return of springtime after the cold of winter. This longing for the blessing of his Friend he described in these lines:

A Fragment

Why do you need love and tenderness
When a fire burns within your breast,
And the whole world of fairy tales
Speaks so clearly to your soul?
When in an azure mist
Your life-path lies before you,
And your goal is won in advance;
Your victory precedes your struggle,
And silver threads link your heart
With lands of dreams;
O you Eternal Gods,
Take away my bitter trial,
And give me back the strength
Of those first showers of Spring!

* * *

Soon after his return from Egypt, Soloviev's friend, Prince Zertelev, introduced him to the latter's aunt, Countess Tolstoi, the widow of Count Alexei K. Tolstoi. The Countess was very kind to Soloviev, and through the years that followed he was a frequent guest at her estate, Pustynka where he found a very congenial atmosphere, ideal for his creative work. More than this, the Countess was deeply interested in his mystical striving, his interest in Jacob Boehme, and above all his experiences with the Sophia. Soloviev's letters to Countess Tolstoi reveal the deep spiritual affinity which grew up between them and was intensified with the passing years.

Soloviev eventually resigned his teaching position in Moscow and moved to St. Petersburg, where he was made a member of the Committee on Education in the Ministry of Public Education. A large part of his time he spent in writing, while his official capacity brought him into contact with many leaders in the intellectual, social and religious life of St. Petersburg and the Empire.

On January 26, 1878 Soloviev began a series of public lectures in the University of St. Petersburg, and also in the Institute of Higher Studies for Women. Among these were twelve lectures on *Godmanhood*; these were a literary and cultural event in St. Petersburg. Leading figures of the intellectual circles of Russia sat enthralled by the eloquence, charm, originality of thought, and above all, by *the warmth of personal experience* that sounded through everything the lecturer said. Later the text of the lectures was printed in a leading church periodical, and Soloviev's name and thoughts became known throughout Russia. Since the lectures on *Godmanhood* have been published in English translation, it is not necessary to discuss their content here.

* * *

In the spring of 1878, Aloysha, the little son of Feyodor Dostoyevski died suddenly. The child was less than three years old, and this second loss of a child was almost more than the parents could bear. Prostrated by the shock of the boy's death, Dostoyevski remained on his knees through the whole night, praying beside the body of his son.

During the weeks following the child's funeral, Dostoyevski remained inconsolable. The manuscript of his new novel, *The Brothers Karamazov*, on which he had worked so energetically in the early months of the year, remained untouched.

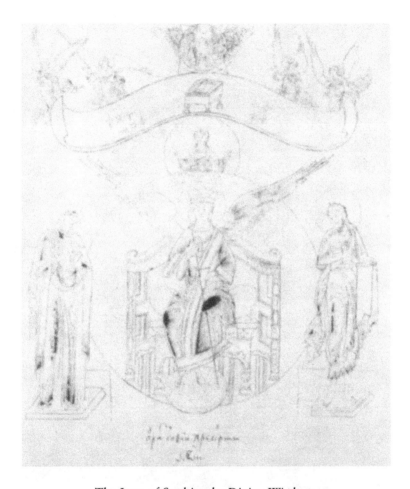

The Icon of Sophia, the Divine Wisdom.
A page from an ancient guide-book for icon-painters

Vladimir Soloviev at the time he took up residence
in St. Petersburg

Finally his wife, Anna Nikolaevna, recalled that for a long time he had cherished the idea of visiting the famous monastery of Optina Pystin, located some one hundred fifty miles southwest of Moscow in Kaluga Province, in order to talk with some of the *Startsi*, Elders, particularly Abbot Amvrosi, friend of Konstantin Leontyev. Therefore she suggested that Dostoyevski make the trip.

However, who could accompany him? Anna Nikolaevna would close the apartment in St. Petersburg and go to Starya Russa for the summer, and he could join her there upon his return. Then together they hit upon an idea: the young philosopher, Vladimir Soloviev, kind, gentle, understanding—he seemed the ideal traveling companion for Dostoyevski. Anna Nikolaevna felt that this impractical, doubtless quite incapable young man would nevertheless instinctively know exactly what to do in case her husband was taken with an epileptic siezure on the journey, how to care for him. Dostoyevski knew that Soloviev was in Moscow at that moment, so—taking the unfinished *Karamazov* manuscript with him to show to the publisher, Katkov, in hope of obtaining an advance—he set out.

Katkov greeted Dostoyevski warmly and, after examining the first chapters of the *Brothers Karamazov*, gave him an advance payment. His financial affairs temporarily in order, Dostoyevski sought out Soloviev in order to persuade him to go with him to Optina Pystin. He wrote to Anna Nikolaevna: "I went to the Neskuchny Garden to see Soloviev... I found him at home; he was very strange, gloomy and weary..." In such a mood it was easy to persuade his young friend to make the journey with him. A letter from Dostoyevski describes their experiences: "Soloviev and I left on Friday, June 23. All we knew was that we had to travel by the Moscow-Kursk Railway as far as Sergievo, five stations beyond Tula, about three hundred versts from Moscow. There we were told it was a thirty-five verst drive to Optina Monastery. But on our way to Sergievo we discovered it was actually sixty versts, not thirty-five. At last we arrived at Sergievo, but there we were told we would have to travel *one hundred twenty*, not sixty versts, and not all the way by the post road, but half the journey was along a side road, which meant traveling with hired horses, which we would have to stop and feed enroute. We spent the nights in villages along the way, and were rattled about in a terrible carriage. But we spent two days and nights in the Optina Monastery. Then we returned with the same horses and again traveled for two days back to Sergievo; altogether it took us exactly *seven days*, including the day we started!"

* * *

Optina Pystin had become increasingly famous as a spiritual mecca for Russians of every class for some fifty years at the time Dostoyevski and Soloviev visited it. Inspired by the example of the famous *Starets* Paisius Velichkovski of Mt. Athos, some of whose pupils had revived ancient mystical practices at Optina at the end of the eighteenth century, the spirituality of the monks and Elders had attracted a whole series of famous men in the first decades of the nineteenth century, among them Ivan Kireyevski, who increased the fame of the monastery by advising the monks on publications, including their remarkable series of translations of the writings of the Fathers of the Church and outstanding works on Hesychasm, the mystical "path of stillness and repose," the way of initiation into the Divine Mysteries.

The Elders of Optina taught and practised meditation on "the Uncreated Light" manifested at the Transfiguration of Christ on Mount Tabor, which, though present in everything and enveloping all things within itself, is hidden from human beings until, through spiritual training, they are able to perceive it.

One of the most significant aspects of hesychast mystical training as it was carried out at Optina and in countless other

MORNING MEDITATION OF
THE ELDERS AT OPTINA PYSTIN

Grant that with peaceful minds we may face all this new day is to bring;

Grant us grace to surrender ourselves utterly to Thy divine Will;

Instruct and prepare us in all things for every hour of this day.

Whatever tidings may come to us this day, may we accept them tranquilly, firmly convinced that everything that happens to us fulfills our divinely-willed destiny.

Govern our thoughts and feelings in everything we do or say, granting us the wisdom when to speak and when to remain silent.

When unexpected, unforeseen things happen, let us never forget for even a moment that everything comes from Above.

Teach and guide us that we conduct ourselves in all sincerity and reasonableness toward every other human being, helping us that we bring neither confusion, doubt nor sorrow to anyone.

Bestow upon us, O Lord, strength to endure the weariness this day's labor will bring, and give us the courage that each of us may bear his full share in all its tasks and events.

Guide Thou our willing, teaching us to pray, to believe, to hope, to bear, to forgive and—above all—*to love.*

This meditation was included by generations of Elders at Optina Pystin in their daily devotions.

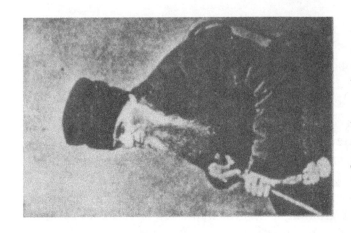

Staretz Amvrosi:
the prototype of Staretz Zossima
in Dostoyevski's *Brothers Karamazov*

The House of Staretz Amvrosi in Optina Pystin.
Here Soloviev and Dostoyevski had their
conversations with the famous Elder.

holy places in Russia, concerns the Prayer of the Heart, which begins as a verbal expression, "Lord Jesus Christ, Son of God, have mercy upon me, a sinner." Eventually, after long practice, this sinks into the heart as "praying without ceasing," whether asleep or awake. This method of prayer is wonderfully described in a little book first published at Kazan in 1884, and more recently in English translation, under the title, *The Way of a Pilgrim*. Both Dostoyevski and Soloviev knew countless men and women, priests, nuns and laymen alike, who had made this mystical experience the object and practice of their lives.

To the saintly Elders of Optina Pystin, as well as to many another monastery throughout the broad Russian land in the mid-nineteenth century and later, streamed the despairing, the infirm, the disillusioned, the disappointed, the shattered in body and soul in the hope that through the advice, the teaching, and above all, the prayers of the Elders they might find consolation and restoration to life. Of the many saintly monks in the history of Optina from its re-foundation in the first decade of the nineteenth century, three rank first in spiritual importance: Leonid (Nagoulkin, 1768-1841), Makarius (Ivanov, 1788-1860) and Amvrosi (Grenkov, 1812-1891). Leonid is remembered for his quickness of wit and friendliness, which made him a great favorite with the peasants who came to him for spiritual advice. Makarius, on the other hand, was a gentle scholar, a translator, a fine musician, lover of flowers and books. His influence was particularly great among educated men and women, to whom he wrote his famous *Letters to Lay People*, published by the Optina monks in 1880, translated and published in English as *Russian Letters of Direction*, 1944. Finally, Amvrosi, an extraordinary judge of character, possessed of a great wisdom and a golden heart, was loved by all who came into his presence. He was at home with the simplest peasant and the most polished diplomat; his friends were legion.

* * *

As the dusty country road wound its way among rolling meadows and fields of wheat, barley and rye, the two travelers could see the monastery from a distance, white against the dark masses of deep forest behind. The white walls, protected from the weather by tiny blue-green tiles, seemed to float upward magically from the gentle meadows surrounding them, rising to a cluster of larger and smaller domes, glowing like flames against the clear blue vault of the sky and topped by bright gold crosses.

A small river, the Zhizdra, still swollen from spring rains, separated the travelers from the monastery, but a crude ferry—a simple platform with railings on each side, guided by a heavy rope, suspended above the water from shore to shore—awaited them. As Soloviev and Dostoyevski, stiff with the jolting of the roads, climbed out of their carriage, a monk greeted them and carefully led the horses and vehicle onto the ferry. Aside from two peasants and a merchant's family, they were the only passengers. Two monks cast off from the sandy shore, bordered with willows and scrub pines. Laboriously, slowly they tugged at the heavy rope, hand over hand. Little by little the ferry edged away from the bank, rocked its way across the stream, and at length was made fast to the opposite shore.

The road led through a mighty forest, carpeted heavily with pine needles. Some of the trees were so huge in girth that four men could join hands around them only with difficulty. The trunks swept upward to dizzy heights; the great columns were topped with dark-green boughs, far above. The silence was broken only by the jingle of the harness of the horses, an occasional snap as a twig broke beneath a carriage wheel, or the singing of birds somewhere in the dim recesses of the forest. The travelers seemed to have entered another world, a world of peace, of silence, where the turmoil and struggle of modern life had never penetrated.

The church in Optina Pystin Monastery

The pilgrims' area in Optina Pystin Monastery

General view of the monastery of Optina Pystin

As they passed beneath the archway with its icon and lamp which burned night and day, they were faced with the small church of St. John, painted pink. Beyond, within the rectangular enclosure they caught glimpses of many low wood buildings, some white-washed, others dark with age. Further off, the ripples of a large fish-pond caught their eye, as did the luxuriant, well-kept vegetable gardens, and the profusion of flowers everywhere. The red of the roof-tiles of the buildings was matched by red-painted porches and entrances, half hidden beneath flowering vines.

On this beautiful June day Soloviev and Dostoyevski were deeply moved by the atmosphere of this famous place, aware that many a fellow-countryman and foreigner had visited this monastery before them. For example, Gogol had come here decades before, and even now some of the older monks could remember his pale face, his long black hair, his pride of intellect. Elder Leonid who was Abbot then, had prophesied that Gogol would lose that intellect at the end of his life, and like Nebuchadnezzar would eat the grass of the field, the herbs of bitterness. And in a sense, he did. All his creative work, all he had accomplished by means of his proud intellect, was brought to nothing. Bitterness overcame his soul, dreariness and melancholia became his daily companions, and even the religion of joy which he had witnessed among the monks here at Optina became in him a twisted fanaticism. Destroying his last manuscripts in the fire, his world sank into the dark gulf of mental collapse. Thus he lived until at last death came to him as friend and consolation.

The two visitors spoke with Elder Amvrosi three times during their brief stay at Optina, and twice Dostoyevski spoke with him in private. And the monastery itself, the life of the monks, the words of Amvrosi, the whole impression of the visit were to appear later in the pages of *The Brothers Karamazov*, somewhat to the dismay of the monks of Optina when the book came into their hands.

In the words of comfort the venerable Father Zossima addressed to the peasant mother grieving over her dead child, it is not difficult to see a reflection of the talks Dostoyevski had with Elder Amvrosi concerning the death of the author's son. In the figure of Aloysha Karamazov, the young monk, one can observe qualities Dostoyevski noted in his young companion on this visit to Optina Pustyn, Vladimir Soloviev.

* * *

In the opening of the second part of *The Brothers Kara-mazov* occurs the celebrated farewell conversation of Elder Zossima:

"Fathers and Teachers: Never until today have I told even him why the face of this youth is so dear to me. Now I will tell you. His countenance has been as it were a remembrance and a prophecy for me. At the dawn of my life, when I was still a child, I had an elder brother who died before my eyes at seventeen... He appeared to me first in my childhood, and here again at the end of my pilgrimage, he seems to have come back to me once more. It is marvelous, Fathers and Teachers, that Aloysha, who has some, though not a great resemblance in face, seems to me so like him spiritually that many times I have taken him for that young man, my brother, mysteriously returned to me at the end of my earth-pilgrimage as a reminder and an inspiration."

Some years after Dostoyevski's death his widow wrote the following words in her copy of *The Brothers Karamazov* opposite the passage quoted above:

"This was how Dostoyevski regarded his intimate friend, the young philosopher, Vladimir Soloviev, who, in his spirituality reminded him of Ivan Shidlovski, the friend who had had such a beneficial influence on the author in his youth."

* * *

The five years between 1877 and 1881 were memorable in the public activity of Vladimir Soloviev. His popularity as a lecturer reached a great height in this period, and at this time he produced three of his major philosophical books. In 1877 his *Philosophical Foundations of Integral Knowledge* appeared. This was followed in the next year by his *Twelve Lectures on Godmanhood*, and two years later by his *Criticism of Abstract Principles*. These three works are of cardinal importance for an understanding of Soloviev's creative approach to religious teaching and philosophical thinking.

* * *

In the last days of September, 1879 word reached Soloviev in St. Petersburg that his father was seriously ill, his life despaired of. The son at once went to Moscow where, on the fourth of October Sergei Mikhailovich Soloviev, the most famous historian of Russia since Karamzin, died. In the afternoon of that day, Vladimir wrote in a letter: "It is a very sad time I am passing through, dear friend."

All night after his father's death, Vladimir remained beside the coffin, reading prayers and Scriptures for the dead. His sister recalled: "In that one night my brother was quite changed." The death of his father, with whom he had never been particularly intimate, nevertheless made a profound impression upon the son.

For the remainder of his life Soloviev made frequent trips to Moscow to visit his mother who, of all her nine children, loved Vladimir the most.

* * *

Impressive as was what he said, *what Soloviev was as a human being* profoundly touched those who heard him speak or came into personal contact with him. The words Dostoyevski put into the mouth of Elder Zossima in his farewell talk with Aloysha Karamazov apply to Soloviev:

> "You will go forth from these walls, but will live like a monk in the world. You will have enemies, but even your foes will love you. Life will bring you many misfortunes, but you will find your happiness in them; you will bless life and will make others bless it—and this is what matters most, after all."

It was this capacity to cause others "to bless life," to accept their destiny, to understand the deep wisdom hidden in all that life brought them, that caused men and women to fill great halls in St. Petersburg and Moscow to hear Soloviev's lectures. For he was unique among public speakers in the Russia of his time: his words worked like magic upon his hearers. For example, he once spoke about conscience and the test for human deeds: "The best criterion of conscience is always close at hand; it is this: Before making any important decision, whether of personal or social importance, call up the image of Christ in your mind. Let it freely stand before your soul, and ask: 'Would he do this?' In other words, 'Will he approve of this action or not? Will he bless me for it or not?' I invite everyone to verify his conscience in this way, for it cannot fail. Whenever you have a doubt, while you are still in a position to reflect and choose, think of your Lord, think of him as living, as he truly is, and place your burden of doubt before him. And he has already taken it upon himself—not, indeed, to relieve you of responsibility for your wicked doings, but so you may turn to him, lean upon him and thus be enabled to reject evil and become an instrument of infallible truth on the most difficult occasions. If all men of good will—private individuals, public figures, Christian leaders—would do this, then already the Second Coming would have begun and the judgment of Christ be prepared, for 'My time is at hand.' Again he described the necessity and inevitability of the coming of the Christ against the course of events in the spiritual history of humanity: "Three steps can be observed in the Old Testament. The first mediators between the Jewish people and God were the ancient Patriarchs: Abraham, Isaac and Jacob. They *believed* in a personal God, and this belief was the content of their own personal lives. Their successors and leaders of Israel: the God-seer, Moses, David, 'the man whom God loves,' and Solomon, the creator of the great Temple, received imperative manifestations of this personal God and worked to imbue the social life and the religious cult of their people with the meaning of these manifestations. God bore witness, face to face, to the outward prophecy and Covenant with Israel. Those who came after them, the third and last step, the Prophets of the Jewish people, realized the insufficiency of this external Covenant, and they felt and prophesied another, inner unification of the Godhead with the soul of the human being in the person of the Messiah, son of David and of God. But they did not envision this Messiah as a leader of the Jewish people only, but as 'a sign to the Gentiles,' as the leader of the whole humanity reborn.

"While the setting for the inhumanization (the Incarnation) was determined by the national characteristics of the Hebrew people, the event itself had to depend upon *general historical developments*. When the concept of an ideal manifestation of the Word (the Logos) became worn out in the Graeco-Roman epoch and was recognized by the human soul as insufficient, when man, notwithstanding immense cultural achievements, saw how lonely he was in a barren, miserable world, when doubts concerning truth and an aversion toward life were springing up everywhere, when the best among the people became suicides out of hopelessness, when, on the other hand, it was believed that ideas in general were clearly insufficient, for the then current ideals had proved powerless in combatting the evil of life—it then became imperative that Truth be embodied in a personal, living force. And when external truth, the truth of people, the truth of the state, became factually expressed in a single living person, in the person of a deified man—Rome's Caesar—then *also* appeared the Truth prepared by the Old Testament manifestations, expressed by the Patriarchs, Leaders and Prophets of Israel—the divine Truth in the living figure of God who became man: of *Christ Jesus.*" In his lectures Soloviev seemed to speak to the innate capacities of his hearers, many times inspiring them to a quite new realization of their possibilities. A case in point is Dostoyevski's reaction to Soloviev's brilliant defense of his doctoral thesis on April 6, 1880 at the University of St. Petersburg: "Recently there took place here the public defense by the young philosopher, Vladimir Soloviev (a son of the renowned historian) of his thesis for the Doctor's degree, and I heard him make this profound remark: 'I am firmly convinced that humankind *knows much more* than it has hitherto expressed, either in science or art.' It is just so with me; I feel that much more exists in me than I have yet uttered in my writings."

An outstanding professor of the University of St. Petersburg expressed the feeling of many on the occasion of Soloviev's defense of his doctoral thesis: "if the hopes of this day come to fulfillment, Russia will again possess a great genius. He is like his father in manner and way of thought, but he will far surpass him. Never before have I experienced such a power of spirit in the defense of a thesis!"

* * *

What was Soloviev like as a person? In his *Three Conversations*, his last work published before his death in 1900, Soloviev describes a man who died "from his own exaggerated social politeness": "Among the duties he imposed on himself was that of reading all letters addressed to him, even from unknown people, as well as books and pamphlets for review. He read all the letters and reviewed all the books. He conscientiously carried out every request addressed to him, and consequently was busy all day with other people's affairs, while his own occupied him at night. What is more, he accepted all invitations and received all corners... and now I am informed he committed suicide because he made a law of social politeness—however, that was not politeness, but a kind of foolish self-sacrifice."

This is a kind of half-humorous portrait of Soloviev himself. A giant in spiritual matters, in everyday affairs he was a veritable child, easily confused, clumsy at the simplest tasks. His kindness knew no bounds; for example, he once passed a whole winter in Moscow without an overcoat because he had given his to a needy student and had no money to buy himself another. His consideration for others was extraordinary: one bitterly cold, stormy winter night, long before the days of central heating, he slept on the floor of the passage outside his hotel room because he had stayed out late, had forgotten his key, and did not wish to waken any of the staff in order to gain entrance to his room. He literally gave all he had to the poor, and when everything was gone he turned to his friends to borrow money and goods which *also* were to be given away.

People were attracted to him wherever he went, seeking a word of advice or charity from the man who was known all over Russia for his kindness. In his relations with others, Soloviev never spared himself. For example, some of the saddest years of his life were the result of his love for a woman who had little in common with him and who—discovering his ardor had cooled—continued to humiliate and persecute him for a long, agonizing time before she finally let him go.

* * *

After leaving his father's house as a young man, Soloviev never had a home of his own. He traveled much, always staying in hotels or in the homes of his many friends. He had little time for himself, and, in fact, seemed unable or unwilling to learn how to plan his daily program of activities.

In response to his deepest insight, Soloviev never ate meat, subsisting principally on tea and vegetables throughout his entire adult life. He once explained his reason for his vegetarian diet thus: "We want to live, yet we die, and we bring death to other beings. Though we cannot preserve life we can destroy it in others, and we do so in order to feed ourselves. And all the time our object in doing this—the preservation of our own life—is an illusion, for at any moment we may die, and die we shall, *however many beings we destroy to keep us alive*. Thus our instinct for self-preservation forces us to *senseless killing*. Moreover, in nourishing ourselves on the bodies of others, humans ... take the life of another to sustain their own ... To accept Nature's laws as the *definitive* rule of life is to accept a law of killing ... and to put ourselves forever under the yoke of death. Humans *as animal* submit to such a fate *in spite of themselves*, but the human heart will not do so, for it has within itself the pledge of *another and different life*." (Italics by Soloviev.)

Soloviev rarely slept in a bed. Like the eighteenth-century Hasid, Rabbi Shmelke of Nicholsberg who, because he did not wish to interrupt his studies for too long a time, always slept sitting up, his head resting on his arm, a lighted candle held between his fingers so that when the flame touched his hand he would be awakened, Soloviev also preferred to sleep in a chair at his table. He worked at night because his days were sacrificed to the demands of others. Children and animals were his most intimate friends; between them and him was an instinctive bond of understanding.

Dostoyevski said of Soloviev, the descendent of priests, through the words of Father Zossima: "You will live like a monk in the world." Those around Soloviev recognized in him a certain solitariness, as though his life was dedicated to an invisible cause, for he seemed to move in an atmosphere of consecration to a power outside himself.

Soloviev's nephew wrote: "The external appearance of Vladimir Sergeyevich was very different in the different periods of his life. If we take his youthful portraits, there one sees that the main features of his beautiful face, somewhat Ukrainian, with black, compressed brows, show his austere purity, energy and readiness for struggle. Unforgettable were his high, pure forehead, long dark hair, thin face, childish, full lips and his light-blue almost grey eyes with strangely enlarged pupils which changed the color of the eyes. The face of Soloviev struck one with its unusualness. In his appearance was something monastic, something of the icons, and at the same time, a hidden fire. He was tall and very thin; his face was colorless, his eyes sad and beautiful."

Humor played a very important role in Soloviev's everyday life. Always ready with a joke, he enjoyed laughing at himself and loved the most delightful plays on words, parodies and puns, concerning even the most serious subjects. Fits of laughter sometimes overtook him in the midst of the soberest discussions. People were sometimes puzzled by this apparent duality in his nature: on the one hand, the profound philosopher, and on the other, the impish, mischievous schoolboy, doubled up in "demonic laughter," as one friend described it.

Soloviev suffered with ill-health most of his life. The moments when he was weakest from physical or spiritual suffering he often took as the occasion to write a few lines in humorous vein to send to one or another friend. Unfortunately these verses lose much of their charm and humor in translation, though perhaps the following "epitaph," expressing his ability to laugh at himself and his sufferings, may be hazarded as an example of this type of writing:

Here lies Vladimir Soloviev, all by himself;
Once a philosopher, only his bones are left!
Friendly he was to most, but to some he was unkind,
His love was often stupid, so in this ditch he lies.
Body, soul and clothes the poor fellow lost,
His soul the devil got, his corpse went to the dogs.
Now you who pass this place, learn from his mistakes:
Avoid Eros' dangers. Spiritual love alone is safe!

Another aspect of Soloviev's nature, a rich inheritance from his childhood years, was described by his friend and pupil, Prince Eugene Troubetskoi: "For Soloviev the forests and mountains were filled with invisible beings. The fairy-tale world with its nymphs, water and forest-spirits, was not only understandable for him, but he was very closely related to it. The life of Nature, its cycles of growth and development, was for him a continuous becoming, and therefore an unfinished, incomplete revelation of another, a higher, supersensible reality. And this understanding of Nature was one of the most powerful sources of his poetic inspiration. The view of mountains and lakes gave wings to his soul; autumn landscapes called forth in him a mood of prayer. In his poetical experiences and expressions his philosophical nature was clothed with flesh and blood. In mystical, poetic intuitions he perceived the soul of the world."

* * *

At the end of January, 1881 Feyodor Mikhailovich Dostoyevski died at his home in St. Petersburg. In him Soloviev lost

Vladimir Soloviev. A photograph made after 1881

Vladimir Soloviev. A photograph made before 1880

Feyodor Mikhailovich Dostoyevski (1821-1881).
A photograph made in Moscow, 1880

one of his best friends, a man who genuinely appreciated him personally, who could accurately evaluate his potentials as a thinker and writer, and who from the first had taken a lively interest in his creative development.

Three months later Soloviev gave three lectures in appreciation of Dostoyevski as man and genius, against the background of the development of art: "In the beginning of human evolution the poets were prophets and priests. Art served the gods. But when civilization developed, art, along with human activities, separated from religion. Artists who formerly had been servants of the gods, now considered art itself as their idol. Priests of pure art were born who regarded the perfection of artistic form the most important factor.

"Modern artists will not and cannot serve pure beauty, and seek only for content. However, since they have been estranged from the former religious content of art, they are now dependent on attempting to imitate reality slavishly, and secondly upon responding to the changing taste of the public, and changing morality.

"Naturally it is easy to utterly condemn the present trend of art, but this is unjust. Behind the facade of the poor art of the present, the promise of divine greatness is hidden. The modern artists more or less consciously wish their art to enlighten humankind. However, *earlier* art offered light and joy to humanity, but modern art draws attention to the evil in life. If art seeks to make this evil life better, it is not sufficient simply to work out of realism.

"In ancient times pure art lifted humanity to the heights of Olympus. The art of the future will return to earth, expressing love and sympathy, not in order to bury itself in the darkness of earthly life, but to help the latter and renew it. However, to work efficiently on this earth for this renewal of art, it is necessary to draw to art *forces which are not of this earth.*

"Art which has been separated from religion must be reunited with it, but in perfect freedom. Artists and poets should become priests once again, but in a far deeper sense than formerly, for they will have to gain control over the idea of religion and consciously direct its earthly incarnation. Even at this moment, the traces of the religious art of the future can be detected in today's seemingly anti-religious art.

"In a certain way Dostoyevski as novelist adapted himself to the manner of other authors, but he is preferable to them because he sees not only the present but also looks far into the future.

"All our authors represent in their novels life as they find it. This is especially true for Goncharov and Count Tolstoi. Goncharov has created prototypes of the Russian land-owner and peasant, while Tolstoi is past master of detail, of a magnificent representation of the *mechanism of the soul*. But both men work with a concrete background, set within rigidly defined limitations. When they wish to transcend the latter, all they can do is revert to nature and to its life which as realism is little subject to change, is *fixed*.

"Dostoyevski's world is the exact opposite of this. Here everything is in movement, nothing is fixed, for he is the only one of our contemporary Russian writers who concen-trates on *movement*. Never influenced by the trends in his surroundings, Dostoyevski nevertheless was always aware of their future development. He saw clearly the far-off, lofty goal of our political movement, but also recognized the mistakes made in the attempts to attain it. What he condemned in it was not the movement as such, but *the means* employed.

"The general significance of Dostoyevski's work is deter-mined by the twofold problem of the highest ideals of human society and the proper means to use in order to attain them. The fully justified reason for our efforts toward social reform is the contrast between the rightful ethical demands of the individual and the prevailing social order. Dostoyevski's deep feeling for the injustice prevalent in human social life is shown in his novel, *Poor Folk*. The social significance of this novel and also of his later work, *The Insulted and Injured*, goes back to the ancient and ever-valid fact that those whose level of ethics is highest are those who, at the same time, society despises most. However, this social injustice was for Dostoyevski far more than merely the theme for a novel. *It was also his life-task.* He observed the happenings in the world around him and condemned them, but he also sought ways to set them right. His first reaction was that those best elements who recognize the injustice at work in human society should unite and transform society according to their points of view.

"When his first naive attempt in this direction brought Dostoyevski before the firing-squad and prison, he soon realized that he should not have attempted to bring about a revolutionary change which only he and his friends saw as a necessity. In prison he came in contact with the perception of reality living in the folk-soul itself. This showed him the mistakes in his revolutionary striving. Even the worst of the convicts who belonged to the lowest classes of society had kept alive what intellectuals generally lose, i.e., the belief in God and the awareness of their sins. These human beings, more or less forgotten and neglected by the church and oppressed by the state, *nevertheless* believed in the former and did not deny the latter.

"Instead of leaving prison in bitterness, Dostoyevski emerged from it morally reborn. He wrote, 'More faith, more unity is needed, and if love has been added, then everything has been done!'

"Returning from Siberia, he was not yet able to fully comprehend a positive, universal ideal, but he *did realise* three facts: that *individuals do not have the right to oppress society in the name of their personal supremacy*; that universal truth is not invented by individuals but *is rooted in the folk-soul*; that such truth has religious significance and is definitely related to *faith in Christ and the Christ-ideal.*

"In his novel, *The Possessed*, Dostoyevski deals with a group of people obsessed by the urge to revolution by force, in order to transform the world according to their ideas. They commit the lowest crimes and die shamefully while the Russian people, healed by their faith, bow before their Savior. This book is extremely important for Russian life, for in it events were prophesied which soon took place.

"Dostoyevski condemns the search for abstract, arbitrary ideals, presenting in contrast the religious faith of the people, based upon faith in Christ. This faith in Christ alone is the positive ideal of a human social life in which the individual is united with all other men. Therefore all those who desire to be leaders in the renewal of the social life must first have the moral strength to unite once again with the people, that is, with the genuine faith still active among them. This is not a question of nationalism, but a matter of religious and ethical importance.

"The socialists wish by force to degrade all people to the purely material level of well-fed, self-contented workers, and the state and society into some sort of common economic association. In contrast, Dostoyevski's "Russian socialism" *lifts all people to a spiritual brotherhood*, to the spiritualization of the entire state and social order through the realization of Christ's truth and life in this state and this social life.

"This universal human ideal is the exact opposite of the ideals of the socialist workers described in *The Possessed*, and so is the way to attain it. In *The Possessed* it is by rape and murder; *here it is an ethical deed of sacrifice*, a twofold act of moral abdication. Individuals must sacrifice, give up their self-constructed assertions of truth in the name of Truth itself and the faith living in the folk-soul. They must respect the belief of the people, not because it is folk-belief, *but because it is truth*. In favor of this Truth the people must also detach themselves from all that does not conform to it, including their national egotism.

"Cosmic, universal Truth demands ethical deeds of sacrifice, not only from the individual, but also from the entire people. This is the universal human ideal which was reached by Dostoyevski, the ultimate word irradiating his work with the light of a prophetic mission." (Italics by Soloviev)

These descriptions of the aims and methods of what in Soloviev's time was called "socialism" become infinitely more cogent and timely if one substitutes the modern word *Bolshevism or Communism* for it. This in no way changes Soloviev's meaning, but, in fact, and from the point of view of twentieth century history, *confirms* it.

* * *

A few days after delivering his addresses in memory of Dostoyevski, an event occurred which radically altered Soloviev's life, his public position and the unfoldment of his creative activity. At the age of twenty-eight years and three months it is as though, having expressed his ideals in philosophical terms, he now is convinced the time has come to bring these ideals into *action*. At the threshold of the fifth seven-year period of his life, against the background of a criminal act which stirred Russia from one end of the country to the other and reverberated throughout the entire world, Soloviev enters upon the stage of Christian *deed*.

Chapter Five

DEED AND CONSEQUENCES

1881–1888

THE FIFTH PERIOD of seven years in the life of Vladimir Soloviev, from his twenty-eighth through his thirty-fifth years,
was a time of crisis and counter-crisis.

In human lives in general, this is the most critical time, for
it marks the half-way point in the average seventy-year span
of human existence on earth. By the twenty-eighth year the
forces of heredity, as well as the impulses given by parents and
early associates have faded away, insofar as external guidance is concerned, or perhaps better said, have been *metamorphosed* into a self-dependent human being. At this time
people find themselves compelled more and more by outer
circumstances as well as by inner urges, to base themselves
upon themselves alone, to witness the unfoldment of their
free egoity, to assume fuller and fuller responsibility for their
deeds, their decisions, their direction.

In another sense, it is as though the physical aspect of their
nature, developed under the nurturing hand of parents and
guardians during their first seven-year span, now—in this fifth
seven-year period—receives a new enhancement, somewhat
like a "second birth," the birth into full maturity. Through
the increasing unfoldment of the ego-forces in these years,
individuals are faced with *responsibility* in the fullest sense.
No longer are they permitted to look to others for direction;
they themselves must now take steps in life-decisions out of

their own responsible insight, accepting fully whatever consequences may result from their actions.

Not all men and women are fully capable of this, however;
one symptom of the critical nature of this period is that statis-
tically it is shown to be a time in the human life-span when
suicide is frequent. Faced with the necessity for action, for
performing a deed for which they recognize they alone must
take full responsibility, the individual may fail, or may delay
until the moment has passed which could have "led on to
fortune." The tragedy of Hamlet is concerned with a man
in this particular seven-year life-period who, faced with the
necessity for action, cannot summon up the force within
himself to act at the right moment, with the result that his
action, "come tardy off," has fatal results not only for himself
but for all those around him.

* * *

Disappointed by the failure of his foreign policies following
the Crimean War, the general inertia, non-cooperation and
misunderstanding among many influential landowners as well
as among the newly-forming industrialist class in response to
the reforms he sought to institute in the post-Emancipation
years, in 1880, on the twenty-fifth anniversary of his acces-
sion to the throne, Alexander II turned over the greater share
of his executive powers to one of his ministers, Count Loris-
Melikov, a self-made diplomat of Armenian ancestry. This
was done just seven days after a Nihilist plot to destroy the
Tsar and his family in the dining room of the Winter Palace
failed, though eleven members of the palace staff were killed
and some fifty others severely wounded by the exploding
dynamite.

This however, by no means satisfied the actively emerging
ultra-radical elements in the country. Finally, on March 13,
1881, following orders from the executive committee of the

Narodnaya Volya, "the Party of the People's Will," conspirators set about to assassinate Alexander II.

In mid-afternoon of that day as the Tsar was driving in his carriage near a bridge over the Yekaterininski Canal, not far from the Nevski Prospekt, the fatal attack was made. An eyewitness reported the event: "A bomb was thrown under the Tsar's iron-clad carriage. Several Cossacks of the escort were wounded; the nineteen year old student Rysakov, who threw the bomb, was caught immediately. Then, though the Tsar's coachman and members of his guard-escort begged him to remain in the carriage, saying he could still be driven despite the damage, the Emperor stepped out. Obviously he felt his human sense of dignity required him to see the wounded Cossacks, to do his best to comfort them, as he so often had done with the wounded in the recent war.

"He approached Rysakov and asked him something, but as he stepped forward he passed close by another young man, Ignati Grinevitski; the latter suddenly threw a bomb on the ground between the Tsar and himself, so that both of them would be killed. There was an immediate explosion; each lived only a few hours.

"Next to his assassin who was unconscious and dying, Alexander II lay on the snow, mortally wounded, profusely bleeding, helpless, his clothing in tatters, abandoned by every one of his official escort. All of them had vanished. It was a group of cadets, returning from parade drill, who lifted the bleeding Tsar from the snow and put him in a sled, covering his trembling body with a cadet cloak, his bare head with a cadet cap. And it was one of the terrorists, Emelianov, with a bomb wrapped in newspaper clutched under his arm, who, at the risk of being arrested and hanged on the spot, rushed with the cadets to help the wounded man!

"The explosion had shattered the body of the Tsar below the waist; the sleigh left a trail of blood in the street; in his room in the Winter Palace, the Tsar died, the draft of what was to have been Russia's first modern Constitution lying unsigned among the papers on his desk nearby. At thirty-three minutes past three on that cloudy March afternoon, with the last breath of Alexander II, a fateful turning-point in the history of Russia had come.

"Soon three other conspirators—Zhelyabov, Kibalchich and Perovskaya—had been arrested, their roles in the murder plot having been established to the satisfaction of the Government."

* * *

The shock and horror that passed over Russia and far beyond her borders was tremendous. Andrew D. White, American Minister to St. Petersburg, declared the assassins' work "the most fearful crime ever committed against liberty and freedom," and his words were echoed in all countries of the world.

The senate of the United States expressed its "abhorrence of assassination as a means of redress for any grievances, and remembering the relations of friendship that have always existed between the people and the governments of Russia and the United States, to the strengthening and maintenance of which the late Emperor earnestly contributed his great influence, the senate extends to the government and people of Russia its sincere condolence in this sad national bereavement."

On the same day the legislature of the State of New York recorded a similar reaction to the assassination of "the friend of the American Union when our country was engaged in a fearful civil war; the emancipator of twenty-three million Russian serfs, who at the time of his death was engaged in the establishment of a constitutional government for the entire Russian people."

* * *

Within Russia the news of the assassination of the Tsar was greeted with disbelief at first. Though there had been numerous attempts on his life, for example, Dimitri Karakosov's shot in 1866, and again in November 1879 when the Tsar miraculously escaped nearly certain assassination when his train enroute from the Crimea to Petersburg was blown up by conspirators, there was almost universal confidence that "the great Liberator" never would be murdered.

Therefore, when upon his assumption of the throne as Alexander III, the terrified, reactionary second son of the late Tsar immediately abolished his father's most recent reforms and destroyed the draft of the proposed Constitution, there was practically no opposition to his actions. It was as though the words of the father of Slavophilism, Alexi Stepanovich Khomiakov, who had died just twenty-one years before, were now whispered into his ear with a new significance and urgency: "Don't talk much about law and rights, and don't listen to those who do talk about them, for *duty* is the only living source of law!" Alexander III announced almost at once his unequivocable, unswerving determination to maintain to the full the power he had inherited from the long line of Russian rulers. As the embodiment of both spiritual *and* temporal law, he demanded that each and every one of his subjects fulfill without question his duty to his Sovereign. The new Tsar proclaimed his intention to make the three fundamentals long advocated by the arch-nationalistic, conservative Slavophils the foundation of his government policies. The first of these was the insistance of a single nationalism within Russia. Under this policy, Western ideas, particularly Western ideas of government, were to be regarded as failures, highly detrimental to Russia, and were to be abolished forthwith. A new policy of isolationism and increasing trade restrictions between Russia and her Western neighbors was established, with emphasis upon the superiority of Russian social and economic life.

Alexander III's second principle designated the Russian Orthodox Church the supreme official church of the nation. Gone was that remarkable spirit of tolerance which, despite his autocratic rule, nevertheless was manifested during the days of the Crimean War under Nicholas I, when the police not unnaturally objected to public prayers being said at the English church in Moscow for the victory of Queen Victoria over her enemies. The chaplain appealed to the Emperor himself, and at once Nicholas personally instructed the police that the English were permitted to pray for anything they pleased. Thus throughout the war the old English families in Moscow continued to meet every Sunday to pray for the victory of their Queen and the downfall of the Tsar whose protection they enjoyed!

In contrast, as a result of the ultra-conservative church policies growing out of Alexander III's second principle, all minority religious groups in the country—including the "Old Believers," Evangelical Protestants and the Jews—became prime targets of vituperative articles in the government-controlled press. Before long these attacks were transformed into outright physical violence, particularly against the Jews, and the notorious *Pogroms*, in which thousands of Russian Jews were butchered without mercy, followed.

The third of the new Emperor's principles was the summary abolition of previous reforms, with the goal of a yet stronger autocratic, centralized government under the Tsar's personal, absolute control. Before long the implementation of this part of the new government's program resulted in increased subversive activity throughout the country. A more violent terrorism—originally confined to a comparative handful of extreme radicals—now spread through great segments of middle-of-the-road intellectuals.

Abroad, this absolutism alienated country after country from Russia, with the result that she found herself more and more alone in the world.

From expressions of horror and indignation at the assassination of Alexander II and deep friendship and sympathy with the Russian people, the tide slowly turned until men like Mark Twain, after hearing an eye-witness account of the abrogation of human rights and the brutal treatment of political prisoners in Siberia, would rise from their seats in public gatherings and exclaim, as he did, their voices trembling with emotion: "If such a government cannot be overthrown otherwise than by dynamite, then thank God for dynamite!"

In less than a decade, Alexander's attempts to turn back the clock, to have yet another try at "the good old days," had created a rising tide of Russophobia in the countries of the West, until in February 1893 it became necessary for the Secretary of the Russian Legation in Washington to publish in *The Century Magazine* one of the weakest defenses of Russian autocracy ever to appear in print. "Autocracy," he wrote, "is as natural and satisfactory to Russia as is the republican form of government to the United States; and that our Government is not felt by the masses of the people to be a despotism is evident from the facts that they submit cheerfully to be ruled by it and that they prosper under it." Such words sounded hollow indeed, particularly in America, where at the time they were written it was known that thousands of Russian subjects, rather than "submit cheerfully" to autocracy, had chosen the horrors of Siberian exile, and that far from "prospering under it," millions of Russian lives were being lost in that country before the relentless onslaught of famine and cholera, sweeping down upon the people. The latter fact was vividly brought home to the American public, who at this very time had dispatched nearly one hundred millions of dollars and five steamer-loads of flour to the relief of the "prosperous" and "cheerful" inhabitants of one of the principal wheat-producing countries of the world. The Tsar's policies bore strange fruit, and strangest of all, perhaps, was the reaction to his "satisfactory" rule on the part of "the masses of the people" under his despotic control.

However, this is to anticipate, for at this point in the life of Soloviev, hardly a voice had been raised within Russia against the avowed determination of the new Tsar to severely punish the murderers of his father.

* * *

On March 26, the day of the opening of the trial of the conspirators, and again on the 28th, Vladimir Soloviev lectured in the hall of the Mutual Credit Society in St. Petersburg. The second of these lectures was titled *A Critique of Contemporary Education and the Crisis in the World Process.* Various conflicting reports concerning this lecture exist, but apparently Soloviev's concluding words dealt with a truth to which the Russian people adhered at that time, i.e., their belief in "the absolute value of the individual person, as a result of their implicit faith in the Person of Christ."

According to one account, Soloviev said, "The people admit that Nature herself has a tendency to absolute oneness, that human nature and external Nature have one soul, and this soul strives to incarnate within itself the divine principle, strives to give birth to Divinity within itself. The people believe in the Holy Virgin and the Christ—and these are the essence of everything."

It was reported that at this point Soloviev expressed ideas which, it was thought, were not his own, for example, that "All men should become Christs, all women holy virgins. So let us say definitely and frankly that we stand under the banner of Christ, and that we serve the only God, the God of Love. Let the people recognize in our thoughts their own soul, and in our conscience, their voice. Then the people will hear us, will understand us, will follow us."

In his memoirs, Lyov Nikiforov, a friend of Soloviev, recalled that the latter then said, "An evil, senseless, awful deed has happened. The Tsar is murdered; the culprits have been captured;

their names are known, and according to the existing law death stands before them as a retaliation, as the fulfillment of a pagan law: 'An eye for an eye, a death for a death.' But how should a truly Anointed One of God behave? The highest among us, the bearer of the impulse of a Christian society—how should one act toward those who have committed so grave a sin? One should provide a national example. One should turn away from the pagan principle of retaliation and the intimidation of people through fear of death, and should permeate oneself with the Christian principle of pity toward the insane evil-doers. The Anointed One of God, without in any way justifying the crime, should remove the murderers of the Tsar from society, as cruel and harmful members of human society. But one should simply remove them without destroying them, constantly bearing in mind the state of soul of the criminals, and should place them under the jurisdiction of the Church, which is the only institution capable of healing them morally."

Another member of the audience, Leonid Slonimski, described the conclusion of the address: "Soloviev spoke slowly, stressing every single word and sentence by means of short pauses, during which he stood quite still, without the slightest movement, his wonderful eyes partly hidden, since his gaze was directed downward, just in front of him. 'The Tsar can pardon them,' he said, with a stress on the word *can*. Then, after a short pause, he continued in a louder voice, 'The Tsar *must* pardon them!'"

A long minute of soul-chilling silence followed. Then pandemonium broke loose, as if a violent hurricane had burst into the hall. The audience exploded into shouts, jeers and screams of emotion: "Traitor!" "Terrorist!" "Murderer!" "Infamy!" "Out with him!" "Tear him to pieces!" And at the same moment were heard equally loud shouts of approval, particularly from the many university students present.

Soloviev mounted the speaker's rostrum once more. His tall, thin figure, his piercing eyes, his pallid face, paler under the stress of excitement, called forth another outburst of mixed fury and approval. He lifted his hand calmly; magically, the entire hall fell silent. After a quiet pause he spoke once again. He assured his hearers they had misunderstood him, that in no way did he condone the murder of the late Tsar-Liberator. But at this moment he was interrupted by his superior at the Ministry of Education, Baron Nikolai who rose from his seat and advised Soloviev for his own well-being to go to his carriage at once, drive to the Premier, Loris-Melikov and give a full account of himself.

This Soloviev declined to do, saying he was not acquainted with the Premier. The Minister replied, "This is not your private affair; it is a public matter, and I advise you to be careful." And as a kind of afterthought he hurled a threat at Soloviev: "It very likely may happen that rather than drive to the Prime Minister you will find yourself forced to travel all the way to Kolimsk!" (Siberia). Soloviev calmly replied, "Well, one can occupy oneself with philosophy even in Kolimsk!"

Suddenly a stout, elderly man jumped to his feet, shouting wildly, "You traitor! You should be the first to be executed! You should be hanged!" But his voice was drowned in shouts of approval from the students who suddenly surged to the platform, crying to Soloviev, "You are our leader! You lead us!" They lifted Soloviev to their shoulders and, forming a solid phalanx, carried him around the hall in triumph. Afterward they seated him in his carriage, formed a guard of honor and accompanied him safely to his lodgings.

* * *

The truth of the Minister's statement that Soloviev's apparent defense of the late Tsar's murderers was a public matter became clear the next morning. Rumors flew thick and fast; the newspapers published accounts ranging from outright attacks to efforts to minimize the whole affair. Soloviev's friends and acquaintances were sharply divided. Some, recalling a sentence he spoke in the opening of his very first university lecture years before: "In every sphere of their activity, and above all else, human beings dream of freedom," concluded that he had always been a doubtful, unreliable person, and turned away from him. Others, more tactful, were "not at home" to him until he himself realized their wish to have no further contact with him. Like every person who attempts to live a great ideal, Soloviev stood more and more alone.

He went to the office of Baron Nikolai and gave the latter his letter of resignation from the Committee on Education. Surprised, the Baron tried to hand back the letter to Soloviev, exclaiming. "But I did not ask you to do this!" Nevertheless Soloviev insisted, and the resignation was accepted, though with regret.

In the early hours of the morning after the lecture, Soloviev had been summoned to the headquarters of Count Baranov, Governor of St. Petersburg, who brusquely ordered him to go home, write out a full report of the affair and submit it to his office for consideration. Having gone from Count Baranov to Baron Nikolai, Soloviev returned to his lodgings, where he wrote the following letter:

Your Excellency:

When I asked you for permission to give a lecture, I said that I would not speak about political matters. Concerning the event of March 1st, I did not say a word, and concerning the pardoning of the criminals I spoke only in accord with a statement of the Tsar that he stands on the Christian principle of all-mercifulness and pardoning, which is the ideal of the Russian people. I concluded my lecture with approximately these words: "The decision concerning the matter is not ours, and it is not for us to judge that of the Tsar. But, as members of society, we would admit to ourselves and proclaim aloud that we stand under the banner of Christ, and that we serve the only God—the God of Love."

Among my eight hundred listeners were many, no doubt, who could easily misunderstand me and could take my words in a wrong sense. On the other hand, I can refer to many well-known and respected persons with whom I am acquainted, who understood the meaning of my remarks in the right way, and who can confirm this statement of mine.

After the lecture, a gentleman unknown to me insistently demanded that I should state my opinion on capital punishment. In reply, I ascended the platform once more and said that in general, capital punishment as practised today, is an unforgivable deed, and should be abolished in a Christian nation.

* * *

Later that same day Soloviev's staunch friend, Nikiforov called on him; afterward he wrote in his memoirs: "When I saw him, the expression of suffering on his face was so intense that involuntarily I drew back in surprise. But the thing that startled me most was a small lock of white hair in the front of his head. This had appeared overnight."

The turning-point in the life of Soloviev had come. The events ahead would tax his strength to the utmost, would intensify his sufferings until finally his premature death would result.

At twenty-eight his hair had begun to change color. Before another decade elapsed, both his hair and beard became entirely grey, his whole appearance resembling a venerable patriarch, worn with care and suffering. But Soloviev was only in the middle years of life.

* * *

While Soloviev appealed to his audience in St. Petersburg for clemency for the murderers of the late Tsar, another attempted to speak to the conscience of the new Tsar himself. From the broad, rolling fields of Yasnaya Polyana, the Shining Meadow, a voice quoted the Gospels: "You have heard it said, Thou shalt love thy neighbor and hate thine enemy. But I say unto you, Love your enemies..." With these words Lyov Tolstoi opened his letter to Alexander III. And he continued: "Your Majesty, if you did that, if you summoned these people into your presence, gave them money, sent them away to some place in America, and wrote a manifesto opening with the words, 'But I say to you, Love your enemies,' I cannot speak for others, but as for myself, poor subject that I am, I would be your very dog, your slave. I would weep for happiness, as I weep now every time I hear your name... I know what a flood of love and goodness would flow from your words, all over Russia... Just one word of forgiveness and Christian love, spoken and carried out from the heights of the throne, only the path of Christian rule, upon which you now must enter, can destroy that evil which is corroding Russia. Like wax before a flame, all revolutionary opposition will melt away before the Tsar-man who fulfills the law of Christ."

It is reported that Constantine Petrovich Pebedonostsev, who meanwhile had become the chief advisor to the new Tsar, refused even to consider presenting Tolstoi's letter to his master. However, it finally came into the Tsar's hand by another means, and it is said that after he read it, he exclaimed, "If this crime were a matter of my personal concern, I would have the right to pardon those guilty of it, but for the sake of my father I cannot do it."

* * *

Like Tolstoi Soloviev addressed a letter to Alexander III regarding the events of March 28, 1881:

Your Imperial Majesty, Most Gracious Sovereign:

Without doubt news concerning my address of March 28 has reached Your Majesty, but in distorted, exaggerated form. Therefore I consider it my duty to give Your Majesty an account of the affair just as it occurred. Confident that the spiritual power of Christ's truth alone can overcome the powers of evil and destruction, which in our time have reached a degree before unknown, confident also that the sound body of the Russian nation exists and is activated by the Spirit of Christ, convinced that the Tsar of Russia is the highest expression and the messenger of the national spirit, carrier of all that is highest in the nation, I had the courage to confess this, my conviction, from a public rostrum.

At the conclusion of my address I stated that the sad conditions of the present offer a totally new opportunity for the Tsar of Russia to manifest the power of the Christian ideal of highest mercy, and that in itself this deed would be a great moral act which would elevate his power to an extraordinary height, and would set his authority on the firmest of foundations.

By extending pardon to the foes of his own power, in opposition to all ideas of earthly wisdom, the Tsar would ascend to superhuman stature, and by his deed would show the divine essence of his imperial rulership, proving that in his person lives the highest spiritual power of the entire Russian nation, by virtue of the fact that in the whole nation no one else would have the ability to perform so sublime a deed.

This is the substance of my address which—to my great distress—was interpreted quite the opposite of my intentions.

Your Imperial Majesty's
faithful subject,
Vladimir Soloviev

Neither Tolstoi nor Soloviev lacked the courage of his convictions. Their testimony was fearless, even before the ruler of their country. They were fully prepared to accept the consequences of their deepest beliefs for, as Soloviev expressed it, "I believe the main point is that one is permeated by the Spirit of Christ to such a degree that one can say with a good conscience whether a deed or undertaking has been done with the positive help of Christ. This is the crucial criterion."

But the Tsar was determined upon an opposite course; the old order was to be bolstered yet a little longer. Severe oppression, cruel punishment, blind reprisals, stubborn reaction—all these became the order of the day.

On April 3, the anniversary of the actual date of the Crucifixion, according to Rudolf Steiner, five of those who had been convicted of sharing in the murder of Alexander II were hanged in a public square in St. Petersburg.

For men like Tolstoi and Soloviev it was clear that revolution was coming, that one day Russia would be torn with civil strife from top to bottom, that reactionary measures of the Government were merely postponing the day of wrath, even compounding its fury. More than this, they were convinced that the highest symbol of justice, the ideal of a merciful, Christian monarch, the head of the church into which they had been born, to which they adhered, failed at the very moment when—in their eyes—a single act on his part would have established him, his country and his church before the world as the highest, most enlightened example of Christian practice.

To Tolstoi and Soloviev, Alexander III not only failed himself, his people, his destiny—he failed his Christ. And both of them were convinced that Russia could not long exist under conditions as they developed from this time onward.

* * *

A reflection of Soloviev's sufferings appears in lines he wrote while visiting his mother in Moscow:

O, in the pure azure, how many, many
Black, black clouds!
How far above me God's clear reflection shines;
Within, how fierce the evil fire, burning!

Within the soul, in unseen struggle,
Two eternal forces mysteriously meet;
The shadows of two worlds, in chaos
Compressing, weave in and out capriciously.

But through the darkness, I believe
Will pass the Word divine, in storms of light;
And the black clouds, in mighty deluge,
Will pour themselves upon the thirsting earth.

Then with glistening dew all things will be refreshed,
The burning of the elemental fire will cease,
The radiance of the heavenly vault will open,
For me will brighten all the beauty of the silent earth.

In reading these lines one is reminded of the words of Faust, describing the struggle between the "two souls" dwelling within the human breast, the "two eternal forces," as Soloviev calls them, mysteriously at work within the human being. These "shadows of two worlds" Rudolf Steiner describes as the two aspects of evil, the one which binds human beings to the earth, shutting out any view of spirit as an ever-present reality, the other, estranging them from their daily tasks, enticing them into a land of dream and illusion. To the first of these Steiner gives the ancient name, Ahriman, the power of darkness, the Satan of the Gospels; the second he calls Lucifer, the figure of the Tempter. Thus the twofold nature of evil appears, and the place of human beings, bearers of the power of the word, of speech, expressing their humanness, is to be seen after the passing storm holding these two forces *in balance*, standing amidst "all the beauty of the silent earth."

The "two eternal forces mysteriously meet," weaving in and out, amid continual soul activity. For the human soul, as Dostoyevski rightly observed, is the battle-ground, the stage upon which the drama of the conflict between the two aspects of evil is eternally being waged. We are under the constant need to so arouse ourselves that we can waken to the temptation of Lucifer to make us "neglect" our tasks and duties on earth, the importance of our life on earth, and to the temptation of Ahriman-Satan which would cause us to "forget" the spirit, to turn our back upon the spiritual world in favor of things perceptible to the senses exclusively.

It is significant that in Soloviev's poetic vision the evil is not destroyed, but is *transformed, metamorphosed* into "a higher good," imaged in the poem as the refreshing dew, the quenched fire, the radiance of heaven, the enhanced beauty of the earth, "silent" before this manifestation of the divine activity.

* * *

Soloviev's reaction to the increasing solitariness he experienced as a result of his courageous deed is expressed in another poem he wrote at this time. The "you" in the poem is he himself.

In a land of freezing storms, grey mists,
You appeared upon the earth;
Alas, poor one, between the warring factions
No shelter's here for you.

But fighters' shouts disturb you not,
Nor clash of arms, nor glint of swords;

You stand there, deeply musing, listening,
Hearing mighty words of old.

In ancient times the highest God to chosen Jew
Promised to reveal Himself,
And the Prophet, aflame in prayer,
In desert silence waited for his God.

A rumbling, far beneath the earth, distant, hollow,
The sun's light slowly faded,
The ground trembled; fear siezed upon the Prophet
—But God was not in the fear.

Then rose a mighty whirlwind, stormy blasts,
A roaring in the heights of heaven;
With it flashing fire, lightning-bolts
—But God was not in the fire.

Now everything grew still; the turmoil ceased,
The Prophet waited not in vain:
A gentle coolness wafted towards him —
In this mysterious breath he divined his God.

* * *

Shortly before his death Dostoyevski pointed to a great future role the Russian people would have to play in the spiritual life of humanity. Soloviev shared this conviction, agreeing completely with Dostoyevski's ringing conclusion: "To be a true Russian is to be the brother of all humankind!"—However, in place of brotherhood, Soloviev saw ultra-conservative religio-political Slavophilism steadily spreading across Russia, backed by a monolithic, reactionary governmental power.

Soloviev recalled the defiant words of Xerxes: "From the East, the light; from the East, strength!"—a battle-cry with which the mighty Persian ruler rallied his forces in preparation for the attack on Greece. But soon the vast horde of slaves fled before a handful of courageous citizens. Therefore Soloviev now addressed his country:

> O Russia, in sublime premonition,
> A mighty decision you ponder;
> What kind of Orient do you wish to be —
> The Orient of Xerxes, or that of Christ?

Russia's ideal of true human brotherhood could come about, Soloviev believed, only if the Russian people were to take seriously what through his spiritual vision he perceived to be their task among the peoples of the earth: "The truth of which I am conscious will sooner or later be known to others, and then by its inner strength it will transform this whole world of deceit, will wipe all injustice and evil from private and social life—and the Kingdom of God will appear in its glory—the kingdom of inner, spiritual relationships of pure love and joy—a new heaven and a new earth."

However, lest this be interpreted as an expression of chauvanism or an invitation to complacency, Soloviev exclaimed:

"Holy Russia demands holy work!"

For, as he reminded his fellow-countrymen: "The idea of every nation is not what it thinks of itself in time, but what God thinks of it in eternity."

* * *

In May, 1883 Soloviev was severely striken with typhus fever. The dread disease progressed alarmingly to the point where his death seemed imminent. His sister, Poliksena

Sergeyevna, the poetess, who was with him, later recalled in her memoirs that on one critical day Soloviev turned to her saying, "Read to me out of the Gospel the story of the Wedding of Cana!" This the sister did, remembering so well the scene in Dostoyevski's *Brothers Karamazov* where the reading of this same passage is described.

For recuperation after the force of the disease had passed, Soloviev went to the country estate of Countess Tolstoi, Pustynka. From there he wrote to his brother, Michael: "I am recovering rapidly now; nevertheless I had real typhus. My hair has come out, and my head had to be shaved, which certainly didn't improve my appearance... And now the young children here run about asking the household, 'Isn't Soloviev a horror? A real horror?'"

That summer Soloviev spent much time reading Dante in Italian. His command of the language grew so rapidly that before long he was able to read the most difficult passages with ease. He also translated the well-known *Epigram* by Giovanni Battista Strozzi, inspired by Michelangelo's Medici Tomb sculpture, "Night," beginning with the words *"La Notte, che tu vedi in Sì dolci atti/ Dorm ire, fu da un Angelo scolpita/ In questo sasso, e perchè dorme ha vita..."* ('Tis Night, in deepest slumber; all can see/ She sleeps, for Angelo did give/ This stone a soul, and, since she sleeps, must live...), and also a long poem by Petrarch.

At this time Soloviev's friendship with the poet, Afanasi Afanasievich Fet was intensified by the appearance of the first of a series of small volumes of poems by Fet published under the title, *Evening Lights*. After a silence of twenty years, Fet now reappeared among the writers of his time as a master of pure lyric poetry. Despite their widely divergent views on philosophy (Fet was an ardent follower of Schopenhauer, a convinced athiest and an active anti-Christian), the two men were drawn together by their appreciation of poetry. Fet, widely known in Russia as the translator of Goethe's *Faust*, deeply appreciated the ancient Roman writers, Seneca and Virgil among them. In the summer of 1887 Soloviev spent many weeks as a guest on Fet's estate in the Kursk Province. Together the two men worked at a translation of Virgil's *Aeneid* at the rate of about eighty verses each day. Soloviev also made a new translation of Virgil's fourth Ecologue at this time. Fet was later to distinguish himself at the age of seventy as the writer of some of the most remarkable, passionate and brilliant love poems in Russian literature.

During their years of friendship, Soloviev was increasingly concerned by Fet's steadily declining health and most of all by his violent hatred of Christianity. For years a severe chronic ailment caused Fet ever-increasing suffering until he determined to end his life by suicide. However, at the very moment he was about to plunge a knife into his own body, he fell dead of sudden heart failure. This occurred in 1892, and Soloviev later said that for a long time afterward he heard almost constantly the voice of Fet calling in torment from the spiritual world.

* * *

In the summer of 1884 Soloviev again spent many months at Pustynka, where the natural beauty of the fields and forests of the estate inspired him very deeply. One day as he was walking along the bank of the Tosna River, Soloviev discovered in a secluded spot a standing stone, covered with moss and lichen. At once he was drawn to this stone which appeared to him like a menhir from ancient days. From that time he went again and again to that place, where he passed many hours in meditation and prayer. One day while he knelt before the stone, many Saints appeared to him in a vision, bestowing upon him their heavenly blessing for his work. From then on, he always referred to that spot as "the place of the sacred stone."

Years later when he was at work on *The Justification of the Good*, he had a similar vision in that place. Again the divine "visitors" appeared before him, once more blessing him, and this time giving him the "leading thought" for his work:

"To justify the faith of our fathers by lifting it to a new stage of rational consciousness—that is my general task." In the autumn when the family left the estate to return to their home in St. Petersburg, Soloviev stayed on at Pustynka, remaining there until late in January: "I live entirely alone in this vast, old, cold house, sleep for the most part wrapped in two cloaks, and work little. I have, nevertheless managed to write a long chapter on Old Testament theocracy."

* * *

This reference to the theocracy of the Old Testament indicates what Soloviev now considered to be the indispensable first step toward the establishment of a universal Church and State, which he called a "Free Theocracy." Such an act he believed would be essential in order to accomplish the future tasks which he saw as being laid upon humanity by the spiritual world.

The "great schism" which had divided the Church into Eastern and Western sections, must be overcome; Christianity must bridge its differences, for "Dogma and cult are not at all the whole of Christianity; there still remain the social and political effects of the true religion, the organization of the collective forces of Christianity, which has as its aim *the rebirth of the world*—there still remains the fighting Church." Again he wrote, "The religious ideal of the separated Eastern Church is not false; it is incomplete. In Eastern Christendom for the last thousand years religion has been identified with personal piety, and prayer has been regarded as the one and only religious activity. The Western Church, without disparaging individual piety as the true seed of all religion, seeks the development of this seed and its blossoming into *a social activity* organized for the glory of God and the universal good of humankind. The Eastern Christian prays; the Western Christian prays *and labors.*"

* * *

Rudolf Steiner gave a valuable indication for a clearer understanding of some of the deeper aspects of Soloviev's thinking in pointing out that something of the ideas and ways of thought present in the great medieval philosopher-mystic, Johannes Scotus Erigena (c.800–c.877) appear again in Vladimir Soloviev.

An Irish monk who had mastered Greek and Latin, Erigena was a teacher in the court of Charles the Bald was grandson of Charlemagne and king of France. Though he was responsible for a revival of philosophical thinking which had remained dormant in Western Europe since the death of Boethius, Erigena had far greater influence as a mystic, both in his own time and later.

Erigena's mystical teachings are embodied in the five books which comprise his great work, *De divisione naturae*, built around his experience of *Natura*, his name for the universal creation, the totality of all that exists.

The ultimate toward which everything moves—no matter how slowly—in the plan of things, is *deificatio, theosis*, the resumption into divine being, the individual man lifted into knowledge of God, where "to know is to be." As God is the *Alpha*, the beginning of creation, He is also the *Omega*, the conclusion, the goal, the end. Therefore, to Erigena the ultimate goal is the restitution of creation's divine nature, its restoration to the Word from which it derived, by which it was made, and is sustained.

In the light of these thoughts of Scotus Erigena one can understand more clearly Soloviev's preoccupation with the reestablishment of the unity of all Christians. Convinced that an error in judgment had separated the community of Christians in the first place, with the result that, in the words of the Epistle which he often cited, "the whole world lies in wickedness," Soloviev was certain that the restoration of the original unity of all Christians was the first step toward "the redemption of all things," the reintegration of all creation into the archetypal divine order of the universe which Erigena had seen in the figure of Natura, and which Soloviev saw in the image of the Sophia.

* * *

To implement this courageous and far-reaching conclusion, Soloviev set to work with all the strength at his command. In lectures, articles and books he spoke more and more openly of the task confronting humanity: the restoration of Universal Christianity, in which there would be "one flock and one Shepherd."

In 1884 appeared *The Spiritual Foundations of Life*, in which he set forth for laymen the essence of Christian living.

In this work Soloviev explains, among other things, that man's hunger and thirst after righteousness take two forms: the hunger for eternal life and the thirst for truth, indicating that these are the two pillars which support religious life-practice. In order to satisfy this hunger and thirst—and *both* must be satisfied if man is to "awake in God's likeness"—Soloviev indicated that three practical steps are requisite. These are *prayer, alms-giving,* and *fasting.*

With reference to *prayer* Soloviev wrote, "When a man joins himself to God in prayer, he also links the souls of others to himself, becoming a link in the chain which binds God and material creation."

Here Soloviev's rendition of the Lord's Prayer can be cited as an expression of the ideal of all prayer: "The Lord's Prayer, which is completely selfless, is also entirely efficient. Each of its petitions already contains the beginning of fulfillment when uttered in true belief. When we believingly say 'Hallowed by Thy Name,' we mean that we wish to receive God, and therefore we first wish that He reveal Himself to us and tell us His Name. By calling for the Kingdom of God, we consider ourselves as already belonging to that Kingdom. When saying 'Thy Will be done,' we mean that we surrender our will to God, thus fulfilling His Will in us. Lastly, the more we restrict our material wants when asking for 'our daily bread' today, the easier we make the fulfillment of our petition.

"By forgiving those who have sinned against us we justify ourselves before God. Recognizing that only spiritual or godly people are subject to temptation, we ask for God's help in our battle against the temptations and impulses of evil powers. By this petition for help, we receive the most efficient aid, for the evil powers cannot be cast out except by *fasting* and *prayer*.

> Our Father Who are in Heaven: Creator of a new and holy life within us,
> Hallowed by Thy Name: may Truth be sanctified through our faith.
> Thy Kingdom come: this is all we hope for.
> Thy Will be done, for it unites all people and all things in a single love; may this be done, not only in the world of those heavenly spirits whose will is Thy word, but also in our own being which has rebelled against Thee.
> Take our earthly life and cleanse it by Thy life-creating spirit.
> Take everything that is ours and make us righteous in Thy Truth.
> Take all our strength and our wisdom, for they are insufficient in our battle against the invisible evil.

And Thyself lead us to perfection on Thy true path—for
to Thee alone belong the Kingdom, the Power and the
Glory
Before time was, and in all Eternity. "

* * *

With regard to *alms-giving* as the second of the three practical steps, Soloviev frequently quoted with approbation the
instruction of the saintly Elder Makarius of Optina Pystin:
"Every time a beggar knocks at your door, try to perceive
Christ himself under the humble disguise. Would you, under
any circumstances, let Christ knock in vain? The moral qualities of the individual beggar have nothing to do with it; that
is Christ's concern, not yours. Who are you to judge your
brother? Christ is using his hand and mouth to test your
compassion. Will you fail him?"

Through prayer alone can the human being receive the gift
of true charity, which is grace—and through alms-giving he
can pass this gift *to his fellow human beings.*

* * *

Fasting—spiritual, intellectual and physical—is "a means
of establishing the supremacy of spirit over the flesh." This,
says Soloviev, "is necessary in order to preserve the dignity
of humanity," because "the principle of true asceticism is the
principle of *spiritual self-preservation.*" Hence in fasting we
apply the gift of grace *to ourselves.*

Nevertheless Soloviev warns that there is a *false* asceticism
which, instead of "preserving the true dignity of humanity"
only plunges people further into the depths of materialism—a
condition resulting from "considering every torment a virtue,
making asceticism an end in itself." The "true protoype" of
this attitude Soloviev identifies as "the devil himself, who does
not eat nor drink and remains in celibacy!"

* * *

The first of Soloviev's "three practical steps" leading to the life of righteousness in terms of human being's relationship with the world *above*—expressed in *prayer*—is an activity of the *spirit*. Establishing their relationship with the world *around*—expressed in *charity*—is an activity of the *soul-*forces of the heart. Bringing about their relationship with the world *beneath*—expressed in *fasting*—is an activity related to the *body*, which in turn has been built up by elements of the mineral, plant and animal kingdoms.

The spiritual path to the heights of the Divine thus involves tasks which people must perform *on earth*. But we may not follow this path solely egotistically and selfishly; otherwise our efforts will fail. It is only when we include an awareness of and gratitude for our relationship with and indebtedness to *all the kingdoms of earth*: mineral, plant and animal— through which we have been able "to climb to humanity's estate"—that our efforts can be crowned with success.

This thought was beautifully expressed by Christian Morgenstern, whose poem, *The Washing of the Feet*, describes the fruit of fasting, the warmth of self-sacrifice, and the spiritual insight that results from devotion:

I thank you, dumb and silent stone,
I bend in reverence to you;
My life and growth as plant to you I owe.

I thank you, fruitful earth and flower,
I bow my head in reverence to you;
You helped me rise to animal's estate.

I thank you, stone and plant and beast,
 make obeisance lowly to you all;
'Tis you have helped me to my human self.

So flows thanksgiving ever back and forth
In the divine Whole, manifold yet One,
Entwining all with threads of thankfulness.

* * *

In 1884 Soloviev again occupied himself with the book, *Characteristics of the Interior Church* by Ivan Viadimirovich Lopukhin which, as has already been said, was widely regarded as a classic expression of Russian mystical striving. The sections regarding the inner path of spiritual development made a strong appeal to Soloviev. Lopukhin states: "In order that the divine kingdom may be perfectly established in our interior center, the force of Love which constitutes its essence must proceed from the Breast of the Godhead, and as it removes the old leaven, must fill the interior with its own spiritual quality. This living light must penetrate like yeast and renew all the three principles of which we are constituted: *spirit, soul* and *body*. For even the body must be filled and clothed in the glory of the children of God, with that clarity of light which is the portion of the immortal body." This process presupposes however that people will take themselves in hand as it were, taking certain steps which are necessary before they can begin to tread the inner path itself. These steps Lopukhin describes in these words: "Before one sows a field one prepares it for the seed. So it is with the sowing of our spiritual birth: the ground of the soul is given a foretaste of its approach by pleasant sensations, emblematic pictures, dreams, visions. But all this is done with the *sole* aim of urging people to strive *onward*, in order to *encourage* them. One must recognize that this takes place only in the *outer* approaches to the soul where the influence of unclean spirits, who all too often transform themselves into angels of light, *also* can enter. This is why experienced mystics advise great care regarding sensations which are inwardly agreeable, above all regarding those which involve the outward senses alone.

"Spiritual immaturity, pride, self-love and ignorance may lead one to mistake these signs for the manifestations of the actual spiritual world itself. In such a case one will then make use of these emblematic figures and pleasurable sensations as food for *spiritual voluptuousness*. In the depths of their hearts such people will be *proud* of these manifestations, *misunderstanding* them and using them solely for *their own* advantage. And thus it is that they will reject the kingdom of God which has actually been drawing near to them. *Thus they increase the obstacles on their spiritual path.*

"The constant exercise of people's inner faculties in harmony with the divine pattern is necessary in order that in their lives they may produce actions in conformity with the will of the spiritual world, for such practice is the means of their initial experience of the inner, supersensible, esoteric life.

"Above all, the love of *one's neighbor* must form one's constant preoccupation. It is by this especially that human nature is shaped and prepared on the inner path to become the dwelling-place of the Divine who is Love alone. People must practice this, concealing in every way possible their striving on the inner path toward the good, taking utmost care lest their striving become an object of self-glorification. In all their good intentions and their steps in carrying them out, they must strive to enter into the esoteric meaning of the words: 'Let not your left hand know what your right hand is doing.'

"Those who thus work at their spiritual development must devote themselves to it in quiet calmness before the Spirit which regenerates can begin to work appreciably within them. Their thoughts are to be turned to whatever brings them to an awareness of the divine presence, all-pervading, all-seeing. Such meditations should end by making people more watchful of themselves, inspiring in them a veneration and love for the Divine. To this goal they should devote the fullest capacities of their souls in greatest simplicity. Here let them also guard against their own imagination, refraining from making pictures within themselves and surrendering to them, for whatever their nature, there is always a danger of their producing fatal results in their inner soul lives.

"Having thus inclined their souls towards the Divine, it is essential that people devote themselves to meditation as regularly and as often as possible, concentrating all their thoughts in the secret place of their hearts, in that inner calmness which, withdrawing them from external things, enables them to enter into the light of the Spirit. On the other hand they are to remember that such meditation should *never* aim at attaining the 'pure Sabbath,' the perfect rest in the spiritual world, the permanence of which belongs *only* to the highest degree of the esoteric life. On the inner path to the Spirit such enjoyment is felt only for a brief moment in order to strengthen and encourage those who thus are striving toward initiation."

Lopukhin's book concludes with a passage embodying motifs from the Rosicrucian alchemical path; at the close it reveals a glimpse of his profound relationship with the images of the whole esoteric way of true Rosicrucianism: "By studying Nature, faithfully striving to ascend her seven rung ladder of Wisdom, sent by Grace from on high, the light of Nature which invisibly gives life to all creation, is discovered. This light with which the almighty word of the Creator, the Logos, impregnated the 'primal matter' (*prima materia*) of all that exists, shines also in the Philosophical Chaos.

"One who thus advances in the study of Nature, enlightened by spiritual Wisdom, searches out 'the interior of the earth' (*interiora terrae*). Happy are those who preserve the good wine of strength and purity in their striving! They will come to know at last how the earth itself was made, and the working of the elements as well. They will resolve them, reducing them to their archetypal essences. Uniting the sun and moon, they will discover the true Medicine, a treasure which will bestow upon them the qualities of a true Philosopher, enabling them to enter the Sanctuary of the Temple of Nature itself.

"The consummation of the great Philosophic Work, the Mirror of Wisdom, wherein is seen all that has been, is and will be, opens the gate of the Sanctuary of the Temple, of the Paradise of Light, the habitation of the New Eden, the dwelling-place of the greatest Sages who possess all the gifts of initiation; of the true Shepherds who perpetually offer pure sacrifice to the Divine, and of the Kings who are rulers of themselves and of Nature.

"Through the reunion of the sun and moon, the active and the passive, results the Unity which is the greatest Mystery of the renewal of the created. This Crown of all the Mysteries of Nature adorns the altar of the Sanctuary itself.

"The Red Rose of the Paradise which begins to open its petals at the very moment a true bearer of the Cross enters upon the inner path of striving toward the renewed, supersensible, esoteric life, blossoms on a new earth, completely vivified. That new earth then becomes for the initiates a place of comfort and rest after they have travelled the dolorous path of the Cross."

* * *

At this time Soloviev re-read the book by Dante Alighieri, *De Monarchia*. From this work by the great medieval Florentine, Soloviev derived the idea that doubtless the best earthly order of things preparatory to the restoration of the unity of all Christians and the ushering in of Universal Christianity, would be a division of rule under a High-Priest, who would have direction of all spiritual affairs, and the administration of a King who would take the lead in affairs of state.

Eventually Soloviev developed his ideal of a "Free Theocracy"—a concept more adapted to ancient times than modern life (in reality a contradiction in terms, as has been pointed out)—to the stage where he envisioned the reunification of all Christians under the leadership of the Pope of Rome, and at the same time saw temporal affairs placed under the authority of the Tsar of Russia. The dual functions of High Priest and King were to be merged in and operated exclusively through the Universal Church. These thoughts Soloviev elaborated in articles and books, the most important of the latter being his *History and Future of Theocracy* (1886), a large work which Soloviev nicknamed "The Leviathan," only a part of which was actually published, and his *Russia and the Universal Church* (1889).

A great contrast exists between the ideal of Church and State which stood before Soloviev as a great vision and hope for a truly Christian future, however, and that conception of the *City of God*, of St. Augustine, which embodied the form and idea of the imperial Roman State. For with Soloviev's dream—and this is the important point—it was the activity, *the life-giving impulse of the Risen Christ*, permeating the entire structure and social life of his Theocracy that was to give the latter its justification and existence. In this Soloviev sought to lead the social solution into a new future, a future permeated by the ideal of the Mystery of Golgotha.

* * *

Soon, however, Soloviev began to realise that his great dream stood little chance of being realized in external life. One sign confirming this was the issuance of an official government document in 1885 titled *Regulations for State Examinations in the Faculty of Laws*, at St. Petersburg. In this publication it was announced that for the first time in history the Russian Orthodox Church had resigned its authority and had placed it in the hands of the Tsar. Soloviev wrote an article in protest, which was published by Ivan Sergeyevich Aksakov in the periodical, *Russ*, for September, 1885. This article was titled *State Philosophy in the University Curricula*, but as Solviev later described it, his was a *vox clamantis in deserto*, for no one else, so far as he knew, made any protest against the Church having surrendered its rights to a temporal power, even though that power was the Tsar himself. To Soloviev, this action on the part of the Church authorities was another example of the spirit of compromise which prevailed more and more in ecclesiastical affairs at that time. It confirmed his contention that only as people find their way to a Universal Christianity can the rule of Christ come about on earth.

* * *

These manifold activities, however, did not alienate Soloviev from the beauties of the world of Nature about him. An example of his devotion to the realities he perceived with mystical vision is this poem he wrote in the quiet country at Postynka on a beautiful day in May, 1886:

Mother Earth, to you I bow my head,
And through the veil of your perfumes
The burning of a kindred heart I feel,
The beating of a cosmic life I hear.

The noontide rays, with ardent joy,
Descend in blessing from the shining heaven;
In happy greeting to the silent light,
The flowing river sings, the forest rustles.

Again I see in sacrament revealed
Marriage of earth's soul to heaven's light,
And in love's fire, all earthly pain
Like fleeting vapor, vanishes away.

This poem reminds one of the ancient Greek legend of the giant Antaeus who, whenever he was thrown to the ground in combat, arose refreshed by his brief contact with his mother Gaia, the Earth. In similar manner, Soloviev's living awareness of the living, nurturing power of earth revealed to him "a kindred heart," "a cosmic life," from which he drew ever-renewed strength for the tasks he had set himself. Pain and suffering disappeared "like fleeting vapor" as he contemplated the mystical marriage between the earthly soul and the light of spirit, the sacrament of renewal.

* * *

In June, 1886, burdened by the demands destiny was making upon him, Soloviev revealed another mood in his poetry. Now it was the voice of his Eternal Friend, the heavenly image, casting its "shadow" upon his life's path, that restored him, giving him new courage and energy for the tasks ahead:

Oppressive dream, amid a host of visions silent,
Crowding and floating round me!
In vain I seek that blessed shadow
That touched me with its wing.

But when to evil doubt I yield myself,
Fear and deaf yearning seizing me,
The wing of her invisible shadow I feel above me,
Again I hear her words, as once so long ago.

Oppressive dream, amid a host of visions silent,
Growing, towering, blocking up life's path;
Yet from afar faintly I hear the shadow's voice:
"Believe not the fleeting! Love—and never forget!"

* * *

In August 1886 Soloviev was in Croatia, enjoying the beauty of the Styrian Alps, not far from places where Rudolf Steiner passed his boyhood years. As a Russian, accustomed to a more level landscape, particularly around St. Petersburg, Soloviev was deeply moved by the majesty of the mountains, and in his poetic fancy he compared their blue outlines to the waves of the ocean, an image used by Ruskin in the memorable world-picture he included in the third volume of his *Modern Painters*: "The silent wave of the blue mountain is lifted towards heaven in a stillness of perpetual mercy."

Thoughts without words, feelings nameless,
Joyfully, mightily surging;
Shores of hopes, of wishes unstable,
In waves disappearing.

Blue mountains nearing, surrounding
A deep azure lake, far away;
Wings of the soul, bright unfolding,
From earth never straying.

Shores of hopes, of wishes unstable,
Soft pearly waves ever plashing;
Thoughts without words, feelings nameless,
Joyfully, mightily singing!

* * *

In support of his ideas Soloviev made a number of trips to the West, notably to Croatia, later to Paris. On his return to Russia in September 1886 after one of his trips abroad he was greeted with the fact that the Procurator of the Holy Synod, a position Peter the Great once described as "the Emperor's Eye," now occupied by Constantine Petrovich Pobedonostsev, had formally condemned his writings and lectures as inimical to the well-being of the country and the Orthodox Church, hence in the interests of the Faithful they had been placed under what was termed "spiritual censure."

Pobedonostsev, whose office had recently suppressed the Society for the Encouragement of Moral and Religious Reading, the old Russian branch of the British Bible Society, who had forbidden continued use of the word *veliki* (great) in characterizations of the French Revolution of 1793, and who was soon to forbid the retail sale in public places of Lyov Tolstoi's *The Powers of Darkness*, was former professor of civil law at the University of Moscow, a Senator in St. Petersburg, member of the Council of the Empire, and former tutor of the sons of the late Alexander II in theory of law and administration. Chief advisor to the new Tsar and now Procurator of the Holy Synod, this "lean, cool-eyed, scholarly looking man" as Dostoyevski once described him, was the very incarnation of reaction in government, religion, social affairs and private life. His basic political and social convictions he outlined in his *Reflections of a Russian Statesman*, 1898. Recognizing that the ideas of the Slavophils were not basically sound, nevertheless he vastly preferred them to what he considered "totally evil" Western ideas: representative government, modern judicial and legal procedures, trial by jury, freedom of the press and public education outside Church control.

On the other hand, Pobedonostsev was an ardent admirer of many Western authors, particularly Emerson, Hawthorne and Lowell, whose works he read in English. He loved Emerson best of all writers, and translated his *Essays* into Russian. He read many Western devotional works also, and made a Russian translation of Thomas A Kempis' *Imitation of Christ*. At the same time, however, he refused to speak any Western language with foreigners except French, which in any case was the official diplomatic language, and consequently was free of any "taint" of Western liberalism.

Pobedonostsev's ban on Soloviev's writings (the former had personally forbidden publication or circulation of the latter's *History and Future of Theocracy*) was extremely comprehensive, for it forbade publication of "everything presented *or to be presented*" by Soloviev for approval by the government censor. In an attempt to save the book, Soloviev drastically revised what he had written, but to no avail; the censor remained adamant.

Soloviev appealed to his long-time friend, Antonius, the Metropolitan of St. Petersburg, even having two audiences with him, but without result. He thought of approaching the Tsar himself personally, but finally gave up the idea. He strove nevertheless to maintain his courage "like a Red Indian who bears himself with all composure, even under torture," as he wrote to a friend at the time. The controlled press took up the attack upon him, and before long Soloviev recognized that insofar as Russia was concerned there was no possibility for his ideas to gain a public hearing.

Again he journeyed to Paris, where he spoke before a number of distinguished audiences on his Universal Church and Free Theocracy ideas. There he also had numerous conferences with leading Roman Catholic churchmen. Fully aware of the stalemate existing in the Russian Orthodox Church, Soloviev hoped that in the West there would be some hearing for his ideas. But this was not to be. Forbidden to publish in Russia by the censor, Soloviev arranged that his works, *History and Future of Theocracy*, his *Russia and the Universal Church, St. Vladimir and the Christian State*, and *The Russian Idea* were issued in France.

Certain Roman Catholic clerics urged him to publish his *Russia and the Universal Church* without the third part on *The Threefold Principle and its Social Application*, which they found doubtful. Had he agreed they would have accepted this as clear evidence of his intention to become an obedient convert to the Church of Rome. However Soloviev steadfastly refused, and the book was finally published as he had written it.

In itself this is important evidence of the fact that Soloviev's attraction to the Roman Catholic Church was but one aspect of his life-long dedication to his Eternal Friend, the Sophia, a path of devotion which led him from one disappointment, one tragic experience, one sacrifice to another for the remainder of his life, until the day was to come when, as he wrote to his friend, Countess Tolstoi, "I myself become ever more a kind of monument to unfulfilled dreams and destroyed illusions."

On his return from Paris, he traveled to Croatia once again at Christmas, 1888 where he visited his friend, the distinguished Croat Bishop of Diakovo, Msgr. Joseph Georg Strossmayer (1815-1905), former member of the Vatican Council of 1870, noted for his powerful advocacy of the unification of the Eastern and Western Churches, his sharp opposition to the excessive claims of the arch-conservatives among the Jesuits and the College of Cardinals, and to the proclamation of papal infallibility as dogma in 1870. Soloviev and Strossmayer were kindred spirits in their idealism, their mutual interests and their hopes for the establishment of a universal Christianity, for as Soloviev wrote, "In reality, a universal Christianity does not as yet exist; thus far it stands only a task still to be undertaken. And how immense is this task, which seems far beyond our human strength to accomplish!"

He wrote his brother Michael afterward from Vienna, enroute to Moscow, that the visit was a great joy, a kind of festival in itself: "In Diakovo we celebrated the Christmas Festival. The village youths played the Christmas Plays in various groups, and sang the charming, naive, Croatian songs. But Strossmayer himself is not well; he is worn and very changed. But with me he was extraordinarily kind, as always... I am very glad I visited Strossmayer, for it is possible we shall never see each other again."

Between the lines of this letter one can sense Soloviev's deep sorrow despite the joy the Christmas Festival at Diakovo brought him. This was because during the visit Strossmayer told him that he had sent a copy of Soloviev's brochure, *The Russian Idea*, to Cardinal Rampolla at the Vatican. The latter gave it to Pope Leo XIII, who had a warm regard for Soloviev, whom he called "the Sage from the East." When the Pope had read the brochure he handed it back to Cardinal Rampolla, exclaiming sadly, *"Bella idea, ma fuor d'un miracolo, e cosa impossibile!"*

Thus his farewell to Bishop Strossmayer meant for Soloviev a farewell to a dream he held most precious, to which he had devoted the last decade of his life. In addition it was a farewell to a wonderful friend who, as he wrote "spoke with me in Latin, French and Croatian, and in all three languages it is pleasant to hear his enthusiastic tones... No people have such a Bishop as he!"

Soloviev memorialized his friendship with Bishop Strossmayer in his Antichrist story, 1900, where the Bishop appears as the prototype of Pope Peter, while by his side stands the saintly *Starets*, John, for which Soloviev's beloved grandfather was the original.

* * *

Soloviev's return to Russia brought even greater attacks upon him. These were caused at least in part by his undaunted defense of the Jewish people in face of the Tsarist-inspired *Pogroms*, a part of Pobedonostsev's policy of "Russification."

In order to keep in active touch with the problems of the Jews of Russia and Poland, Soloviev attended numerous meetings of Jewish organizations where various aspects of contemporary Jewish cultural and social life were discussed. There he made many friends among Jewish leaders who profoundly appreciated the fact that a prominent Christian philosopher and writer had voluntarily chosen to ally himself with their tragic destiny at this fateful hour in their history.

For example, at this time a group of young Jewish intellectuals and professional men, under the leadership of Alexander Yakolevich Passover (1840-1910), the brilliant St. Petersburg jurist, organized themselves to study Jewish culture, including history, customs, literature and Old Testament backgrounds. Vladimir Soloviev was a warmly welcomed guest at these meetings, and there gave a series of outstanding lectures on the Old Testament Prophets, which were deeply appreciated by his audience.

In these months Soloviev spent long hours in earnest conversation concerning the persecution of the Jews with one of his close friends, the well-known St. Petersburg financier, philanthropist, educator, patron of the arts and Jewish community leader, Baron David Guenzburg (1857-1910). A linguist of extraordinary ability—it was said he was the only man in Russia who could translate any Middle Eastern or European language into any other of the same stock—he was, despite the official prohibition against Jews occupying governmental posts, the official translator in the Foreign Ministry in St. Petersburg. As a teacher he was noted for his profound knowledge of the history of the Near East, of Hebrew, Arabic, Turkish, Aramaic cultures and languages. And although as a Jew the law prevented him from occupying a professorial chair in these areas of study, he was nevertheless constantly consulted by the University of St. Petersburg.

Baron Guenzburg's magnificent personal library numbering some fifty-two thousand volumes, among them extremely rare books and manuscripts on many subjects, over and above an equally impressive collection of periodicals, was considered the second largest private collection of books in the world, that of the King of England being the first. Later, the library of Vladimir Soloviev was also incorporated in this extraordinary collection.

A man of remarkable objectivity, modest, simple, even shy, (it was well known that he never asked favors from officials for himself) Baron Guenzburg was able to intercede successfully with the government again and again on behalf of his fellow-Jews. He was a forceful speaker and vigorous leader of the Jewish community in St. Petersburg, a champion of those suffering from governmental anti-Semitism.

His relationships with Jewish circles and outstanding Jewish leaders like Baron Guenzburg brought upon Soloviev bitter attacks in the newspapers, attacks which weighed heavily upon him, as he wrote in a letter to Tolstoi: "I stand in great need of consolation and encouragement, dear friend, and I strive not to be discouraged."

Soloviev considered entering a monastery as a monk at this time. At the Troitsa he had many serious talks concerning the matter with the well-known clairvoyant *Starets*, Father Barrabas. However, despite the spiritual friendliness and love with which he was received by the monks, it was entirely clear that they by no means wished him to join them unless he first recanted his ideas of the Universal Church and the Free Theocracy.

Soloviev now felt that the moment had at last come when he was forced to make a clear public expression of his personal religious principles. The Western and Eastern Christians alike had entirely misunderstood his ideas; now he must state his position. This he did in a letter to the editor of the *Novoye Vremya* and in a similar statement to the ultra-conservative Russian Orthodox *Church Herald*: "I remain, and I hope always to remain a member of the Eastern Orthodox Church, not formally, but actually, in full conformity with my Confession, and fulfilling all the religious duties connected with it."

In similar vein he had written to his friend, the Archmandrite Antonius, later the Metropolitan of St. Petersburg: "I shall never convert to the Roman Church!... I have returned from abroad and know both the good and the bad sides of the Western Church, entirely clearly... and above all, I can say that I have returned to Russia as fully Orthodox as I was before my journey."

Despite his obvious sincerity, it was abundantly evident that the forces of bureaucratic conservatism in both government and clerical circles had no intention to accept Soloviev's statements. Instead, the government-controlled press became even more vituperative in its attacks upon him.

* * *

In face of disappointment and discouragement, Soloviev wrote the following lines:

Though centuries of evil deeds spoiled everything,
Though nothing pure and spotless has remained,
The voice of conscience stronger is than doubt,
The fire within my soul has not yet died away.

The Great Event that happened once, was not in vain,
Not in vain did Heaven bend itself to earth;
Not in vain did God come down to humanity on earth,
Not in vain did the Eternal Gates stand opened wide.

In depths of cosmic consciousness, by eyes unseen,
Yet lives the Source of Truth eternal;
And through long centuries of human shame
Still sounds its Word, like solemn funeral bells.

Light on Earth was born, but Darkness received it not,
Yet Light still shines in Darkness, where good and evil
    meet;
Not by power external, but by the Truth itself
This world's Prince condemned is, together with his deeds.

Chapter Six

BEFORE THE ICON OF THE SOPHIA

1888–1895

THE YEARS BETWEEN thirty-five and forty-two are the time when human beings can unfold their greatest capacities during their life on earth. For this reason they have been called "the high summer of a person's life." As the years of childhood and youth represent the "springtime," the period when the human being is incarnating ever more deeply into earth-existence, the years *following* this particular seven-year span represent the onset of a gradual withdrawal, an excarnating process, leading eventually to the "winter" of earth-existence, and finally to the death of the physical body and a "birth"—a return—to the spiritual world. Therefore the "high summer" years, the years when a person tends to breathe most deeply the atmosphere of this earth, and is fully "at home" here, present great possibility and challenge.

The possibility of these years lies in the fact that now the *physical* forces have reached their greatest capacity. On the other hand, the challenge is: How will one *use* these forces? Will one apply oneself to the tasks that life's destiny brings at this time, or simply "flex one's muscles," as it were, giving way to a warm sense of well-being, and let it go at that? There is also the danger that the tasks—both mental and physical— which this turning-point brings will be so confusing that instead of recognizing their importance and purpose in one's life-experience, one will, in the words of Dante, "Midway upon the journey" of one's life, find oneself "within a forest dark, the straightforward pathway having been lost."

The test of these years is how one will react to the fact that one now faces a great turning-point. From now on, the forces of one's body will diminish little by little, and their place will be taken by a continual growing, an *increase of the powers of soul and spirit*. Will one be able to summon sufficient *maturity* to accept the gradual dying away of the physical, and on the other hand, sufficient insight and wakefulness to learn to *work with* the gradually increasing power of the spiritual? Upon this depends one's fruitfulness as a human being, one's contribution to humanity, one's capacity to live a truly worthwhile, constructive life. The challenge of these years is whether or not one can come to say "Yes" to a great direction in one's life, to the influx of the spiritual, which in itself opens the doors to a richer, fuller contact with one's fellow human beings, to the experience of *community* with other human beings, a relationship based upon mutual respect and freedom.

Out of the ruins of his ecumenical hope for the reunification of all Christians and the establishment of a Free Theocracy, Soloviev experienced a new inner freedom, a kind of "new birth." From his failure to reconcile the irreconcilable, involving him in the struggle between the form and the spirit of Christianity, Soloviev experienced the birth of *his individual faith*. Out of the fire of his personal suffering came a new view of life, a new world conception. The optimistic, universally utopian outlook Soloviev formerly shared with many men and women of the nineteenth century, had burnt itself out. However, from the ashes, phoenix-like, arose a new view of humankind and of humanity's future. Leaving behind his former interest in the "institutional" aspect of religious experience, Soloviev saw unfolding before him what he called "the religion of the Holy Spirit," revealing itself to him in the light of the Divine Wisdom, the Holy Sophia.

One must not imagine that this inner development and increased spiritual insight came about quickly. Like all processes of birth it involved a certain period of gestation, a time of delay, of apparent reversal of direction, of painful experiences, but the years between 1888 and 1895 brought ample evidence that the light of his Eternal Friend was shining upon his path more clearly than ever before.

* * *

As we have seen, his concern for the reunification of all Christians had highlighted for Soloviev the destiny of the Jewish people and their tragic sufferings. Already in 1864 his article on *The Jews and the Christian Problem* had presented Soloviev's basic convictions. There he described the persecution of the Jewish people as "actually confirming my contention that Christendom *has never regarded them in a Christian way.*" He condemned the indifference of Christians towards the sufferings and persecutions of the Jewish people as clear evidence of "an absence of warmth" which he called "the moral freezing-point, *the cold of spiritual death.*" With incisive logic he argued: "If Christ is not God, the Jews are not more guilty than are the Greeks who killed Socrates. But if we acknowledge Christ as God, then we must acknowledge that the Jews are *a God-bearing race.*

"The idea of *holy flesh* and the concern to realize that idea plays an incomparably greater role in the life of Israel than among any other people. A considerable part of the law of Moses concerning the distinction between pure and impure, and the laws of purification, is connected with this.

"If we consider the Jews' striving for the materialization of the divine principle and their care to purify and sanctify the bodily nature, we shall easily understand why it was that the Jewish people presented the most suitable setting for the inhumanization (Incarnation) of the divine Word... For both reason and piety compel us to admit that besides a holy and virginal soul, the vessel of a pure and holy body was needed for God to be made man.

"Firmly believing in the living God, Israel could enter into a personal relationship with Him, could make a covenant with Him, could serve Him as an active ally in the final realization of the spiritual principle, through purifying material nature. In its own midst Israel thus prepared a pure, holy vessel for the incarnation of God, the Word.

"This is why the Jews are God's chosen people; this is why Christ was born in Judea."

Turning to the future, Soloviev points out that the ultimate goal is the same for Jews and Christians alike, namely, "the realization of divine law in the human world, the incarnation of the heavenly in the earthly." For Soloviev the Jewish people have not only a great mission and task in a *historic* sense. They also have a vital task *for the future as well*. In the light of present-day developments, particularly with regard to the State of Israel and her role among the nations of the earth, these words of Soloviev are weighty with prophetic insight:

Once upon a time the flower of the Jewish race served as a receptive ground for the divine inhumanization, and in the same way the *Israel of the future will serve as an active medium for humanizing material life and nature, and for creating the new heaven wherein righteousness dwells.*

* * *

The brutal persecutions, the mass murders of Jewish people that broke out in Russia in the 1880s and 1890s of the last century, Soloviev regarded not only as a crime against individuals, but as an unspeakable offense against the dignity of humanity as such. For him, "The peculiar horror and evil of murder lie, of course, not in the actual taking of life, but in the inner rejection of the basic moral law, in the decision to break, on one's own initiative and by one's own action, *the bond of universal human solidarity* with regard to this concrete fellow human being who, like me, bears the image and likeness of God."

In 1890 Soloviev proposed to Lyov Tolstoi that the latter, as one of the most widely known and respected of Russia's humanitarians, prepare the text of a protest against the terrorism then being condoned by the Russian Government against its Jewish subjects.

Tolstoi's reply expresses the cordial relationship and understanding existing between the two men. Tolstoi suggested that not he but Soloviev prepare the proposed text because "I know in advance that if *you*, Vladimir Sergeyevich, write what you think about this matter, you will also express my own thoughts and feelings, because the basis of our revulsion regarding the suppression of the Jewish people is one and the same, namely, our mutual awareness of the brotherly link which must exist between all nations and peoples, and most of all with the Jews, among whom Christ was born."

Soloviev drew close to the spirit of the Jewish people, learning Hebrew not only in order to read the Scriptures in the original tongue, but because of his intense interest in the profound esoteric secrets of the language itself. Years before in London he had studied the noted book by Henry Cornelius, Agrippa of Nettisheim (1487-1535), *De Occulta Philosophia* (Antwerp, 1531). Soloviev had been particularly impressed with this passage from Book I, Chapter 74: "The omnipotence of God has by His Providence divided the speech of men into various languages... but above all languages, the writing of the Hebrews is the most sacred... *The twenty-two letters* (of the Hebrew alphabet) *are the foundation of the world* and of all creatures that exist, for every saying and every creature are in those letters and (from them) receive their Name, Being and Virtue. Therefore one who will penetrate into them must, at each joining together of the letters, examine them until the voice of God is manifest... For it is from the latter that (Hebrew) words have efficacy in magical works... because it is known by all wise men that the Hebrew letters are the most efficacious of all because they have the greatest similitude with the Celestial (script) and the (created) Universe."

These ideas were developed further in the teachings of Rabbi Israel Baal Shem Toy (1698-1760), founder of the Hassidic movement, as expounded by Rabbi Schneur Zalman (1745-1812) of Ladi, in his *Shaar Hayihud Vehaemunah*, "The Portal of Unity and Faith," the second part of his *Likute Amarim*, "Selected Sayings" (*Tanya*): "It is written 'Forever, O Lord, your word stands firm in the heavens' (Ps. 119:89). Israel Baal Shem Toy, of blessed memory has explained these words thus: 'Let there be a firmament in the midst of the waters' (Gen. 1:6)—these very words and letters are forever standing firm in the heavens, giving life and existence to the heavens, as is written: 'The word of our God shall stand forever' (Isa. 40:8). For if the letters were to remove themselves and return to their Source, even for an instant, everything would return to nothingness, just as it was before the Creation... And so it is with all created things in this world: the name by which anything is called in the Holy Tongue is a vessel for the life-force contained in the letters of that name as it has descended stage by stage from the divine Words of Creation until it reaches that particular created thing and gives it life. The creature cannot receive its life and existence from the ten divine Words of Creation of the Torah directly, for the life-force as it issues from the latter would be infinitely greater than the capacity of the creature to receive. Hence the name by which the created thing is called in the Holy Tongue is a vessel for the life-force contained in the letters of that name as it has descended stage by stage, diminution by diminution, from the Divine Words of Creation to the created thing in the world, sustaining the latter in earthly existence."

From their side, Soloviev's selfless intervention in defense of the Jewish people won him their love, respect and appreciation. The Russian Zionist, Frederick Goetz, wrote what is perhaps the best expression of their regard for this remarkable man: "One can state positively that since Lessing there has been no scientist or writer of Christian faith who has been regarded by the Jews with such respect and warmth, who was so widely popular and so sincerely loved by them as was Soloviev. And one can say that in future, among the most noble Christian defenders of the Jewish people, along with the names of Abbot Gregoire, Mirabeau, Macaulay, the illustrious name of Soloviev will ever be remembered with all love and thankfulness by the Jewish people."

Forbidden by the Government to give public lectures, to teach in the University, or to publish books within Russia, Soloviev's economic situation at the beginning of the 90s was serious. In order to find employment he sought out the circle of liberal "Westerners" in St. Petersburg, since most of his conservative Russian Orthodox friends had turned away from him, either convinced that he had become a convert to Roman Catholicism or was no longer to be regarded as a "reliable" member of their particular level of society. On the other hand, Soloviev did not share unreservedly the spiritual and cultural ideals of the Westerners, but in contrast to the repressive acts of the Government of Alexander III, their social-political views appealed to him. In a short time Soloviev's articles began to appear in the liberal *Vestnik Evropi, The Messenger of Europe*. At first there was no reaction from official circles, but before long the periodical received a "first warning" from the censors for having published Soloviev's article, *The History of Russian Consciousness*.

In 1890 work was begun toward preparation of what was to become the celebrated *Brockhaus-Efron Encyclopedia*, ultimately the authoritative source of information on Russia and everything Russian. Soloviev was appointed editor of the theological and philosophical sections of this work. He contributed over fifty articles to the encyclopedia on a wide range of subjects, including Mysticism, Theosophy, Gnosticism, Early Christian Philosophy, the Ante-Nicene Fathers, Neoplatonism, Eastern Wisdom, and so on. He also wrote articles for other reference works, including the famous *Dictionary* compiled by Vengerov. His contributions to these scholarly publications show the broad range of Soloviev's knowledge, the depth of his perception, his capacity for research and for the reduction of most complicated material to cogent, easily accessible form. In this one sees a marked similarity between his abilities and those of his historian-father.

* * *

The vision of his Eternal Friend remained an ever-present need in his life, as expressed in this poem he wrote in 1890:

Heat without light, clouds without vapor,
Noises of the city's vanity;
In the yearning heart, thoughts fruitless,
Palpitations of a wingless dream.

I wait for the clouds to move onward,
Then will my thoughts flow in tears;
And over my mourning abandoned,
Your face like the sun will appear.

* * *

During these years Soloviev migrated between the estate of Pystinka, some fifty miles outside St. Petersburg, where he loved to walk along the beautiful Tosna River, the Hotel Rauka in Finland, his mother's home in Moscow and the apartments of friends and relatives in St. Petersburg and Moscow. Once he stayed as a guest in the barracks of the Imperial Guard Regiment in St. Petersburg. Afterward he wrote jokingly to his friend Stasaulevich: "I suppose that in my future necrology and in the dossier devoted to me in the biographical library of Pavlenkov will be written, 'The best, most mature years of this remarkable man were spent under the hospitable roof of the barracks of a battallion of the reserve infantry regiment of the Guards, and also in the cool and quiet shelter of the carriages of the Tsarskoie Selo Railway!"

* * *

In September 1887 the Yellow River overflowed its banks, and more than a million Chinese lives were lost. Two years later a terrible famine swept over China, leaving twelve million dead in its wake. With the beginning of the 1890s ominous rumors of the advance of Asiatic cholera across Siberia and into European Russia began to reach St. Petersburg. Serious and repeated crop failures were reported in outlying districts of Russia itself.

Watching these developments, it seemed to Soloviev that they were symptoms of a revolt of Nature against humankind, who increasingly regarded Nature merely as something to be exploited, as an instrument which could be fashioned to work their will. He expressed his reaction to this in a short verse:

Nature does not permit you to strip
The garment from her beauty;
With machines you will not wrest from her
What your spirit cannot divine!

In lines like these one sees how Soloviev's spiritual sensitivity enabled him to detect trends which in our own time have become urgent for the entire world as the consequences of the disruption of the ecological balance of the world of Nature have become alarmingly apparent.

* * *

Soloviev believed that a proper relationship between human beings and Nature can come about only as people undertake their tasks in the light of true Christianity as the ultimate of their spiritual striving. For Soloviev recognized that the triad presented in the ancient Mystery Wisdom as the proper arrangement of all knowledge and life—Science, Art and Religion—must once again be brought into a rightful balance in human affairs, for the good of humankind and the evolution of the earth. Using the term "Philosophy" to denote humanity's love of a living wisdom, a living Sophia, as the highest of all *Art*, and the term "Theology" to denote awakened spiritual perception (*Religion*) Soloviev gave this important indication regarding a properly balanced conception of the world:

"It is necessary to place Theology in an inner relationship with Philosophy and Science, and thus to organize the entire field of true knowledge into *a complete system of free and scientific Theosophy.*"

He recognized, however, that to accomplish such a rearrangement of human knowledge, it would be necessary for people to come to a clear recognition of what Christianity really is. This point he discussed in a letter to Ykaterina Romanova: "Human beings let themselves be led by their convictions, and for this reason it is necessary to work on these convictions, to convince people of the Truth, of Truth itself, that is, Christianity—of course, not that semblance of Christianity which, as we know it from the different catechisms, is only subjective. The question is really this: How can this Truth be led over into the general consciousness? For at the present time it still is something completely foreign and incomprehensible to many. So first of all the question arises: Where does this estrangement, this present-day thinking in regard to Christianity, come from?

"For most people Christianity is only a subjective, half conscious faith and indefinite feeling, which doesn't say much to intelligent thinking and cannot be accepted by it. After the modern human intellect developed, modern people rubbed against this half-conscious Christianity and rejected it.

"But the time has now come to raise Christianity, to resurrect it. The task stands before us to lead the eternal content of Christianity into a new form which would be right for it, that is, a form which can be taken up *by modern thinking*, by the intellect. To achieve this, everything must be used which has been achieved within the last centuries by means of this intellect.

"And when Christianity is poured out in a new form, when it appears in its new configuration, then everything will vanish which until now has hindered Christianity from penetrating into universal consciousness. Its apparent contradiction to human thinking will gradually disappear."

Now Soloviev's goal emerges as the effort to find the way to true Christianity in its most all-embracing sense as a Wisdom of God, a *Theos-Sophia*, involving a reorientation of human knowledge, and out of this a Christianity with which modern thinking, feeling and willing can find a satisfying and satisfactory relationship, without compromise. His thoughts on this subject he was able to share with others when the invitation came for him to give a private lecture before the Moscow Psychological Society. His theme was *The Collapse of the Medieval World-Conception*, and the effect of his presentation upon his hearers has been likened to that of an exploding bomb. He started with the challenge essential Christianity places before modern humanity: "True Christianity is the regeneration of humankind and the world in the spirit of Christ, the transformation of the kingdom of this world into the Kingdom of God, which is not of this world. This regeneration is a long and complex process. It cannot be simply a natural process or one which happens by itself, unconsciously. It is *a spiritual process*, and it is necessary that humanity participate in it *by means of a person's own faculties and mental forces.*"

From this beginning, Soloviev developed his theme, point by point until he arrived at the climax, which is staggering in its implications: "The Spirit of Christ blows wherever it wills. Indeed, *even its foes* may serve it. Christ has required us to love our enemies, and therefore He not only is able to love them, but certainly realizes *how to make use of them* in His work. Those unbelieving workers in the cause of modern progress have nonetheless worked for the good of Christianity. They could not harm Christ by their lack of belief, *but they have hurt material Nature*, with which many of them were working. They express the false view that Nature is lifeless matter, a machine without a soul. In return, Nature, as if insulted by this twofold lie, *refuses to feed humanity.* It is this common danger which should unite both believers and unbelievers.

"It is time human beings realized their oneness with Mother Earth and rescued her from lifelessness, so they also can save *themselves* from death. But what oneness can we have with the earth, when we have no such oneness, no such moral relationships *among ourselves?*

"It is easy to blame others, to hamper them. Seek to do better yourselves to bring about a living, social, universal Christianity. If we are truly Christians *in deed* and not only in name, *it depends upon our efforts that Christ in his humanity will rise from the dead.*"

This theme is developed a step further in the last of a series of articles which Soloviev wrote for the privately published journal, *Philosophy and Psychology*, issued after Soloviev's

death under the title, *The Meaning of Love*, by many considered to be his masterpiece.

In this essay Soloviev indicates that while religious faith and
performance of good works have preserved human beings and
their integrity in spite of materialism, *they have not enabled
them to defeat 'the last enemy'—death itself.* Then he postu-
lates an example, "not entirely fantastic," of two human beings
who have so ennobled their spirit by "consistent concentration of will and consciousness," and their bodies by ascetic
practices that at last they have succeeded in the restoration
of "the true integrity of human individuality, the attainment
of complete spiritualization *and immortality.*" Now Soloviev
asks whether this extraordinary pair will be able to *enjoy* their
deathless state, in view of "the milliards of people who gave
their lives for others, whose bodies rot in their graves." This
query he answers in the negative, pointing out that "Human
beings cannot accept such a gift if they are not able to rob
death of *all* its prey. If they cannot do this, it is better that
they turn their backs on deathlessness (for) our regeneration
is indissolubly linked with *the regeneration of the universe, in
which humanity should participate actively.*"

This concept, "not entirely fantastic," of the regeneration of
human beings and universe, thus robbing death of its "prey,"
was not original with Soloviev. It was the fruit of his friendship with a man whose ideas have been almost forgotten with
the passage of time—Nikolai Feyodorovich Feyodorov.

In February, 1878, long before he wrote in *The Meaning
of Love*, "*True spirituality is the regeneration of the flesh, the
rescue of it, the resurrection of it from the dead,*" Soloviev
heard of Feyodorov for the first time.

One day Dostoyevski received a manuscript in the mail,
accompanied by a note from a certain N.V. Petersen, who
described himself as "a friend of the author." After reading
the manuscript, Dostoyevski gave it to Soloviev to study; in
it the latter found a "Plan" so significant, so fantastic in its

Vladimir Soloviev. From the Portrait by Kramskoi

Nikolai Feyodorovich Feyodorov (1825-1903).
From a drawing made by the painter Pasternak in the library
of the Rymantsev Museum, Moscow

implications, that it made a profound impression upon him. The manuscript contained an element which later was to form a vital part of what Soloviev called his Religion of the Holy Spirit. Of the latter he wrote: "The Religion of the Holy Spirit which I profess is broader and more embracing in content than *all* individual religions. It is neither the totality of all of them, nor is it their extract, in the sense that the complete human being is neither the totality nor the extract of individual organs."

Actually Soloviev did not live to work out the details of this Religion of the Holy Spirit in its entirety, but as an outline or a first "sketch" it is clear that what he had in mind was and is one of the most inspiring and far-reaching developments of Christian thinking in modern times.

Soloviev's reading of Feyodorov's manuscript gave him a key-thought which played an important role in his future thinking; *the interdependence of all human beings.*

In a letter he wrote to Feyodorov, Soloviev described his first impression of the former's work: "I read your manuscript avidly and in a ravenous spirit. For this reading I took a whole night and a part of the morning, and for the next two days, Saturday and Sunday, I thought a very great deal about what I had read. Your Plan I accept absolutely and without question. We should talk, not about the Plan itself, but about some of its theoretical fundamentals or presuppositions, as well as about the first practical step toward its realization. For the present I will say only that *since the appearance of Christianity* your Plan is *the first forward movement* of the human spirit on the way of Christ. From my side, I can only acknowledge you as my teacher and spiritual father. Remain in good health, my dear teacher and comforter."

Dostoyevski was no less appreciative of the contents of the manuscript, for he wrote Petersen, a teacher, later to become a collaborator with Lyov Tolstoi in the latter's school for children at Yasnaya Polyana: "Fundamentally I fully agree with these thoughts; I read them as my own—concluding, "Soloviev and I believe in real, literal, individual resurrection, and that it will occur on earth."

Not long after his initial study of the manuscript, Soloviev met Feyodorov in Moscow. Feyodorov has been described by those who knew him in his position as deputy librarian at the famous Rumyantsev Museum in Moscow as "a tall, wizened, slightly bent, but energetic figure of an old man, clad in tatters, whose eyes sparkled with all the liveliness, fire and energy of youth." Soloviev found him a person of genial, friendly ways, was struck with the unusual originality of his character, and—as he wrote to Strakhov—"he completely charmed me so that even I think his strange ideas are not far from the truth."

* * *

Nikolai Feyodorov was born in 1825, the natural son of Prince Feyodor Gagarin, grandson of Prince Alexievich Gagarin, one of the leading Russian Freemasons in the time of Catherine II. Nikolai, his brother, his sisters and their mother —described as a captive Circassian woman—lived on his father's vast estate in South Russia as a boy. He was educated in Tambov and Odessa, finally becoming a teacher of history and geography in state schools in central and north-central Russia for about fourteen years, beginning in 1854, the year after Soloviev was born.

N.V. Petersen, who later sent Feyodorov's manuscript to Dostoyevski, described his first meeting with Feyodorov which took place in the town of Bogorodsk in March 1864: "I went to visit Nikolai Feyodorovich. He was a bachelor and lived as an ascetic. He did not have a bed, not even a pillow, and he ate what was given him by his landlord. In his talk with me he developed his world conception, according to which it is necessary 'to unite all men in labor.'"

In 1868 Feyodorov was appointed deputy librarian in the Tschertkov Library in Moscow. Later he accepted a similar position in the Rumyantsev Museum which was housed in a great mansion on the Pretschistenka not far from the beautiful Church of the Redeemer, with its five gilded domes and lavish facade of magnificent marbles. The Rumyantsev Museum contained a remarkable collection of old paintings, fine sculptures, prints, a large mineral collection, while its ethnological collection represented with great accuracy of detail the various peoples included in the Russian Empire. In addition, the library of the Museum was famous for its seven hundred thousand books and nearly three thousand rare manuscripts. It was not long before Feyodorov—thanks to his remarkable memory and excellent scholarship—developed an intimate acquaintance with the volumes and other materials in his charge.

For twenty-five years Feyodorov presided over the reading room of the Rumyantsev Museum, and was well known to the host of professors, students, writers and visitors who came to the library. As he sat in the corner of the reading room with its two rows of tall windows, Feyodorov seemed the epitome of a scholar and friendly librarian-counsellor. Whenever he saw that a student was seriously interested in a particular line of research, Feyodorov spared no pains to help him, often selecting books for him, advising him and generally encouraging him in his work.

In his last years Feyodorov was librarian in the Ministry of Foreign Affairs where he was active at the time of his death in 1903 at the age of seventy-eight.

Feyodorov never earned more than four hundred rubles (about two hundred dollars) a year, not through necessity, but by choice, since under the law any man who earned more than that amount was liable for jury duty. Feyodorov firmly refused to serve as a juror, for he did not wish to be a judge over his fellow human beings. He was a true ascetic. His bed was a bare convex plank, while some sort of hard object served him as a pillow. He slept only about four or five hours each night. He possessed no clothes other than the tatters he wore constantly; often he was mistaken for a beggar. For the most part he lived on tea and pretzels, with the rare supplement of a piece of old cheese or salt fish. For months on end he had no warm food at all.

Feyodorov's dislike of money amounted almost to physical disgust. He felt there was something impure about coins and paper money and did not wish to have them in his pockets. After he had paid for his extremely modest needs he gave away all the money left from his salary—often presenting it to needy students whom he met at the library. But, despite his generosity, he often exclaimed, "You may spend all you want of the stuff, but try as you may, there's still some of that accursed money left over every time!"

A Professor Linechenko, who knew Feyodorov for many years, recalled that "He lived the life of an heroic ascetic, but not of a hermit. Nikolai Feyodorovich greatly enjoyed people and social life. I remember him as a very old man, but he was amazingly alert, full of life, sometimes capricious and hot-tempered. He was thin, slightly bent, of middle height, almost completely bald. His face had a noble quality about it, and his eyes shone with a wonderful radiance. Winter or summer he wore the same very old coat and always rubbers. He was exceedingly kind and compassionate, but sometimes he took a dislike to certain persons. In such instances, no reason or proof one could bring forward would persuade him to put aside his antipathy. He had a remarkable sensitivity for people."

One day a young writer appeared at the library. Feyodorov was very cool to him, almost rude, hardly speaking to him at all. When someone remonstrated with him concerning his abrupt treatment of the young man, Feyodorov exclaimed impatiently, "He amounts to nothing; he only writes for money!" Asked to prove what he said, he could not do so, for he did not know the young man personally at all. Nevertheless he clung tenaciously to his estimate of him. Later the young man became a journalist and was well known for his aggressiveness and avarice, just the opposite of his appearance in earlier life. Feyodorov had perceived this trait in him years before it became evident to others.

Tolstoi and Feyodorov were well acquainted, and one afternoon Feyodorov took advantage of the novelist's presence to show him some of the rarest books and manuscripts in the library collection. Tolstoi looked at everything, and then with a shrug of his shoulders exclaimed, "Well, there are many stupid things written by people, to be sure, and all this rubbish should have been burned long ago!" Feyodorov struck himself on the forehead with his open palm in a fervent gesture, exclaiming in exasperation, "I've seen many fools in my life, but such a one as you I never met before!" With this, Feyodorov rushed out of the room, overcome by emotion.

Tolstoi, of course, was deeply sorry he had obviously hurt Feyodorov by his remark, and later went to the latter's lodgings and apologized to him. As a matter of fact, Tolstoi had a very high regard for Feyodorov and later said to the poet, Fet, "I am proud to live in the same century with such a man!"

Feyodorov's knowledge was truly encyclopedic; his capacity for remembering even the smallest details was amazing. Once some engineers were consulting in the library about some topographical details connected with a certain spot in a wilderness area of Siberia where they were planning to construct a section of the Trans-Siberian Railway. They showed Feyodorov the detailed map they had obtained, but he pointed out that it was incorrect, saying, "Between those two little hills there is a small stream which the map doesn't show." They didn't believe him, particularly when he told them that never in his life had he been in that remote place in Siberia. But later, after the engineers had visited the site, they returned to the library to tell Feyodorov that he was entirely correct: a stream did, in fact, exist exactly where he told them it did, and the official topographical map was inaccurate.

The well-known painter, the father of the late Nobel prize-winner, Boris Pasternack, author of *Doctor Zhivago*, knew Feyodorov, and wished to paint a portrait of him. However, he realized that the latter would almost certainly never consent to sit for him, for doubtless a portrait would not be compatable with Feyodorov's ascetic habits. Therefore Pasternack went to the library one day, took some books from the shelves, and, under pretence of making notes from his reading, quietly sketched the aged Feyodorov while the latter sat at his desk, entirely oblivious of what was going on. This portrait by Pasternack, reproduced in this book, reveals a famous artist's impression of this highly original thinker.

Feyodorov was exceedingly modest and self-effacing where his writings were concerned. He shrank from any form of publicity, even the simplest; his friends signed his letters for him; he refused to allow his manuscripts to be printed during his lifetime. Therefore it was not until 1906—three years after his death—that a little group of his devoted students published his writings at Vernyi in Central Asia. They appeared in two volumes in an edition of 480 copies which—in line with Feyodorov's ideas—were not sold, but were distributed freely to anyone who asked for them, the publishers having renounced all rights to the books.

* * *

The principal work of Feyodorov, *Filosofiya obshchevo dela*, *The Philosophy of the Common Task*, is the expression of the single thought which occupied him for years; like Pushkin's *Miser Knight*: "He possessed but a single vision, incomprehensible to the mind." In the nineteen sections of Feyodorov's book is contained the outline of a "Task" which is startling in its implications. From one point of view, Feyodorov's idea appears morbid, grotesque, breathing an atmosphere of sorcery, of macabre fantasy. But this is only *one* aspect. From another point of view his idea and his exposition of it—since they appear to contradict the teaching of traditional Christianity which views resurrection solely as the gift of God, not as something which can be accomplished by human exertion—brand Feyodorov a heretical thinker, whose idea leads straight into the morass of black magic, crass materialism, even madness.

But there is nevertheless *another* aspect of Feyodorov's idea and his development of it. This is reflected in Tolstoi's estimate of him, reported by his son, Ilya Lvovich: "My father considered Feyodorov a pure Christian, for the latter seemed always to radiate goodness. It is remarkable that father, who always grew excited and easily lost his temper in arguments, would listen to Nikolai Feyodorovich with complete attention and never lost his temper with him. Father said, 'If there are saints, they must be just like him!'" Other famous people in many walks of life also considered Feyodorov an entirely righteous man, even referring to him as "an uncanonized saint."

When Soloviev first read Feyodorov's manuscript, his fullest attention was aroused by passages like this: "Nature as she exists today—due to humankind's ignorance and immorality—cannot be considered God's creation, for in her His intentions are partly unfulfilled and partly distorted... The world of Nature is blind today, moving toward destruction and chaos, for man's faith in Satan has resulted in *knowledge without action*. The Tree of Knowledge has been changed into the wood of the Cross. Men are called upon to be instruments of God in that through the unifying power of the wood of the Cross, they can transform *knowledge into activity*.

"The teaching destined for *all* of us, not only for scientists alone, can be related only to a Task which is absolutely universal, common to all humanity, including all, understandable by all, *necessary* to all. Such a cause can be only the *perfecting and restoring of life.* It is necessary to begin with changing the relationship between human beings, and also the attitude of human beings toward Nature and of Nature toward human beings. Our relationship with Nature should be supplanted by a conscious, powerful regulation of Nature by an all-embracing, perfect will of all humanity, directed *toward a lofty moral goal.*

"The scientists who have separated Science into many separate sciences, imagine that the calamities which fall upon us are not a matter common to everyone. This blind force of Nature apparently demands nothing from us except what this force does not have, i.e., a ruling mind regulating it. For example, regulation of meteorological processes is necessary, not only to secure a harvest, but also to bring to an end the hard, underground toil of the miners who dig for coal and iron. This regulation is necessary in order to substitute for this manner of obtaining power, a way of obtaining locomotive forces directly out of atmospheric currents, out of the solar force. In the governing of this meteorological process is included the solution of agricultural and industrial questions."

In words which sound remarkably descriptive of our contemporary world, Feyodorov points out that: "Today everything is in the service of war; no invention or discovery exists which has not been considered by the military from the point of view of its possible use for war... Even the channels of communication themselves exist only for military strategy, for commerce, for war-making or profit... Today science is dominated by industrialists and business men... In earlier times the servant of theology, today science is the servant of industry.

"The aim of all human effort is to secure for everyone a healthy, moral, happy existence, including the victory over hunger, over disasters caused by the elements, illness, imperfections in the human organism, and finally *over death itself.*

"But the fulfillment of this Task common to all humanity is not limited to winning immortality for the living. With

The Elder Amvrosi (1812-1891), the original of Father Zossima, Staretz of Optina Pystin whom Soloviev visited, 1878

Vladimir Sergeyevich Soloviev.
From a photograph taken in Moscow

God's help the future generations, with the power of universal knowledge, with a united will, *have no right to leave in the captivity of death all those who gave them life, that is, their ancestors. The restoration of life to the ancestors* is the highest moral obligation of the future generations who are called by the Savior to be perfect as their Father in Heaven is perfect. The fulfillment of this duty does not run counter to the will of God. On the contrary, with God's cooperation it will be the fulfillment on earth of the Will of our Heavenly Father who is a God, not of the dead, but of the living.

"The message of life, of immortality and of resurrection, is the essence of the teaching of the Savior because Christ is the Resurrector. The unavoidable condition for resurrection is that the believers, patterning themselves after the model of Christ, shall not have faith alone, but shall enter into the very work of salvation itself. *Then humanity will become an instrument of life, a life-bearing force.*

Christ's resurrection demands a general resurrection... "

This bold vision of the resurrection of all the departed ancestors, through a common work, united in love, seemed to Soloviev and Dostoyevski a glorious prospect *at first.*

However, Dostoyevski soon put his finger on a basic difficulty. This he did in his first letter to Feyodorov after his initial reading of the latter's manuscript. He suggested that what Feyodorov no doubt was indicating was the resurrection, not of physical, earthly bodies from their graves, but *spiritualized* bodies, similar to that of Christ in the period between Easter morning and Ascension Day. Soloviev also shared this impression at first, but after many long conversations with Feyodorov, he became perplexed and confused. He felt in the insistence of Feyodorov upon "a material, visible, palpable" resurrection of the dead, something of a refined materialism. He seemed to detect some sort of unholy magic in the manipulating of the forces of Nature proposed by Feyodorov. Finally he asked himself: What if the dead were really to rise from their graves, *and were quite unchanged in their inner nature*, beset with their sins, infirmities and limitations as before in life, *would that be real progress?* Would that not rather indicate an extension into an unbearable eternity, of human errors and weaknesses, and not a real transformation, a genuine, positive spiritualization of humankind? Were such a "Task" successful, what then would be the significance of the Mystery of Golgotha, the Deed of Christ, particularly his having united himself with the earth, whereby the latter has become the Body of Christ? What about the institution of the New Adam in place of the old, which had been accomplished by the Resurrection of Christ?

After much consideration, Soloviev wrote to Feyodorov: "The plain physical resurrection of the dead cannot be an aim in itself. To resurrect human beings in the same state, in which they try to devour each other, to resurrect humanity on the level of cannibalism, would be as impossible as it would be absolutely undesirable. If humankind were to cloak their activities with divinity, then God would not be visible behind them. We do not conceal God because the divine action (grace) shows through our activity... In a positive religion... we have not only the beginning and prototype of the resurrection and the coming of the future Kingdom of Heaven, but also the real, practical, actual way to this goal. Therefore our 'Task' should have a spiritual, not a scientific character; it should rely on methods of faith, not on intellectual arguments."

Careful reading of Feyodorov's book will show that to some extent Soloviev misunderstood his meaning. However, Feyodorov certainly gave ample cause for such misunderstanding, though he denominated Soloviev's objections "Nonsense."

Soloviev and Dostoyevski, gifted with unusual spiritual sensitivity and perception, sensed in Feyodorov's idea an emergence of something pre-Christian out of the ancient, pre-Slavonic subsoil of Russia. From unknown depths, from a long-forgotten past, "something" had forced its way to the surface and touched the mind and heart of a scholar of saintly heart, filled with longing for a broader, deeper community relationship with his fellow human beings on spiritual grounds, in whose thoughts the dead were constantly present. Through him, this "something" took the outer guise of a noble ideal, a selfless objective, expressed in the philosophical-religious language of late nineteenth century Russia.

It is evident that a direct connection exists between the darker implications, the pre-Christian side of Feyodorov's "Task," and Dostoyevski's premonitions and portrait of the Antichrist.

On the other hand, the positive aspects of Feyodorov's idea are reflected not only in Soloviev's *Meaning of Love*, but even to a greater extent in his *Justification of the Good*, which he began writing in 1894. In October of that year Soloviev first experienced concern over "Panmongolism":

"Panmongolism" — the word sounds strange,
But it suits my ear
As of a premonition to be fulfilled,
A great, divine destiny.

Numberless like locusts,
Insatiable,
But guarded by a force from Beyond,
The tribes are moving toward the north.

O Russia, forget your past glory,
The double-headed eagle lies crushed,
And the tatters of your banners
Are playthings for the yellow children.

Humbled in trembling and fear
Will be those who forget the aim of love;
The Third Rome lies in dust —
Never will there be a Fourth.

The death of Alexander III in November 1894 increased Soloviev's anxiety for the future of Russia, typified in Moscow, "the Third Rome," as it had been called. Like the apocalyptic storm-clouds of vengeance looming up on the horizon in El Greco's unforgettable painting of Toledo, Soloviev saw a severe destiny approaching Russia.

* * *

Feyodorov's *Philosophy of the Common Task* brought into focus three points in the thinking of Soloviev. *First*, it directed his attention to the dangerous materialism disguised as "modern progress" with its goal of *heaven on earth* as an enormous threat to the future of humanity. *Second*, it helped him to develop as a positive Christian element in his "Religion of the Holy Spirit" the goal of *community* as an association of free human beings motivated by common work for the well-being of humanity. *Third*, it caused Soloviev once again to take into account, this time at an even more conscious level, perhaps, the eschatological aspects of Christianity: the restoration of the unity of all Christians and the resurrection of all humankind in the light of the Mystery of Golgotha.

To Feyodorov, Soloviev owed, to some extent at least, the increasingly clear realization of the implications of the Deed of Christ for Christian life and thought, which form a dominant place in the writings of his last years. For it is this Deed of the Death on Golgotha and Resurrection—entirely inexplicable to any mind limited by the "boundaries of knowledge" and the materialistic outlook characteristic of nineteenth century thinking—which gives Christianity its essential meaning. In the light of the Resurrection, the "simple man of Nazareth" disappears from human consciousness, giving place to the cosmic proportions of the Risen One present with humanity, having united himself with earth-evolution to the end of the aeon.

Vladimir Soloviev. A photograph made about 1885

The Cathedral of St. Sophia in Novgorod, built 1045-52.
From a photograph, 1880

Out of this point of view Soloviev wrote Tolstoi in August 1894: "All our disagreement consists in only one point: the Resurrection of Christ. The spiritual power in relation to material existence is not constant—it increases. It attains freedom in humanity, and stands revealed. The ultimate victory of the forces of the inimical power of materialism is death... Death is the victory of absurdity over reason, chaos over cosmos... Immortality to a human being is the same as reason to an animal, i.e., *human*. The meaning of humanity is an immortal, i.e., *Christ*. Just as the animal kingdom is drawn toward reason, so humanity is drawn toward immortality.

"Upon what is based the belief in the actual Resurrection of Christ as the first-born of the dead? I have three grounds: 1) The victory over death is the inevitable, natural sequence of inner spiritual perfection. The image of complete spiritual perfection is Christ, and because of this, this spiritual, perfect man is the first-born of the dead, *and there is no reason to await another*. 2) When behind the planet Uranus, the astronomer Leverrier discovered the orbit of another planet, which is Neptune, on the basis of his mathematical calculations alone he first said, 'It must be there,' and then he observed it, he saw it. In this manner the Holy Scriptures and the Prophets foretold the coming of Christ, and like Leverrier, so afterward the Jews saw that a perfect man had risen from the dead. 3) The fact of the quite extraordinary enthusiasm of the apostolic community would be without any basis if the fact of the Resurrection did not exist."

* * *

At about this time Soloviev occupied himself with the age-old questions concerning the significance of Art in relation to human life, as well as to the world of Nature. This consideration was perhaps stimulated by the fact that the wealthy railway builder and Moscow merchant, Savva

Ivanovich Mamontov, well-known patron of the arts—he was among those who for years contributed lavishly to opera, ballet and theatrical companies, among them the Moscow Art Theater—had co-founded with Princess Tenishev, a new and very beautiful periodical titled *Mir Iskusstva*, The World of Art. Directed toward improvement of the general public's appreciation of the arts in general and modern art in particular, the magazine included among its permanent contributors Dimitri Merejkovski and Sergei Diaghilev, the latter to become famous in the West for his ballet group.

Soloviev found a place among the contributors to this periodical, partly as a reviewer. One of his reviews describes a certain new book of poems as a production which "has undoubted merit, for it burdens its readers with neither bulk nor content."

Another article in a more serious vein discusses some of the fundamental aspects of a work of art: "The aesthetic connection between Art and Nature consists not in the repetition, but in the continuation of the artistic work done by Nature—in a further and more complete solution of the same aesthetic task.

"Just as a ray of light plays upon a diamond to the delight of the spectator, but without producing any change in the material composition of the stone itself, so the spiritual light of the absolute ideal, refracted in the artist's imagination, illuminates the dark human reality without in the least altering its essence.

"The ultimate task of perfect Art is to realize the absolute ideal, not in imagination only, but in very deed—to spiritualize and transfigure our life. If it be said that such a task transcends the limits of Art, the question may well be asked: *Who has laid down those limits?*"

* * *

This period of Soloviev's life was rich in poetic expression. Among the poems he wrote at this time are the following:

Shining rays in abundance
Grant us the new spring day
While in silence, night-shadows
Strengthen the fortress of ice.

Dark earth appears amid the snow,
But its sad color brings us joy,
As it is flooded with victorious light
Of the new-born spring.

Aboard the steamer *Torneo* Soloviev wrote a poetic impression of the sunrise:

Behold, the thin moon slowly pales,
Faintly shines the star of Aphrodite;
The new light touching the wave's soft crest
Awaits with me the rising sun.

Behold, like pouring streams of blood,
Overwhelming forces of the darkness,
The ancient struggle begins once more,
Once more the Sun, the Sun is victor!

In a brief verse Soloviev pictures the ancient theme of the lily and the rose:

 Zion's mighty fortress stands impregnable,
Roses of Sharon bloom in deathless beauty;
Upon the water of life, in the mysterious grotto,
The sacred lily floats, immaculate and pure.

Ever and again Soloviev returns to the mystical meeting with his Eternal Friend in the desert, now hovering before him as a beautiful dream of long ago:

The dim light of a well-known radiance,
The scarce-heard echo of a song from far away,
And the world of the past, in undimmed splendor
Rises once again before my responsive soul.

Titled *A Portent*, the following poem reflects Soloviev's prophetic vision, a mystical picture of the fate which was to overtake Russia, the country Dostoyevski once called the woman clothed with the sun":

One, forever one, even if in the sleeping temple
In the darkness, hellish glare, thunder in silence;
Everything may lie in ruins, our banner will not waver,
Our shield will yet remain upon the ruined wall.

Fearful, half-awake, we hurried to the holy place,
Stifling smell of burning filled our temple;
Fragments of melted silver lay scattered,
Black smoke clung to the charred carpets.

But the Sign of the Eternal Covenant
Between heaven and earth, stood as before;
On the Virgin of Nazareth the light of heaven shone
— And on the serpent's vain poison.

Titled *Immanu-el*, the following poem gives Soloviev's impression of the inner meaning of the Christmas Event, not only for the past but for our present as well.

Into the darkness of ages has vanished
That night, when weary with evil and fear,
Earth rested in heaven's embrace,
And God-with-us was born in the stillness.

Today many things happen no more:
The face of heaven the Kings no longer scan;
Alone in the desert the Shepherds no longer hear
The angels speaking of God.

But the Eternal, revealed in that night
Still is untouched by passage of time,
And the Word, once born in a manger,
Today is reborn in your soul.

God-is-with-us, Yes, but not under the heaven,
Nor afar beyond star-boundaries infinite;
Nor in the dark fire of evil, nor fevered emotions,
Nor in sleeping memories of ages long gone.

Now and *here* He is present!
Amid world-illusion,
In the turbulent stream of life's daily concerns,
Lives your own joyous secret:
The Evil is vanquished,
And we are immortal —
for now God-is-with-us!

The following poem which Soloviev wrote in 1892, is one
of his best-known and most loved. Often cited as an example
of his Platonist conception of the world, it is a beautiful
expression of his mystical view of the relationship between
humankind and Nature.

Dear friend, do you not see
That whatever we look upon here
Is but reflection, merely a shadow,
Of what is invisible to our earthly eyes?

Dear friend, do you not know
That the jarring noises of the world
Are but an echo distorted
Of triumphant harmonies?

Dear friend, do you not sense
That in all the world is only
What one heart says to another
In silent greeting?

In the ancient city of Novgorod stands the Cathedral of St. Sophia, the latter founded in 1405 by Vladimir, son of Yaroslav, Grand Prince of Kiev, who had built the Cathedral of St. Sophia there only a decade before. Held in devout veneration by generations of Russians, the Novgorod Cathedral of St. Sophia was an important object of pilgrimages throughout the centuries.

Soloviev was much attracted to an icon in this cathedral, called the *Sophia Premúdrost Bózhia*, Sophia the All-Wisdom of God. Inspired by the scriptural word-picture, "Wisdom (*Hokhmah, Sophia*) has built her house, she has hewn out her seven pillars" (Proverbs 9:1), a striking female figure wearing red robes is shown seated upon a throne, rising out of the golden background of Eternity. At the right and left of this figure stand the Virgin Mother and John the Baptist, each on a slight elevation. Above the central figure, the Christ appears in his cosmic glory, while in a yet higher sphere angelic beings surround the Word of God represented in the form of an open book.

Soloviev frequently visited the Cathedral of St. Sophia in order to study this icon about which there was considerable mystery. It is said that in the fourteenth century a Russian nobleman inquired of the Archbishop of Novgorod the meaning of the name: "the All-Wisdom of God." The Archbishop replied that he did not know. But in a number of parts of Russia through the centuries, cathedrals and many churches were built in honor of what Soloviev described as "the most exalted, all-encompassing form, the living soul of Nature and cosmos, one with God from all Eternity... an all-encompassing, divinely-human completeness, revealed to us by Christianity... the actual, pure, perfect humankind."

Variations of the *Icon of Sophia* exist, but the basic elements, in conformity with the strict traditional requirements governing iconic art, are always present. One can observe that four levels are clearly depicted, spheres of consciousness, degrees of spiritual exaltation. First, is the region of the Virgin and John the Baptist; second, the enthroned Sophia, staff in hand; third, the living Christ in glory; fourth, the eternal, archetypal world of the divine necessities, recorded in the writing of the everlasting Gospel, inscribed in the starry heavens, figured in the angelic hosts.

From the *Icon of Sophia* streamed a divine power and grace, for—in the words of Ivan Kireyevski, the early Slavophil,— "This icon, century after century has absorbed the currents of passionate exaltation, the prayers of grieving; unhappy people. It must have become filled with energy, have become a living organ, a meeting-place of humanity and Creator."

Described by Prince Troubetskoi as "meditations in color," the forms of the icons bear witness to the love of the *beauty* of Christianity, characteristic of the Russian people from the very beginning of their Christianization. Reflecting the words of the Psalmist, "Lord, I loved the beauty of Thy house," the Russian priest at the end of the Liturgy repeats the prayer, "Sanctify those who love the beauty of Thy house."

One of the early Eastern Fathers, John Damascene, said, "The icon is *an image of a mysterious, heavenly vision*, a hymn of praise, *a manifestation*." Thus the forms of the icons bear the impress of the spiritual world; in them lives an echo of the clairvoyance of ancient times when spirit and matter were not entirely separated, when a "picture" was not merely material, but was touched by the spirit, something spiritual-physical.

Images of "a mysterious, heavenly vision," the icons were born out of the spirit; their chief characteristic is *timelessness*. Utterly calm, they are a "threshold" for the reverent soul, a window opening upon the world of spiritual archetypes, "guides" to the spirit-beings they represent. Every icon has its own inner architecture, its own mystical dynamic, its musical, harmonic unity which nothing can disturb, weaken or destroy.

In the presence of an icon one stands face to face with Eternity, with the divine order of things. The icon requires of us that we "lay aside all worldly cares," as the Liturgy urges, freeing ourselves from the spell of our subjective concerns, in order that the icon can speak to us. When it finally *does* speak, however, it will impart to us the greatest joy and peacefulness through its visions of matchless color.

Through the living drama they embody, the icons are heaven's answer to the sorrow of humanity. As Prince Troubetskoi wrote, "At last, through suffering in our time we have come to understand all the suffering which has gone to make the icon—all the age-long soul of the people, all the tears shed before the icon, and how powerfully the icon gives answer to these tears! Its language cannot be understood by those filled only with dreams of material well-being; it becomes real when these dreams fade, and the pit opens beneath humanity's feet. It is *then* that we need an unshakeable support; it is *then* that the joyful vision of the icon becomes our daily bread. In ancient Russia, in 'days of great tribulation,' this vision was a great sustaining power; it is no less vital for us today, when the danger of the world is still greater."

In the calm, quiet faces, the hands speaking the language of tranquillity, the ordered, balanced gestures, the clear-seeing eyes, the absence of shadows because here the divine light permeates all things, the flowing garments—in all this speaks the language of the Everlasting. Thus things have been ordered from before time was. Thus it will be when all that is has disappeared, swallowed up in the evolving aeons.

The icons present neither "realism" nor physical characteristics as such, for naturalistic representation cannot convey the profound sensitivity, the "weightlessness," the spiritual "refinement," the "divine proportion" of the world of the Eternal.

Before the *Icon of the Sophia, the Divine Wisdom*, one may well ask: What is the meaning of life? What is the reason of our existence? What makes life worthwhile? And perhaps these are among the most fundamental questions one can ask, after all.

The painters of the icons, who have answered these questions, if only we can read their answers, were by no means philosophers nor men of keen intellect. They were spiritual sages, adepts, and their answer to these questions was not given in words but in pictures. To these questions they replied in form and color, revealing a vision of a new dimension of truth, a new world. In a kind of "priestly writing," like the hieroglyphs of old, they set before human beings a vision of the divine reality which completely possessed their souls. And today we can *learn* to "read" these hieroglyphs, these artistic presentations, these meditations upon spiritual realities.

In the icons the asceticism of the figures, their non-naturalistic restraint, their spiritual "reserve," as it were, serves to emphasize the spiritual life and light streaming from the eyes with overwhelming strength and intensity. This light, concentrated in the eyes, is a kind of symbolic expression of the absolute power of spirit over the physical body. For the vision of the icon can replace for humans "the worship of the beast" with a vision of the transformation, the transfiguration of all things in the light of spirit. This transfiguration is a process having as its initial step the transformation of the individual human being.

In the *Icon of the Sophia*, as in all icons, everything bears the impress of law and wisdom, the manifestation of the primordial world of eternal archetypes, far removed from the world of everyday. Here is the Eternal Silence, the world of the Father, the Ground of all existence, the all-encompassing divine Wisdom, out of which everything has conic, in which all things exist, to which all will return.

The Son, the Christ in his eternal, cosmic, universal aspect, reveals himself in the Light of Mount Tabor, the "uncreated Light," forming the spiritual content of the meditations of untold generations of monks of Athos and Russia... With lifted hands the Light of the World blesses all that is, for through Him, the Logos, all creation has come into being, has significance, is capable of divinity.

Enthroned, the divine Sophia, face radiant with Seraphic wisdom, clad in eternal aspiration and the green-gold life of hope, holding the staff of intention, purpose and authority, marks the boundary between Past and Future, the threshold of the eternal Now, across which the new grows eternally out of the old.

From the Sophia's throne of power and majestic clarity stream the gold-permeated rays of wisdom, the gold-green shining glory, central hue in the eternal Sign in the heavens, everlasting token of God's covenant with humanity.

The golden streams of life flow from the supernal Wisdom into human hearts and all creation. Her divinely regal aspect calls forth the highest in human beings, awakening in them renewed aspiration toward the Heights, one end of her staff resting upon the earth, the other pointing upward to the starry script of the eternal Gospel. For she is the bridge, the impelling power, "the Eternal Feminine" in all human beings, drawing them upward and onward into the spheres of the Divine.

Soloviev described the Sophia Icon of Novgorod in these unforgettable terms: "This majestic female figure... receiving adoration from the last representative of the Old Testament and from the progenitress of the New Testament, is the actual, pure, perfect humanity. It is the most exalted, all-encompassing form, one with God from all eternity, and in the temporal process finding oneness with Him and uniting to Him everything that exists. *Beyond any doubt this is the true significance of this majestic Being.*"

Standing before the *Icon of the Sophia* in Novgorod Soloviev felt himself once again in the presence of his Eternal Friend. But, he asks, "How many Christians of the past or present have known or even *desired* to know this genuine essence of Christianity?"

With this question Soloviev touches clearly upon the heart of his life-task. To help others to know "this genuine essence of Christianity," this Divine Wisdom, this Isis-Sophia, became his central aim for the remainder of his life. It led him to investigate and discuss aspects of Christianity he had not touched upon previously in such detail and clarity: the consummation of creation, the role of Christ in the new heaven and the new earth, and—*The Antichrist*.

Chapter Seven

THE CONSUMMATION OF ALL THINGS

1895–1900

THE SEVENTH SEVEN-YEAR period in the life of Vladimir Soloviev was cut short by his death at the age of forty-seven. Born
prematurely, Soloviev was convinced that his death—which
considerably before the event, he clearly saw approaching—was also to be premature, brought about, he was confident, by his first-hand experience with *the evil*.

Already in 1894 Soloviev was preoccupied with visions
of the approaching end of the old order of things, particularly as they had existed in Russia during his lifetime. He saw
the country about to be "punished" catastrophically for her
sins by a great future advance of "barbarism" coming from
"the Mongolian East," sweeping all before it. His fears were
entirely fulfilled when the mighty Empire of the Romanovs
was humbled in defeat before the Japanese, only a few years
after his death.

Despite the unsuccessful efforts of friends like Princess
Zinaida Volkonskaya, who in 1886 had introduced Soloviev to
the Roman Catholic Bishop Strossmayer and Canon Racki of
Diakovo (Dalmatia), with whom he had had a long and spirited
correspondence and a number of interviews on the subject of
the reunification of all Christians, and the hostility of the two
Russian Jesuits living in Paris who had turned their backs on
Soloviev and his "Free Theocracy" ideas after a brief period of
friendship and cooperative interest, Soloviev determined once

and for all to make one more attempt to bring these ecumemical ideals before the world. Therefore he decided to fulfill *in his own individual person* what he had not been able to so much as begin for humanity on a larger scale. Therefore, on February 18, 1896, Vladimir Soloviev, in the presence of witnesses, read aloud the Creed: "In the form adopted by the Roman See for Christians joining the (Roman) Catholic Church," and afterward took Communion at the hands of a Uniat priest, Father Nicholas Alexievich Tolstoi.

Soloviev's action has caused a certain amount of confusion among students of his life and writings. The Roman Catholic writer, d'Herbigny, for example, sees in him "the Russian Newman," referring to the conversion of the Englishman, John Henry (afterwards Cardinal) Newman to the Roman Catholic faith. A very different view is taken by many Russians, and by Russian Orthodox believers in particular. They are convinced that while Soloviev doubtless was sincere in taking Communion according to the Roman rite, his action was more of an "intellectual" one, while in his heart he remained always a completely dedicated adherent of the Russian Orthodox Church of his ancestors.

The letter Soloviev wrote in May, 1896, to the French Roman Catholic author, Tavernier, gives a clue to the real significance of Soloviev's action of less than three months before: "*Respice finem*. On this matter there are but three certain truths, to which the Word of God bears witness: 1. The Gospel is to be 'preached to the world,' that is, the Truth must be proclaimed to all humankind. 2. The Son of Humanity will find 'hardly any faith on the earth,'—in other words, in the last days the true believers will be an insignificant minority and the remainder of humanity will be *followers of Antichrist*. 3. However, after a short, fierce struggle, the evil will be vanquished and the Faithful will be victorious."

Soloviev was convinced therefore that the most vital task of "the faithful remnant" would be to join forces on the side of the Christ in "the short, fierce struggle" with the Antichrist. For the great test of humankind is to be *Christ or Antichrist?* Upon this the entire future of earth and humanity will depend.

The rallying point, the focal center for "the faithful remnant" who will *not* join with Antichrist, Soloviev believed would be found in the Pope at Rome, in whom he saw "the spiritual center of universal Christianity." *It was to this center—not to a dogma nor "in submission to ecclesiastical power"* that Soloviev united himself in February 1896.

* * *

Soloviev's major creative accomplishment during this period was doubtless the completion of his book *The Justification of the Good* in 1896. This work presents in philosophical terms the means by which humanity can attain spiritual maturity and at the same time metamorphose the experience of death. Through the aid of Sophia, the Divine Wisdom, human beings can achieve Godmanhood ultimately, and at the same time can bring about in very deed—though in a much higher, far more spiritual sense than visualized by Feyodorov—the resurrection of the dead.

The human being's attainment of spiritual maturity Soloviev bases first of all upon the teaching of the Eastern Church Fathers to the effect that though we "fell" from the divine state in which we bore "the image and likeness of God," we fell only insofar as our "likeness" to God is concerned. Humanity's *archetypal, "image" nature* in relation to God has remained intact and unspoiled, despite the Temptation and "Fall." The Eastern mystics showed how, as an individual, one can regain one's "likeness," and so restore one's divine condition. However, for Soloviev, this was not sufficient. In his view, *humanity as a whole* must find salvation, must find regeneration, complete reunion with the Divine, through the agency of the divine Sophia.

Vladimir Soloviev. A photograph made in St. Petersburg, c. 1890

(l. to r.) Vladimir Soloviev, Prince Sergei Troubetskoi, Nikolai Grot, Lyov Lopatin. A photograph made c. 1895

Soloviev had already dedicated years of effort toward making this goal clear, as has been shown. He had sought to awaken in his fellow human beings their need for "A free and universal Theocracy, the true solidarity of all nations and classes, the application of Christianity in public life, the Christianizing of politics; freedom for all oppressed, protection for the weak; social justice and good Christian peace." He was unable to achieve these all-important objectives, though he outlined in them a new future and a goal *in education* which *could* enable human beings to rise to these great attainments at some future day. Here again the ideas of Feyodorov achieve a new significance, a positive dimension: "The absolute worth of human beings—their capacity to be the bearers of eternal life and to participate in the divine fullness of being—which we religiously revere in the departed, we morally educate in the coming generation by affirming that the two are connected by a bond that triumphs over time and death. The technique of education belongs to a sphere of its own, but *if pedagogy is to be based on a positive, universal principle*, it can find the latter only in the indissoluble bond between generations which support one another in furthering one common task—the task of *preparing for the revelation of the kingdom of God and for universal resurrection.*"

* * *

In his *Justification of the Good* Soloviev mentions with appreciation the mystical writings of Swedenborg, Thomas Lake Harris and Laurence Oliphant, though Soloviev was able to express his own spiritual ideas and experiences with much greater philosophic depth than either of the last two, particularly with regard to the roles of the Eternal Feminine, the Sophia, and the Unity, the Oneness of all things in history and in individual experience.

But neither history nor individual experience have meaning, in Soloviev's view, without the recognition that, in his words, "Christianity possesses a distinctive content which is independent of all the elements contained in it. This content is simply and solely Christ. In Christianity we find Christ and Christ alone. *This is a truth which has often been stated, but very little assimilated.*"

The Logos, the Pancreator, who has moved "from being the center of Eternity to become the center of history," is for Soloviev the focal-point of all his spiritual striving, the motivation of his entire mysticism, which can be termed *Christocentric* in the highest degree. For him what humankind experience as Christ in our time is by no means the fullness of Christ, but is *only a beginning* in that direction.

Soloviev makes emphatically clear that Christ would be meaningless for humanity unless the existence and cooperative activities of a divine *and* a human nature in a concrete, organic *oneness* are taken into account. What Soloviev points to as the significance of Christ in our day is like a glorious dawn—but only a dawn—which directs our gaze and our hope toward a later time, another age, another civilization to come. Thus we can best understand Soloviev's philosophy and, above all, his vision of the nature and significance of the Christ for human and cosmic evolution, when we see in his teaching something of a seed-like element, picturing for us a Christianity and a future as yet unborn.

* * *

In *The Justification of the Good* is described the process whereby the divine manifests itself in the material world through five "kingdoms"—Soloviev emphasizes the latter term—the mineral, vegetable, animal, human *and God's kingdom*. And Soloviev reminds us that "the last and highest stage is usually not taken into account at all."

Indicating that these five kingdoms represent "clearly defined *grades of existence*," he continues, "Stones and metals are distinguished from all else by their *extreme self-sufficiency and conservatism*; had it rested with them, Nature would never have wakened from her dreamless slumber. But, on the other hand, without them her further growth would have been deprived of a firm basis or ground. Plants in unconscious, unbroken dreams *draw towards* warmth, light and moisture. Animals by means of *sensations and free movements seek* the fullness of sensuous being: repletion, sexual satisfaction and the joy of existence. Natural humanity, in addition to these things, rationally strives to *improve* its life by means of the sciences, arts, and social institutions, actually does improve it in various respects, and finally rises to the *idea* of absolute perfection. Spiritual humanity, or humanity born of God, not only understands this absolute perfection with the intellect, but *accepts it with the heart as the true beginning of what must be fulfilled in the consummation of all things*."

As human beings rise to this higher stature they cease "to be merely human, and form part of *a new and higher plan of existence* in which their purely human ends become the means and instruments for another final purpose," despite the fact that those human beings who have attained some degree of spiritual maturity, and to some extent—however small—have become "bearers of the Kingdom of God, apparently do not seem to differ in any way from human beings of this world, though the Principle of a new order of being lives and acts within them."

This "Principle" to which Soloviev refers is the Christ—but *not* the Christ of narrow dogma, traditionalism or misguided exclusiveness, characterized by the utterly blind, mistaken opinion that through his Deed of Golgotha and Resurrection, Christ has united himself with the Earth only for the sake of Christians, whereas in reality he came for Jews, Buddhists, Hindus, Mohammedans—for the future evolution of the Earth, *including all humanity*, regardless of race, creed or status. Moreover, as Rudolf Steiner pointed out, "Though Christianity *began* as a religion, it is infinitely greater than all religions," all dogmas, all limited, sectarian views and opinions.

John Ruskin once wrote that "Humanity's use and function is to be the witness of the glory of God, and to advance that glory." Soloviev amplifies this by pointing out that "The God-man not only accurately understands but actively realizes the meaning of everything, while embracing and uniting all things by the living, personal power of love. The highest goal of humanity and the human world is to gather the universe together *in thought*. The goal of the God-man and of the Kingdom of God is to gather the universe together *in reality*."

Here Soloviev's thoughts are similar to that mystical insight which expressed itself in *The Ode to God*, written by the eighteenth century Russian poet and mystic, forerunner of Pushkin, Gavrilla Romanovich Derzhavin (1714-1816), translated by John Bowring:

> Though but an atom midst immensity,
> Still, I am something fashioned by Thy hand!
> I hold a middle rank 'twixt heaven and earth,
> On the last ridge of mortal being stand,
> Close to the realm where angels have their birth,
> Just on the boundaries of the spirit-land!
> The chain of being is complete in me;
> In me is matter's last gradation lost,
> And the next step is Spirit — Deity!

The reference to the atom in this poem is reminiscent of Soloviev's essay, *Concerning Atomism*, in which he made the significant statement: "Atoms are not a part of matter; they are the forces which create matter."

Prince Eugene Troubetskoi, friend and pupil of Soloviev, wrote in his book on Soloviev's teachings: "As sons of the earth, human beings receive from it a lower life, according to their nature. But it is just by this that their task as mediator is created. It is their task to give back to the earth this life, by transforming it into light and into life-creating spirit. When the earth can be lifted to heaven through human beings and through human reason, then through them, through their work, heaven can come down to earth and fill it. Through them the whole world, which still remains outside the Godhead, must become the united, living body, the sole incarnation of the Divine Wisdom, the Sophia. It is not difficult to come to the conviction that this teaching of Soloviev represents a clear, classic expression of deep, religious sentiment. What Soloviev thought, he experienced to the innermost depth of his soul; through his mouth speaks the man for whom God is All, is everything, the man who has really dedicated everything to God:—his heart, his reason, his will and his feeling."

* * *

As the century drew toward its close, many people—Soloviev among them—were convinced that history itself was nearing a climax, that a totally new era was about to dawn with the coming of the twentieth century. This conclusion was confirmed for some by interpretations based on the mystical-historical writings of the Renaissance thinkers, Agrippa of Nettisheim and the latter's friend and teacher, Trithemius of Sponheim.

Soloviev felt that time itself was accelerating, and as the century came near its end, his entire soul-calmness was changed into a tension, a kind of unrest, of mystical expectation. For example, in a poem he titled, *The Waking Dream,* written in the mid-90s, he expressed this mood: "The end is near and the unexpected will soon fulfill itself." In another poem written in these same years Soloviev observed:

Something longs to be put into words —
Something still remains unspoken —
Something is happening —
But it is neither here nor there.

Soloviev's mysticism passed through three distinct phases, growing more personal, more original, increasingly less dependent upon Church tradition or ascetic discipline. Apocalyptic pictures of cataclysmic events and demonic visions came increasingly to the fore in his experience. The calm visions of the Sophia which began in his childhood were paralleled by mystical experiences of "the Fathers at the stone," and finally in the last years of the century were accompanied by manifestations of dark forces in various guises. The last brought with them what Soloviev described as "a consciousness of the not too far distant image of pale death."

This growing consciousness etched itself upon his countenance during this last decade, as one of his brothers recalled: "The face of Soloviev changed very strikingly in the last years. On it appeared something of the other world, a deep sorrow and a clear message, a light from the Beyond." —It is not to be wondered at that some of Soloviev's most ardent admirers now began to look upon him as a sort of Messiah, a source of spiritual light in the midst of gathering darkness.

The portrait of Soloviev by Kramskoi, reproduced in this book [page 181], is generally regarded as one of his best likenesses. When Soloviev went to the painter's studio for sittings, he was often accosted by the little daughters of the concierge, who ran to him with cries of delight, siezed the skirts of his overcoat and exclaimed joyfully, "Little Father! Little Father!" They thought he was a priest.

This "priest-like" appearance, which became more and more pronounced in the last years of Soloviev's life, carrying with it something of an atmosphere of "mystery," was noted by many. Among the crowds of visitors, beggars and admirers

The handwriting of Vladimir Soloviev, February 27, 1895

Vladimir Soloviev. A sketch by Ilya Efimovich Repin, August 1896

who streamed to his rooms at the Hotel Angleterre in St. Petersburg where he generally lived when he was in the capital, were many who regarded him with the veneration usually accorded a respected member of the clergy.

In Finland, the coachman who usually drove him from his hotel to the station, had a deep respect for him. When he noticed that everyone addressed Soloviev as *"Herr Professor,"* he decided to better this, and called him "Father Parthenson," for he saw in Soloviev a close resemblance to a well-known, saintly Archpriest of the Old Believers.

Once Soloviev was walking with a friend when an old man came up to him, took off his hat, bowed very deeply and asked, "How are you, Father?" When Soloviev gently suggested that the old man had undoubtedly mistaken him for someone else, the latter exclaimed, "But you *are*—you *must* be Father John!" He had taken Soloviev to be the famous priest, John of Kronstadt.

Saintly and priest-like though Soloviev appeared to many people, it would be an error to conclude that his nature was entirely that of a Christian saint. A genuine mystic, profoundly devoted to his Eternal Friend, the divine Sophia, bearing within himself an ideal of the Christ far surpassing the general conception of him at that time, dedicated to the vision of a future for humanity beyond the comprehension of many a leading theologian, statesman, scientist or artist of that day, nevertheless in Soloviev there also existed a quality of earthiness with which he wrestled manfully on his spiritual path. This wrestling, this struggle he described in these words: "In order to manifest the spiritual idea in the material world, it is necessary to be free and detached from that world. However, the highest aim of spiritual striving is not ascetic detachment from the natural life, but *its hallowing, its perfecting*. The goal is not to *destroy* earthly life, but *to raise it to God Who comes down to meet it*. The task of spiritual striving is not to weaken the flesh, but *to strengthen the spirit for the transfiguration of the flesh*."

Like the German mystic, Heinrich Suso (1295-1366), Soloviev at last became the gentle mystic of the heart, the kindly servitor of the Divine Wisdom, the Sophia, in whose cause he learned, as Suso long before him had expressed it, to "Receive suffering willingly; bear suffering patiently; learn suffering in the way of Christ." Out of his bitter experiences came the Soloviev of the last years, a man whose gentleness and spiritual greatness were an inseparable part of his nature.

* * *

Near the end of his life Soloviev returned to the study of a love of his youth—the study of Plato. He translated several passages from the Greek philosopher's works, and in 1897 published his essay, *The Tragedy of Plato's Life*. In the following passage from this essay an unmistakably autobiographical note is evident: "The entire world is filled with evil; the body is the grave and prison house of the soul; society is the sepulchre of wisdom and truth. For the philosopher, life is a continual death. But this death to the affairs of daily existence does not make way for emptiness, but to a better life of the mind, which contemplates what by and in itself is absolute."

In another passage Soloviev describes a task of the philosopher: "The analysis of *various types of organic manure* is of interest to the farmer. For us, two facts are of importance: first, that every kind of manure is the result of decomposition, hence only worms and not human beings can subsist on such decomposing matter; and second, that by their spiritual work people can and ought to extract from this putrifaction *the beautiful blossoms and deathless facts of life*."

These words echo the saying of the Christ in the Gospel of John: "Unless a grain of wheat falls into the ground and dies, it remains alone; but if it dies it brings forth much fruit" (John 12:24).

Soloviev's lines, referring to his Eternal Friend, whose mystical roses have accompanied him through the years, are contained in his essay on Plato:

Light out of darkness,
The blossoms of your roses
Cannot rise above the dull clod
Unless their dark and hidden roots
Pierce the gloomy depth of earth.

And he comments: "Indeed, such is the law of the soil."

This "law of the soil" of which Soloviev writes, points to the significant connection of the Russian people with the Earth itself. The spiritual qualities of the Russian earth, its permeation by the sun in a quite special way, and the consequences of this for the Russian people and their development, have been discussed by Rudolf Steiner. This remarkable relationship between the Earth and "the law of the soil" out of which Russians find their connection with the spiritual world, was wonderfully depicted in Dostoyevski's *Brothers Karamazov*. In that novel is described the spiritual rebirth of the young Aloysha through the death experience of the Elder Zossima, which reaches its climax in the former's mystical exaltation: "His enraptured soul was craving for freedom, space, openness... The silence of earth seemed to melt in the silence of the heavens; the mystery of the world was joining with the mystery of the stars... Aloysha stood gazing, and suddenly, as though his legs had given way, he threw himself to the ground. He did not know why he kissed it, why he had such an irresistible desire to embrace the whole of it. But kiss it he did, weeping and sobbing, watering it with his tears, passionately vowing to love it forever, till the end of all time... But every moment he felt distinctly, even palpably, that Something as certain and unshakable as the wheeling of the stars was entering into his soul. Some idea had taken hold of him, and it would remain with him for the rest of his life, and forever after. He was a weak youth when he fell to the ground; he stood up a resolute champion, and he felt and knew this all at once, at the very moment of his ecstasy."

Tschaikovski also had a similar relationship with the Russian earth: "Why is it that the poorest Russian landscape, a stroll on a summer evening through Russian fields, forests, and across the steppe in the night can touch me so that I have fallen to the earth feelingless, overpowered by a surge of love for Nature, by the indescribably sweet atmosphere that wafted to me from forest, steppe, stream, village, the little church—everything that makes up our poor Russian landscape. Why?"

Soloviev's maternal ancestor, Grigori Saavich Skovoroda, to whom we have already referred, once described a like experience in a letter to his pupil, friend and biographer, Kovalinski: "I went out into the garden for a walk. The first feeling that arose in my heart was one of deliverance, of freedom, of joy. Overwhelmed by a sudden great surge of warmth within me, I was almost instantly pervaded with extraordinary strength. A sweet fire filled me; everything around me seemed to burn with fervent heat. The world itself disappeared; I was entirely immersed in a transport of love, of peaceful rest, an awareness of eternity round and about me. My eyes shed tears of joy; I was filled with ecstasy, surging through me like a tender wave."

* * *

From the autumn of 1891 to early in 1893 Soloviev lived in Moscow for the most part, though he made journeys to visit friends in the country and also in Finland. In July, 1893 he sailed to Finland, thence to Sweden. From Stockholm he wrote to his brother: "The voyage here was glorious. Finland is much more beautiful than Italy, especially the entrance to Abo!... The first night I watched the sunrise from the deck and wrote a poem of my impressions; the second night I slept on the deck beneath the eternal stars..." From Sweden he crossed into Norway and from there to Scotland.

In these Northern lands, amid the great natural beauty of silent lakes, granite rocks, mysterious fjords, forests of birch and pine, clear, fresh mountain air, Soloviev found peace of soul and poetic inspiration.

On his way north from Stockholm to Upsala, burial place of the ancient kings, Soloviev wrote:

Wherever I look, everywhere are stones,
Mighty cliffs and pines;
Why is it that this poor land
Has become so dear to me?

Amid endless struggle with Nature,
The human spirit grows,
And from the raging seas
Man hurls defiance to the skies.

Among misty shadows
Upon rocky crags,
In the glow of Northern Lights,
The portal of the spirit-realm appears.

It was not in vain that from Kashmir,
From the far-off Southern Seas,
To this land, at the world's beginning,
Hosts of heroes wandered.

In these Northern lands and on Northern seas Soloviev was constantly mindful of his Eternal Friend. He described his awareness of her presence in a poem he called *On the Deck of the Frithiof*:

I scarce could whisper one name
'Ere the star fell into the sea;
No time to wish, and now it is too late;
Everything has vanished, both joy and sorrow.

 The shore has left us long ago,
Around me lonely deeps of the sea;
Within my solitary soul another vastness
Spreads round, before, behind me.

In Scotland Soloviev experienced the Mysteries of the
ancient Celtic world and the presence of the dead, with great
intensity. The poem he wrote describing his impressions he
titled *Moonlight in Scotland*:

In the high mountain valley
A moonbeam crept in at my window;
"Come out! Come out! Don't sleep!"
It cried. — Besides, I couldn't sleep.

Brighter than clearest dream
All the valley lies in moonlight,
I call no one to go with me:
Let the waterfall speak to me alone.

Higher, higher, where a lone fir
Stands far above the rocky cliff,
A stream invisible slips among the stones
Where gnomes live underneath the earth.

Wider, farther spreads my view,
Clearer, fair in shining moonlight;
Wavering forms of mountains grey
Reflect themselves in Lomond's deeps.

Why is the beauty of this night
Like a wordless phantom, lorn and sad?
From above pours down a cold, clear light,
And the earth lies as drear as the moon.

A shining pall unfolds itself
Over coffins of ages long past;
In the moonlight I stand quite alone
With an invisible host of the dead.

Deep into my soul, penetrating,
The moon-cold is flowing about me;
In the clear, enveloping silence
What is moving and clamoring round me?

Rough voices of dark, hidden fighters,
Wild shouting and echoes unearthly;
Horns sharply blowing, drums fiercely rolling,
And the pipes skirling round me in fury.

Now lo! The lone fir slowly wakens,
Its branches soft sighing and moaning;
The mute rock with life moves and trembles,
Mysteriously the moss-covered granite is stirring.

In the spring of 1898 Soloviev decided to visit once more
the land where he had met his Eternal Friend so long ago,
the land of Egypt. On his journey there he had a mysterious
experience which seems to have changed his attitude toward
the evil in the world. He wrote about this in the preface to his
Three Conversations:

Is *evil* but a natural defect, an imperfection which disappears by itself as the good increases, or is it a genuine
power, controlling our world by means of temptations,

so that in order to combat it successfully, help must be obtained in another sphere of existence?

I soon felt how important the problem of evil is for everyone. Some two years ago a change in my spiritual way of life brought about in me a strong and definite wish to clarify in some manner the principal aspects of the problem of evil, a task which must be of concern to everyone."

The *Three Conversations*, with their climax in the *Narrative Concerning the Antichrist*, which concludes the book, was Soloviev's contribution to the clarification of "the problem of evil which must be of concern to everyone."

* * *

Sitting at his writing-table late one June night in 1873, Dostoyevski startled his secretary by suddenly exclaiming, after a long period of silence, "These so-called liberals haven't even a ghost of an idea that the end of everything is just at hand! They don't realize that *the Antichrist himself* has already been born on the earth, and that soon he will appear among us!" Then he slapped the desk fiercely with his open hand, shouting, "The Antichrist is coming! He's coming, I tell you! The end of our world is near at hand! It's closer than most people imagine!"

Shortly before his death in 1841 the Russian poet and novelist, Mikhail Yurevich Lermontov also had a prevision of the coming of the Antichrist who, in his words, "Will not only be a warrior but will also be the executor of dismaying cruelties and terrific castigations. That tardy avenger will be allowed to give the world a long-premeditated and well-prepared blow. His mission will be to fight and chastise at the same time. He bears two swords: one of them is the bloodstained sword of battles, the other is the axe of the executioner."

The handwriting of Vladimir Soloviev,
Moscow, November 25, 1898

Vladimir Soloviev. The last photograph, 1900

Already at the close of the eighteenth century Ivan Viadimirovich Lopukhin in his book, *The Interior Church*, to which we have already referred, described those who will join the Antichrist as coworkers: "The chief members of the kingdom of the Antichrist will be the false workers of wonders, the unjust just, and the writers who, proclaiming the mystery of the spirit of darkness, array themselves in the glitter of deceitful light... Those who are in greatest danger of serving the Antichrist, thus attaining the ultimate in depravity are those who have given themselves up to *spiritual voluptuousness*, devoting themselves to the occult sciences, not from love for the truth but from motives of self-conceit. Among them are also those who from idle curiosity, self-interest and vanity seek after hidden knowledge of Alchemy in order to 'make gold,' and to discover the means of prolonging their criminal lives. With them are included all who are concerned only with *the letter* of Theosophy, Kabbala, Alchemy and the other esoteric arts, for this leads directly to the works of the powers of darkness. Among these disciples of spiritual voluptousness are those who know nothing of the spirit but cling to the letter alone, which has the *appearance* of a mystery.

"The mightiest workers in the kingdom of the Antichrist will be those spiritual hypocrites who hide their self-love, pride, lust, cunning and love of domineering under the cloak of humility, fasting, chastity and charity. Among these are founders of those pernicious sects whose rule has every *appearance* of love for the good. But the most active of all intermediaries of the kingdom of the Antichrist are the new philosophers who strive to prove that the soul is mortal, that self-love is and ought to be the root of all actions, and that Christianity is merely fanaticism. These philosophers carry the ignorant with them in their ideas, laboring to persuade people that there is not even any God.

"The field where the evil spirit of the Antichrist will reap a formidable and terrible harvest is tilled by those miserable men who steep their hands in their brothers' blood and those slaves of their senses who strive to fill to the brim their cup of sensuality, drunkenness of the passions, and inordinate lust."

Konstantin Nikoleyevich Leontyev (1831-1891), Russian diplomat, traveler, author and physician also had a premonition of the approach of a great spiritual climax. In 1880 he wrote: "Who knows if we Russians are not about to take the path that was once taken by the Jewish nation? The latter did not expect that the Master of the new Faith would come out of their midst. It is therefore entirely possible that our Russian nation, at first silent and then deprived of her churches, will at length give birth to *Antichrist!*"

In June, 1897 Soloviev told his friend, the poet Velichko, "*Something* is making itself ready. *Someone* is coming. You can guess that by Someone, I mean *the Antichrist*. The end of the world is not far away. I feel it as a traveler who is nearing the sea feels the breath of the salt air long before he reaches the shore."

This premonition of a coming crisis, a climax in the world development related to the advent of Antichrist, is connected with the change in his conception of evil which came to Soloviev as a result of an experience he had on his journey to Egypt.

In his earlier life Soloviev was inclined to discount the role of evil in the world-process. He didn't believe in the "traditional devil," nor in hell. The view of Augustine that evil is without substance, existing only by permission of the good, had found ready acceptance in his thinking. However, in the early 90s he began to speak about Antichrist, first in a collective sense, but then as a being incarnated in a single body, the being the Scriptures call "the Son of Perdition." *Now* he stood before evil in a form sinister in its impressiveness.

Two accounts of Soloviev's experience enroute to Egypt in the spring of 1898 have been preserved. One of these was reported by his brother, Mikhail, the other by one of his friends whom Soloviev told about it.

One day Soloviev entered his steamer cabin and saw "the devil sitting on a pillow in the form of a furry beast." Instinctively recognizing that this was the devil, Soloviev asked, "Do you know that Christ is risen?" whereat the devil suddenly raised himself and pounced upon Soloviev, who later was found unconscious on the floor of his cabin.

The other version varies slightly: "I was traveling on a steamship bound for Egypt at Easter time, 1898. Suddenly I felt something pressing itself against my shoulders. I saw a white, misty spot, and heard a voice exclaim in triumph, 'Ah, I have you, tall one, I have you!' At once I repeated the most powerful conjuration that exists: 'In the name of Jesus Christ, the Crucified!' At once the devil disappeared, but for a whole day afterward I was utterly exhausted."

Soloviev's poem, *Archipelago at Night*, was doubtless written under the influence of this curious experience:

I saw in the sea-foam,
The play of dark evil magic,
To me no illusion; indeed
The dread mist carried peril.

There gathered and rose
A host of hellish spirits,
And the curse of evil words
Echoed shrilly round me.

In a longer poem Soloviev once again repeated the same theme of his personal meeting with the powers of darkness, which he imaged under the guise of evil sea-devils. The poem is called *The Eternal Feminine*, and is subtitled "A word of admonition to the sea-devils."

The sea-devils grew fond of me;
Everywhere they traced my steps.

Yesterday in the Bay of Finland,
Today in the Aegean they lie in wait.

Clearly the demons seek my death,
As becomes them, befitting their nature;
God be with you, O devilish ones,
But I'll not let you devour me!

It's better that you listen to me,
For you I have some good advice:
— To become once more God's flocks,
Dear devils, — this depends on you.

Do you remember, near this sea
Where once stood Amathunt and Pathos,
The first unexpected grief in life
You once had to experience?

Do you remember roses and white foam,
Purple reflection upon blue waves,
Do you recall the body beautiful,
And your confusion, trembling and fear?

Know you now: the Eternal Feminine
Comes to earth again in form supernal;
In deathless light of the new goddess
Heaven unites itself with watery depths.

To approach her would be in vain,
O clever devils; Why should you complain?
What all Nature awaits with yearning,
You'll not delay nor conquer!

O you proud, courageous devils,
Don't you know: To fight with any woman

Brings dishonor to a man, and so,
Dear devils, do surrender soon!

* * *

Though Soloviev had no new meeting with his Eternal Friend in Egypt, his awareness of her spiritual presence was very pronounced during his whole visit there. His impression of the country he wrote in a letter to his friend, M.M. Stasyulevich in Russia: "Here we found winter fields ready for harvesting (as we have them in Russia at end of July), and a wonderfully greening summer wheat. Before we arrived there had been a parching drought, but we brought the north wind and a pleasant coolness. Thanks to the British, Egypt is like an orderly city. Even the trains run according to the timetable, and not arbitrarily as when I came here for the first time twenty-two years ago."

Leaving Egypt, Soloviev's travels took him to the French Riviera, where at Cannes he began to write what was to be his last work, *Three Conversations*, concluding with the *Narrative Concerning the Antichrist*.

In a letter Soloviev had pointed to the ideal of thinking permeated by the Christ as a great goal for humanity: "But when such consciousness has come, humankind will stand *before severe trials*, testing their willingness to serve Christ with all the forces of their will." Soloviev now took with profound intensity the words of Christ in "the little Apocalypse" reported in the twenty-fourth chapter of the Gospel of Matthew: "Nation will rise against nation, there will be pestilences and earthquakes... but all these are *but the beginning of the birthpangs*... They will torture and kill you... False prophets will appear and lead many astray... but he that endures to the end will be saved... There will arise false Christs... who will produce great miracles... in order to deceive the very elect... At once after the tribulation of those days, the sun will be darkened and the moon will not give her light, the stars will fall from the heavens, and the mighty ones of the heavens will be shaken. *Then* shall all peoples of earth wail, and they shall see the Son of Man coming on the clouds of Heaven with great power and glory."

In the light of these words, Soloviev realized that "the consummation of all things" is not to be a peaceful, harmonious development, leading to the establishment of a "Free Theocracy" on earth. He relinquished his former vision of the world peacefully evolving to a cosmic embodiment of the Christ under the guidance of the divine Sophia, and a complete unification of all humanity in a condition of Godmanhood. In contrast with his earlier impressions, Soloviev now pictured the consummation of all things, involving the completion of the historical process, as an event involving mighty catastrophies. Only a tiny handful of Christians will remain faithful, and the Second Advent of the Christ will occur only after a great purgation of humanity.

But before this Second Advent can take place, "Another" must first appear. Before the coming of the Anointed One in his glory, "Another" must come *in his own name*. Before the glorious reign of Christ can begin, there must be the reign of *Antichrist*.

In his *Antichrist Narrative* Soloviev presents an apocalyptic vision; his inner experience of the Eternal Feminine in the human soul, of the Sophia, the Divine Wisdom, as "the guardian angel of the soul, overshadowing all creatures with its wings as a bird its little ones, in order to raise them into true being" has now broadened to *a cosmic prophecy*. What will lead humanity to the star-crowned Virgin, whom he described as "the all-embracing mother, *'mater-materia'*, the cosmic mother-matter of the Pythagoreans and Plato, whom the Greeks called Urania, the heavenly Aphrodite, the queen of the azure, starry heaven, as she stands on the moon, clad in blue robes, crowned with stars of gold"? It is only through the power of

Christ working in human hearts, in their thinking, in their will, through the activity of the Sophia, the Divine Wisdom, that the ultimate unity of all humanity can come about.

* * *

Soloviev was confronted with a question: How can the Antichrist be depicted in modern times? In the form of human or superhuman, in distorted animal guise, or in some unearthly representation, designed to convey a sense of the awe-inspiring nature of this being? Shall the representation of Antichrist bear the image of an ugliness unimagined, unbeheld on earth before, or shall it manifest a beauty unparalleled in all history? These questions have confronted creative artists in every age, and their response has been in terms of their individual experience, the consciousness of their historical period, their talent and medium.

Medieval painters, and before them the Byzantine artists represented the Antichrist as the incarnation of all ugliness and animality. In later Gothic times the artists represented him in a grotesque, parti-human guise, an externalization of the human metabolic, digestive processes, as it were. People seemed "to turn themselves inside out" in their effort to depict the ultimate of evil.

With the dawn of the modern age in the Renaissance, human consciousness underwent a tremendous change of direction and insight. With the birth of the modern time people concentrated their attention on the physical world of the senses. Heaven seemed increasingly remote, earthly concerns more and more absorbing. In harmony with this new trend, artistic representations—even of the most spiritual beings—became more and more identified with the physical earth, with the creatures of the environing world of the senses. In harmony with this development of consciousness, the Antichrist representation became more "literal," as it were, as though artists attempted to extract from their limited, personal conception of evil something they could magnify to a kind of superhuman— but always *basically individual* proportion. Thus the extra-human dimension, the non-spatial quality of the Antichrist figure vanished more and more at the hands of the Renaissance artist, until he became a more or less magnified 'man' with a perpetual scowl of anger on his face.

A consciousness of the *levels* in the spiritual world, typified by the supra-human figures, the "Persons" of classic Greek drama, depicted by the animal-plant-human figures of medieval artists, understood so well by Gothic sculptors and painters, slowly disappeared until in the Age of Enlightenment in the eighteenth century the Antichrist became little more than a human figure of only slightly heroic proportions, muscular, dark, somewhat sinister, but scarcely an expression of the totality of the Forces of Darkness, the Prince of Abomination described in the Scriptures.

The greyness of modern mediocrity in artistic conception, born of the absence of a living awareness of the levels of spiritual proportion, has lost an understanding of the "greatness" of evil as well. The majesty, the supra-human might of the eternal *"NO!"* epitomized in the figure of the Antichrist, has disappeared in the face of a contemporary demand for "equality" in all things—even in the spiritual sphere.

The "new understanding" of the Gospels resulting from nineteenth century materialism with the Christ depicted as the human "teacher and friend," rather than in his cosmic grandeur as the incarnated Word, also carried with it a loss of appreciation of the Antichrist figure as well. On the other hand, has this perhaps resulted from people having lived *in the presence of the Antichrist* for so long that they have grown accustomed to him? Might it not be that the disappearance of the cosmic greatness of the Christ from the general thinking life of humankind has been in itself a kind of preparation for the appearance of Antichrist on earth?

Today people are beginning to realize more and more—and Soloviev's courageously prophetic *Antichrist Narrative* can be a great help in this direction—that in reality the Antichrist is not a single figure, manifesting itself in the world. As "the mystery of iniquity" the Antichrist is *a power* manifesting itself in countless forms, presenting itself in a myriad of guises, working in limitless ways. Its activity is by no means confined to those situations where Christ is attacked or individuals willfully turn their backs upon Him. Through Soloviev's prophetic insight we can recognize the Antichrist as *an impersonal, a suprapersonal power*, operating as an inevitable accompaniment to the particular nature of our modern consciousness. It is a concomitant of the apocalyptic character of the age in which we live today.

From the standpoint of its prophetic accuracy, Soloviev's *Antichrist Narrative* is recognized as one of the very greatest creations of Russian spiritual thought, without equal in Russian literature. This achievement is all the more remarkable when one realizes that Soloviev knew *from personal experience and insight* the immensity of his task: to reduce to a single, individual entity an impersonal power and to express in artistic form "the conclusion of our historical process of evolution, consisting in the appearance, the glorification and the destruction of Antichrist."

* * *

Soloviev was under no illusion concerning the reaction his exposure of the activity of impersonal evil in the world would bring to him personally. He recognized that in removing the mask from evil—even though presented in the form of fiction—he had entered into "a struggle with death." In revealing the true nature of evil operating *under the guise of good* in the world, Soloviev was convinced he had shortened his own life. He returned to Russia from the Riviera with the manuscript of *Three Conversations*, including the Antichrist story, ready for publication, and at Easter, 1900 the work appeared for the first time.

* * *

That Soloviev was entirely conscious of what lay ahead for him personally and for humanity as well is revealed in a significant conversation he had at this time with his friend Velichko, who later reported it in an interesting monograph titled *Vladimir Soloviev, his Life and Task*: "Speaking of his *Narrative of the Antichrist* Soloviev asked me, 'What do you think I'll get for having written it?' 'From whom?' I asked. He replied, 'Naturally, from that one whom the story concerns! *From himself!*' Sensing his meaning I replied, 'But that won't happen so very soon!' After a moment's pause he answered with quiet earnestness, 'Sooner than you think.' He also told me he was filled with a particularly strong religious fervor... but 'I have the premonition of a rapidly nearing epoch when Christians will again be obliged to hide themselves in catacombs while the faith will be persecuted. Yes, it will once again be persecuted, but this time it will be in a less apparent and direct way than in the age of Nero, for the methods will be more refined and more cruel. Lies and many other subterfuges will be used. But tell me, don't you see who is approaching, who is coming? I see him, I see him! I have seen him for a long time already!'

"Soloviev's voice was trembling, his eyes were filled with sorrow. '*Now*,' he repeated with great anxiety, '*the time is near.*'"

It was at about this time that Soloviev wrote in a letter to a close friend: "I am conscious of the not too distant image of pale death." And his premonition was not incorrect.

* * *

At Easter, 1900 Soloviev read his Antichrist story to a group of invited friends in the apartment of his brother Michael in Moscow. Among those present at the reading was the writer, Andrei Bely. In his memoirs titled *Arabeski*, Arabesques, published in Moscow, 1911, Bely described the occasion: "Soloviev looked sad and tired, with the same imprint of death and awesome greatness that had settled upon him during the last months in particular. It was as if he had beheld something nobody else had seen, and lacked words to communicate his knowledge.

"Soloviev began to read. As he read the words, 'John stood up like a white candle,' he also made a movement as if to get up. He stretched himself in his armchair. Through the window one could see the flashing of sheet-lightning. Soloviev's face was trembling in the lightning glare, as though touched by inspiration."

The famous Russian artist, Ilya Efimovich Repin, who painted a whole gallery of portraits of the best-known men and women of Russia of his time, including statesmen, nobility, artists, scientists, musicians and literary personalities, as well as historical subjects of unusual interest, also made a pencil sketch of Soloviev. This drawing, reproduced in this book [page 222] shows Soloviev as he appeared at the time of his reading of the Antichrist story. As an accompaniment to Repin's sketch, Andrei Bely's word-picture of Soloviev is of interest: "His enormous, fascinating grey eyes, his bent back, the long, weak arms, his beautiful head with grey, ruffled strands of hair; his large mouth with protruding lip, his furrowed face... A giant with powerless arms, long legs, a small body, inspired eyes... a powerless child with a lion's mane."

When one examines Repin's sketch and reads Bely's description, it is difficult to remember that at this time Soloviev had just passed his forty-seventh birthday.

* * *

Soloviev's preoccupation with his vision of the advent of Antichrist was accompanied by an intensified awareness of the presence of his Eternal Friend as he described her in the preface he wrote for the third edition of his poems, then being published: "The more perfect and the nearer to us the revelation of the true beauty enveloping Divinity, and which through its power leads us to deliverance from suffering and death, the sharper is the line separating us from its false likeness, that deceiving and powerless beauty which only makes the eternal kingdom of suffering and death. The Woman clothed with the Sun is already in labor, and there the ancient Serpent gathers against her his last forces and strives to drown her in the poisonous floods of the beautiful lie of deception in the guise of Truth."

* * *

One day at the beginning of July, Soloviev visited the editorial offices of *Vestnik Evropi* and spoke with his collaborators on the staff. Leonid Slonimski, who was present, reported: "Nothing foretold his approaching end. He looked the same as usual, alert and clear in spirit, but tired and weak in body. He spoke about the articles he intended to write for the magazine in the autumn. He read us a short essay about the situation in China, which he intended to print in a certain periodical. After a brief discussion, he decided to develop the concluding part of the article further in order to print the whole thing in our *Vestnik Evropi*."

On July 14 Soloviev journeyed to Moscow and there was overtaken with sudden illness. He learned that the President of the Moscow District Court, Nikolai Davidov was about to visit Ozkoie, the country estate of Prince Pavel Troubetskoi, and decided to accompany him. Davidov later wrote, "As I returned from the court at about three o'clock in the after-noon of July 15 I noticed that on the coat-rack in the ante-room another coat was hanging beside mine. Soloviev was lying on the couch in my private study, his face turned to the wall. He was very much changed due to the fact that he had cut his long hair, and his face was deathly pale. When I asked, 'What ails you?' he replied that just a short time before he had begun to feel nauseous and must continue to lie down for a little while."

Davidov telephoned Ozkoie to inform the Troubetskois of the situation, and when he returned to his study he found that Soloviev drank soda-water from time to time in a kind of preoccupied way, but soon began to talk. Among other things he said he had received an advance payment for an article from the editor of *Questions*, and that this was very welcome, for it compensated for the illness that had come over him... "The time passed but Vladimir Sergeyevich asked to be allowed to lie still a little longer. It was already after five o'clock; I proposed that we postpone the trip to Ozkoie, that he stay the night with me and that we go there early the next day. But he would not agree to this, saying that if I did not wish to go there now, he would go alone. At that moment he stood up, trembling with weakness, and walked into the ante-room. I did not think it right to force him to stay with me, and I preferred to drive him to Ozkoie myself. He had nothing with him except a few books, and I couldn't get out of him whether he had taken lodging somewhere in Moscow or not. He only repeated, 'Tonight I must be with the Troubetskois.'

"I hired a fast carriage, and with considerable difficulty helped Vladimir Sergeyevich to get into it. It was necessary to close the top because it began to rain. As we walked out on the porch, a beggar rushed up to him and began to kiss his hands, saying, 'Angel, Vladimir Sergeyevich, it's your name-day!' From his pocket Soloviev took some paper money, and without even looking at it, give it to the beggar.

At one point on the way Vladimir Sergeyevich asked that we stop so he could have a little rest, adding, 'Otherwise I shall just die right now!' And judging from his weakness it seemed as though he very well might. Yet a little while later he asked that we continue, saying that he felt 'like a plucked sparrow,' adding, 'of course something like this can't happen to you!'

"Despite his weakness and suffering, from time to time he started joking about himself and begged my pardon that through his illness he had made so much trouble for me.

"It was quite late when we arrived at Ozkoie. Soloviev was so weak that he had to be lifted bodily from the carriage. He was placed on a couch in the study, was very happy that he had arrived at the Troubetskois, and asked that he be allowed to rest quietly.

"The next morning he told Troubetskoi that in the night he had had a dream in which he saw quite clearly Li Hung Chang, the Chinese statesman, who spoke to him in classical Greek, telling him that soon he would die. He was distracted, but made many jokes, though his memory was already weak and he couldn't recall where he had left his baggage upon arriving in Moscow. Later his things were discovered in the restaurant of the Slyanski Bazaar.

"As she saw me off, the wife of Troubetskoi said that in spite of what her husband thought, Vladimir Sergeyevich would not recover. Then she told me that once when she was saying Goodbye to Vladimir Sergeyevich, he corrected her, saying, 'Not Goodbye, but *au revoir*, for we shall surely meet again! *Before my death I shall come to you.*'"

* * *

The physicians found Soloviev in a serious condition. His metabolic system was nearing complete collapse, sclerosis of the arteries was far advanced, there was involvement of the kidneys and uremia was also present. He was in considerable pain at first; later this passed away. He was often half-conscious, and there were periods of delirium.

Prince Troubetskoi wrote: "During the first week he still talked a good deal. He asked me to read him the dispatches in the newspapers, spoke quite a bit about the Chinese situation, and said, 'I think everything has come to an end. The main current of world history which branched out into the ancient, medieval and modern age, has ceased. The professors of world history are out of step; their object has lost its vital meaning for the present time. Everything is finished.'"

Shortly before this, at the end of the last letter he was to write, Soloviev had observed: "The historical drama is over, and only the epilogue remains, though—as with Ibsen—it may be prolonged into five acts."

Soloviev spoke increasingly about death as his illness advanced. Prince Troubetskoi related, "On the seventeenth he said he would like to confess to a priest and take Holy Communion, 'not with the reserved Sacrament usually given to the dying, but tomorrow, after Mass.' Then he prayed for a long time, repeatedly interrupting himself to ask if dawn was near and when the priest would arrive."

The priest, the Reverend Father Sergei Belyaev, came to Soloviev early in the morning. In his recollections of the occasion, later published in the *Moscow Journal*, Father Belyaev wrote: "Vladimir Sergeyevich confessed with true Christian humility. The confession lasted not less than half an hour. Among other things he said he had not confessed for three years because the last time he did so (I do not recall whether it was in Moscow or St. Petersburg), during the confession he had a dispute with his confessor about a dogmatic question. Vladimir Sergeyevich did not say what the specific question was, but at that time he was not admitted to Holy Communion.

"After the confession I asked Vladimir Sergeyevich whether he could remember any other sins. He replied, 'I shall think and try to remember.' I told him to think about this, and prepared to leave in order to go to the church to celebrate the Liturgy, but he stopped me, and asked me to read the Prayer of Absolution over him because he was afraid of losing consciousness meanwhile. I read the Prayer of Absolution over him and then went to church to celebrate the Mass. Afterward I returned to him with the newly-consecrated Holy Sacrament and asked him, 'Did you recall any other sins?' He replied, 'No, Father, I prayed about my sins, asking God to forgive them, but I didn't remember any more.' I then gave Vladimir Sergeyevich the Holy Communion. With us were Prince S.N. Troubetskoi and his wife."

The dispute with his confessor of three years before, to which Soloviev referred, took place in his mother's home in Moscow. In 1897 while he was visiting her, he suddenly fell ill and asked for an Orthodox priest in order that he might confess to him. Accordingly, his former teacher at the Troitsa Theological Academy, the kindly and learned theologian, Father Alexander Mikhailovich Ivantsov-Platonov, was called. In the house at the same time was an intimate family friend, a Mme. Yeltsova, sister of Soloviev's life-long friend, Professor Lyov Mikhailovich Lopatin (1855-1920). In her recollections which appeared in *Contemporary Notes*, Paris, 1926 she wrote: "Father Ivantsov Platonov stayed with Vladimir Sergeyevich for a long time, engaged in an extended conversation with him. Nevertheless, coming out afterward he said he had not given him the Sacrament, that there was nothing dangerous in his condition, and furthermore, since Soloviev had eaten something earlier that morning, he had not given him Communion. Alexander Mikhailovich, a man of great intellect and amazing kindness—one could even say, holiness—seemed, however, to be worried, even depressed about something as he went out. At least that was my impression. At that time we were entirely satisfied with his explanations, but afterward it came to my mind that perhaps they had had a dispute between them over the dogmatic question about which Soloviev later confessed and repented before a priest in his final confession just before his death."

Returning to Father Belyaev's account of Soloviev's last confession, his having taken Communion in the Roman Catholic faith in February 1896, and his later insistence of the rightness of what he had done in his confession to Father Ivantsov-Platonov, Soloviev now said to Father Belyaev: "The priest was right, and I disputed with him out of zealousness. After that he and I had a correspondence on the question, but I didn't want to give in, although I fully realized that I was not right. Now I am entirely aware of my error and wholeheartedly repent it." Thus Soloviev repented his insistance on his "Universal Church" idea, received Absolution and Communion, and died a member of the Russian Orthodox Church.

After receiving Communion, Soloviev grew steadily weaker. As Troubetskoi recalled, "He spoke less, and those with him tried to speak with him as little as possible to save his strength. He continued to pray, either aloud, reading the Psalms and Church Prayers, or silently, making the sign of the Cross from time to time. He prayed when he was conscious, even when he was half-conscious. Once he said to my wife, 'Don't let me fall asleep; make me pray for the Jewish people; I have to pray for them!' He began to read a Psalm in Hebrew.

"He wasn't afraid to die, but he was afraid his life would be prolonged needlessly; therefore he prayed that God would give him a speedy end.

"On the twenty-fourth his mother and sisters arrived. He recognized them and was happy they had come, but it was clear that his strength was declining with each passing day. On the twenty-seventh it seemed as if he felt a little better; he was less delirious. He turned on his other side with less effort and answered questions more easily. However, his temperature began to rise sharply and next day clear signs of approaching death set in; on the following evening at half past nine he silently passed away.

"In his last days he said, 'Probably I worked too much at one time in my life.' On his deathbed he said, 'The labor for God is hard.'"

* * *

The funeral of Vladimir Soloviev was held in the Chapel of the University of Moscow where he had beheld his first vision of his Eternal Friend, decades before. As the coffin was carried beneath the archway of the main portal of the church, which bears the inscription, "The Light of Christ enlightens me!" one could recall the verses Soloviev had written not long before:

On a path secret, sorrowful and dear,
You near my soul, and so I thank you!
Sweet it is to touch, with saddened memory,
These calm, death-shrouded, silent shores.

With mysterious threads my deepest heart
To images vague is bound, to weeping shadows;
Something yet unspoken is longing to be said,
Something yet to happen, but neither here nor there.

Moments pass with soundless steps,
O draw near me and unveil my eyes;
One who is eternal, inseparable, appears before me,
And the years gone by are but a single hour.

* * *

On August 3, 1900 Soloviev's body was buried beside those of his father and grandfather in the Cemetery of the

Novo-Devichi Convent in Moscow, thus fulfilling what he had told Prince Troubetskoi during his last illness was the purpose of his trip to Moscow: "...I came in order that I might be with my dead ones."

In his funeral eulogy, Professor V.N. Guarrier, a long-time friend of Soloviev and his family, referred to Soloviev's relationship with his Eternal Friend: "Everywhere you brought joy and hope with you, dear Vladimir Sergeyevich. The radiant vision upon which you existed, and from which you received consolation, was not in vain!"

Could he have replied from beyond the threshold of death, looking backward over the years of his earthly life, it well might be that Soloviev would have echoed the words of another great striver for the spirit, another lover of the Eternal Friend, Giordano Bruno—words spoken by the latter on the occasion of his departure from the University of Wittenberg in 1588:

> "The divine Sophia have I loved and sought from my youth; I have desired her to be my spouse. Ever have I loved her beauteous, radiant form. Ever have I prayed that she might be sent to abide with me, that she might work with me to the end that I might know what I lacked and what in me God would find acceptable. And since she has ever known and understood me, has guided me in all my life's activity, I am persuaded that even after death she will ever keep me safe, wrapped securely in her watchful, constant love."

The truth of these words is attested by the concluding verses of Soloviev's poem, *Three Meetings*, his loving expression of gratitude for his mystical encounters with the Sophia. It is as though now he looks forward eagerly to yet a fourth and even more glorious meeting with his Eternal Friend, a meeting which can come about only in the moment of his death:

Triumphant over death in premonition,
The bonds of ages overcome in dream,
Eternal Friend, I will not call upon you,
Though indeed you will forgive my feeble song!

Though still enchained amid the world's futility,
Beneath the weight of matter's heavy crust,
My soul beheld your everlasting splendor
And came to know your radiance divine.

My spirit wakens now, and here around me,
Arises once again the azure mist, as long ago,
While the sea of earthly life, conquered by your beauty,
In silence has receded, far away.

The study of Prince Troubetskoi at Ozokoie,
the room where Soloviev died

Chapter Eight

Epilogue

Vladimir Soloviev died at the very moment a new dimension had entered the spiritual history of human evolution with the ending of the *Kali Yuga*, the Dark Age, and the dawning of the new Age of Light. The first twenty-six years of his life paralleled the momentous events taking place in the spiritual world, sometimes called the War in Heaven, almost from the latter's inception just a decade before his birth to the victory of Michael and his hosts in 1879, when Soloviev had reached the zenith of his popularity as a lecturer, able to fill great halls in Moscow and St. Petersburg to capacity. Just thrice seven years after this, Soloviev died.

Though they never met personally, the lives of Vladimir Soloviev and Rudolf Steiner paralleled each other in a remarkable way, from the birth of the latter at Kraljevic, Austria (today in Yugoslavia) in 1861, the year before Soloviev's first "Meeting" with his Eternal Friend occurred in Moscow. In 1873 when Soloviev published his first article, *The Mythological Process in Ancient Paganism* and was graduated from the University of Moscow, Rudolf Steiner was a student at the Realschule in Wiener Neustadt; the following year Soloviev successfully defended his Master's thesis, *The Crisis in Western Philosophy* and was appointed a Fellow of the University of Moscow in the Faculty of Philosophy.

At the beginning of 1878 Soloviev gave a series of public lectures in St. Petersburg on *Godmanhood* in the presence of a distinguished audience including Tolstoi and Dostoyevski, having recently returned from England and Egypt, where he had had his second and third "Meetings" with his Eternal Friend. In the autumn of 1879 Rudolf Steiner entered the *Technische Hochschule*, the Institute of Technology, in Vienna, and the following April Soloviev brilliantly defended his doctoral dissertation, *A Critique of Abstract Principles* at the University of St. Petersburg.

In 1881, when Soloviev reached "the turning-point of his life" as a result of his remarks concerning the assassination of Alexander II, Rudolf Steiner, having recently read Goethe's *Faust* for the first time, was attending lectures by Karl Julius Schroer on Faust at the *Technische Hochschule*. In 1884, when Soloviev was at work on his utopian *History and Future of Theocracy*, Steiner, on the recommendation of Schroer, his "fatherly teacher and friend," entered the Specht home as tutor, this innaugurating a new phase in his pedagogical activity.

In 1886, as a part of his preparatory work for the editing of Goethe's Natural Scientific Writings for the Kuerschner edition, Steiner wrote his *Theory of Knowledge Implicit in Goethe's World Conception*. In the same year Soloviev was forbidden by the Russian censorship all public lecturing and writing as a result of his expressed interest in Roman Catholicism. In 1888 Soloviev visited Paris and Vienna in support of his ideas concerning universal Christianity, and Steiner traveled from Vienna to Weimar to visit the Goethe-Schiller Archives in preparation for his work as independent collaborator in the editing of *Goethe's Natural Scientific Writings* for the Weimar Edition of Goethe's works, then in preparation.

In 1891 Rudolf Steiner received his doctorate at the University of Rostock, his thesis being *Wahrheit und Wissenschaft*, [Truth and Knowledge]; in the same year Soloviev gave a private lecture on *The Collapse of the Medieval World Conception* before the Psychological Society in Moscow, with

marked success. In 1894, in the midst of intense inner struggles, Soloviev wrote his essay on *The Meaning of Love* and
began work on his *Justification of the Good*, and Steiner's
Philosophy of Spiritual Activity was published in Berlin.
Under the profound impression made upon him by the
German philosopher, Nietzsche, Steiner published his book,
Friedrich Nietzsche, Fighter for Freedom, in 1895, and the
following year, in an attempt to exemplify universal Christianity in his own person, Soloviev received the Sacrament
for the first and only time from a Uniat priest in Moscow,
an action which has been interpreted in certain quarters as
evidence of his "conversion" to Roman Catholicism. In 1897
Soloviev visited Scandinavia and Scotland, the year Steiner
published his *Goethe's Conception of the World* and undertook the editorship of the *Magazin fuer Literatur* in Berlin.

In 1898 Soloviev made his last visit to Egypt, and the
following spring began to write his *Three Conversations* at
Cannes. At about this same time Rudolf Steiner experienced
a severe inner struggle, an inner testing which ultimated
successfully because, as he stated in his *Autobiography*,
he had been able "to stand in spirit before the Mystery of
Golgotha in most inward, most earnest solemnity of knowledge." This occurred in the same months when Vladimir
Soloviev was profoundly occupied with the problem of the
Antichrist.

At Easter, 1900 Soloviev's *Three Conversations*, including
his Antichrist Narrative, was published. In those months, in
addition to his editorial work, writing and lecturing, Steiner
was giving adult education courses to young people in the
Workers' School in Berlin.

* * *

A few weeks after Vladimir Soloviev's death, in response
to an invitation from Count and Countess Brockdorff,

Владиміръ Соловьевъ.

ТРИ РАЗГОВОРА

О ВОЙНѢ, ПРОГРЕССѢ И КОНЦѢ ВСЕМІРНОЙ ИСТОРІИ, СО ВКЛЮЧЕНІЕМЪ КРАТКОЙ ПОВѢСТИ ОБЪ АНТИХРИСТѢ И СЪ ПРИЛОЖЕНІЯМИ.

ИЗДАНІЕ ВТОРОЕ.

Съ портретомъ автора.

Изданіе Спб. Т-ва Печатнаго и Издательскаго Дѣла „Трудъ".
С.-Петербургъ, Фонтанка, 86.
1901.

Title page of Soloviev's *Three Conversations*
with the *Antichrist Narrative*, St. Petersburg, 1901

Rudolf Steiner began lecturing at the Theosophical Library in Berlin. His first lecture concerned Nietzsche. His second, titled *Goethe's Secret Revelation*, was a study of the latter's fairy tale of "The Green Snake and the Beautiful Lily," an artistic representation of the working of the Divine Wisdom, the Sophia, in the life of modern humanity. *This inaugurated Rudolf Steiner's public presentation of Anthroposophy, the science of spirit.*

In the ensuing years Rudolf Steiner referred repeatedly to Vladimir Soloviev, characterizing him from a number of points of view, for example, as one who, out of his clairvoyant faculties, was able to forecast events to occur in the twentieth century (June 29, 1909); as one whose highly developed spiritual conception of the Christ is like a rosy dawn announcing the advent of a later development of civilization (June 16, 1910); as one whose "beautiful meditations" point the way to a great vision of the Advent of the Christ in the Etheric World, which will appear to humanity in the course of the twentieth century (October 7, 1911); as a true clairvoyant whose vision embraced future events of immense significance for the evolution of humanity as a whole (September 19, 1911), and so on. Rudolf Steiner also spoke about the past earthly incarnations of the eternal entelechy of that individuality known as Vladimir Soloviev in a lecture given at Dornach, September 19, 1924. (For further details see *The Writings and Lectures of Rudolf Steiner—a Bibliography*, compiled by Paul M. Allen, New York, 1956; *Das Vortragswerk Rudolf Steiners*, by Hans Schmidt, the Goetheanum, Dornach, 1950; *Rudolf Steiner, Das Literarische und kuenstlerische Werk*, Rudolf Steiner-Nachlassverwaltung, Dornach, 1961.)

Further clarification of the nature of the Sophia, the Divine Wisdom, which as has been shown, played a vital role in Soloviev's spiritual experience, was given by Steiner in a lecture at Hamburg, May 31, 1908, and in another at Dornach, March 26, 1922.

When a series of translations of principal works of Vladimir Soloviev in German by Harry Koehler (the pseudonym of Harriet von Vacano) titled *Vladimir Soloviev, Ausgewaehlte Werke*, appeared through the publishing house of the Kommende Tag, Stuttgart in 1921/22, Rudolf Steiner wrote an introductory essay for one of the volumes, titled "Vladimir Soloviev, a Mediator between East and West." In that essay he characterizes Soloviev as one who, as a representative of the true spiritual life of the European East, can contribute much to the deepening of East-West understanding. In a preface to another volume in the series, Rudolf Steiner pointed to Soloviev's world conception as something from which streams a wonderful quality of warmth of soul, a philosophy which works as religious meditation, and religious ideas which are like philosophy experienced in the inner life of modern humanity.

In connection with the development of eurythmy, the art of movement inaugurated by Rudolf Steiner, he created eurythmy forms for twelve poems by Vladimir Soloviev, translated by Marie Steiner into German. One of these poems was included in the eurythmy performance given at the Goetheanum (the building created by Rudolf Steiner at Dornach, Switzerland) on New Year's Eve, 1922/23, one of the last events which took place in that remarkable structure before it was totally destroyed by fire that same night.

The next evening following the fire, when Rudolf Steiner continued his lecture course, he opened his consideration with words of encouragement to those gathered in the wake of that catastrophic event, and then read *once again* the poem by Vladimir Soloviev which had been presented in Eurythmy the previous day.

Thus Vladimir Soloviev is linked with perhaps the severest test Rudolf Steiner had to face on his spiritual path, a test which he endured and surmounted, thus opening the way to the enormous achievements of the concluding years of his life.

Soloviev's Three Meetings

VLADIMIR SOLOVIEV

MOSCOW—LONDON—EGYPT 1865–1876

Triumphant over death in premonition,
The bonds of ages overcome in dream,
Eternal Friend, I will not call upon you,
Though indeed you will forgive my feeble song!

Heeding not the world's own vain illusions,
Through the heavy dullness of this mortal sheath,
Amid the glorious, uncreated ether-light
I came to know your radiance divine.

Thrice you revealed yourself to sight of humanity,
Not in shadowy imaginings of the mind;
In prophetic joy, in help, in grace vouchsafed,
To my soul's call your image came in answer.

I

The first time, — how long ago it was!
Thirty-six years have passed away since as a child
I felt the first burning darts of sudden love,
All confused and baffled by darkening clouds.

I was nine, she too was nine; it was in Moscow
On a day in May, I spoke to her, confessing

My ardent love, but she made no reply!
Have I a rival then? I thought — a duel there must be!

So ran my thoughts, when in the Service
On Ascension Day my soul was stirred with anger;
"All earthly cares... to lay aside... in peace serene..."
The choral anthem sounded, echoed, died away...

The altar stands revealed, but where is the Priest,
The Deacon, the throng of people worshipping?
My passion's flood has ebbed, has vanished,
And now around me and within, the azure infinite.

Enwoven with gold-blue, in streaming light,
Bearing still a flower from far-distant lands,
Beckoning to me, you stand with radiant smile,
And then, as silently, you vanish from my sight.

My childish love grew distant, far removed,
Blind to all earthly things became my soul,
When urgently my little German nurse
Tugged at my sleeve: "Volodinka, alas, how stupid
    he's become!"

II

The years too quickly fled; now Master and Fellow,
I traveled abroad the first time; now Berlin,
Now Hanover, now Cologne, one after the other
Drew near and quickly vanished from my view.

It was not Paris, gay center of the world,
Nor dreamy Spain, nor glamorous Far Eastern lands —
The British Museum was my long journey's goal,
Nor indeed were my dreams and hopes deceived.

Blessed months, could I ever forget you?
Though not because of beauty's phantoms fading,
Nor human passions, nor Nature's grandeur,
But because my soul was filled with you alone, Beloved!

Despite the toiling millions in the city,
The machines' fire-breathing, heavy throbbing,
The massive, soulless buildings towering high,
A sacred quiet here surrounds me — I am alone.

Alone, yes, cum grano salis.
I was lonely, true,
But nonetheless by no means a hater of humankind;
People there were in all my aloneness,
But among them, whom shall I name by name?

I cannot here recount their names and titles,
Nor describe their appearance, their strange tongues;
Suffice it to say that among them were a few Britons,
And two or three from Moscow — all scholars like myself.

Most of the time I was alone in the great Library,
And, believe it or not, but God is my witness:
Mysterious powers led me to choose for reading
Everything possible concerning Her.

And if, by chance, my erring whims suggested
That from the shelves I take down other books,
Such strange things happened then
That, quite confused, I left for home.

Once in days of Autumn
I said to her, O Flower divine,
I feel your presence here! But why
Have you not appeared to me since childhood?

Hardly had I thought these words
When suddenly all was filled with golden azure,
And you were there in heavenly radiance;
There I saw your face, your face alone!

That single moment brought me years of happiness,
No worldly matters could distract my soul;
But were I to mention more of this,
My words would empty seem, and meaningless.

III

I said to her, you once let me see your face,
But your noble image I yet long to see;
The gift you granted to a child,
To a grown-up man you'll surely not refuse!

Within me now I heard the message: "Be in Egypt!"
To France then, and to Southern countries lies my road;
My feelings struggled not at all with reason,
And reason — like one dumb — said not a word.

To Lyons, Turin, Piacenza, Ancona, Ban,
Then from Brindisi's quay, across the shimmering
Deep-blue, broad Mediterranean flood,
A British steamer safely bore me.

Granted willingly in Cairo were credit and lodging
At Hotel Abbat — vanished long-since, alas!
Modest, comfortable, best in all the world;
Russians were staying there, even some from Moscow!

A retired, tenth-grade General entertained us
With memories of his old Caucasus days;

It is right that here I tell his name,
For long ago he died.

He was the illustrious Rostislav Faddeyev,
Story-teller extraordinary, fabricating
Frivolities, courtesans, vast cathedrals —
His flights of imagination boundless.

Twice daily at the table d'hote we sat together,
Gaily and long he romanced and discoursed,
Ranging through his ample store of doubtful anecdotes,
Varied by his unique philosophizing.

Meanwhile I waited for the promised meeting,
Till finally in stillness of the silent night,
Like a cool breeze I heard the whisper,
"I'm in the desert; you'll surely find me there!"

But to go on foot? — Ah well, it can't be helped!
One is not transported from London to the far Sahara
All for nothing; My pockets were as empty as could be;
And for days on end I'd been living there on credit.

Where I was to go, God only knew — yet I set out
One fine day, like the famous Uncle Vlas
In old Nekrassov's tale,
Without money, without provisions.

Doubtless you smiled as I started,
Wearing my warm overcoat and over-high top-hat;
Mistaking me for a devil, the brave Bedouins
Took fright and swiftly ran away.

But I barely saved my skin when,
Bound hand and foot like any captive slave,

Loudly wrangling sheikhs of neighboring tribes
Took council what best to do with me.

Finally they let me go — a generous gesture;
I went in haste, laughing silently with you,
For gods and men alike smile and laugh
At misfortune — when it's safely over!

Meanwhile, silent night descends to earth
All at once, without twilight;
Around me, only silent darkness,
Above me, night and shining stars.

Lying on the sand I look and listen,
Somewhere, far away, a jackal howls;
Probably he would devour me,
For quite unarmed I'm lying here.

Yet worse than jackal is the piercing cold,
The day was hot, but now the air is chill;
The cold glitter of the stars above,
The bitter frost below, conspire to banish sleep.

Long I lay there, until at last
A gentle whisper: "Sleep, my poor friend!" —
I fell asleep, and upon awaking,
Celestial vault and earth with roses breathed.

In radiance of heavenly glory,
Your eyes aflame with azure fire,
Shine forth like ethereal dawning
Of cosmic creation's primal day!

Everything that was, is, and ever will be,
One moment's fleeting glance encompassed;

Distant forests, seas and rivers far below me,
Snowy mountain-heights, enwrapped in shimmering
    blue.

I gazed upon it all, and all was fair,
In form of Womanhood, embracing all in one;
The infinite encircled there, yet limitless,
Before me and within me — You alone!

O radiant Countenance, you have not deceived me!
Your fullest glory I beheld amid the desert waste;
Ever will your heavenly roses bloom within me
Where'er my stream of life may flow.

It lingered but a moment, then the vision faded,
The sun rose glorious upon the eastern sky;
The silent desert spread around me; my soul was
    praying
To the blessed sound of chiming bells within.

Though my spirit was all awake,
For two days and nights I'd eaten nothing —
My eyes grew dim. Alert though the soul may be,
Starvation, as the saying goes, one cannot play with!

Once again, towards the Nile I plodded,
And as the day drew near its close,
I entered Cairo, your smile still glowing in my soul,
But in my shoes huge holes were worn!

Viewed objectively, it looked extremely foolish;
As the General ate his soup in silence,
I told the barest facts — of vision I said nothing;
At last he spoke with fitting gravity, eyes fixed firmly on
    me:

"While, my dear sir, intelligence gives one the right to
  be stupid,
It is surely better not to abuse the privilege;
Dull-witted, common folk have no monopoly
In displaying various types of madness.

"Therefore, if you would not be ashamed,
Should others think you a madman, or worse, a fool,
Take my most serious, well-meant advice,
And of this inglorious adventure never speak again!"

Triumphant over death in premonition,
The bonds of ages overcome in dream,
Eternal Friend, I will not call upon you,
Though indeed you will forgive my feeble song!

Though still enchained, amid the world's futility,
Beneath the weight of matter's heavy crust,
My soul beheld your everlasting splendor,
And came to know your radiance divine.

My spirit wakens now, and here around me,
Arises once again the azure mist, as long ago,
While the sea of earthly life, conquered by your beauty,
In silence has receded, far away.

The Work of the Human Being for the Earth

VLADIMIR SOLOVIEV

THINKERS BEMUSED BY collectivism regard the life of human-kind as merely a struggle between classes of human beings, considering individuals insignificant, transient elements of society, without rights of their own, who at any moment may be brushed aside in the interest of "the general welfare." But what can come from a society composed of moral zeros, of rightless, non-individual creatures? Would that be *human* society? Where would its dignity and inner value come from? How could such a society long maintain itself? It is clear that this is nothing but a sad and empty dream, which neither could nor should be brought into existence.

Social life is not a condition *added* to the individual life, but is implicit in the very character of personality. The latter is basically a rational, moral power which can act only in the life of a community.

Fundamentally, society is not the outer boundary of the individual, but is actually an inner fulfillment. Society is not the mathematical sum of the individuals comprising it, but is the indivisible whole of the community life. This communal life has been preserved from the *past* in the continuing *social tradition*; it is realized in the *present* through *social service*; in *social ideals* living in the best of people, lies its hope for continuing into the *future*.

It is only in a community that personal achievement is fruitful, but *in a community which develops*. Unconditional surrender to any limited, fixed form of social life is far from being the duty of any individual. More than this, it is positively wrong, for such surrender can only be detrimental to the human dignity of the single person.

As such, each person is a moral being, that is, a being who, apart from a social function has absolute worth and the absolute right to live and freely develop positive, constructive abilities. From this it follows that *under no circumstances nor for any reason can a human being be regarded as a means for a purpose external to himself or herself*; cannot be merely an instrument for the good of another person or for the well-being of a group or even for the so-called common welfare itself, that is, the welfare of the majority of human beings. This general welfare, this common good has *no claim* upon a person as an individual, but upon the person's work or activity to the extent that that work, being useful to the community, at the same time secures a worthy existence to the worker. The right of each human being is based on the human dignity inherent in and inalienable from the person, upon the fact that every human being is unique and individual, and therefore must be an end and not merely a means or an instrument. This right of each person is *unconditional*, while the rights of the community with regard to the person are conditioned by the recognition of the individual's rights.

* * *

The first impulse to work is given by material necessity. But for a person who recognizes the absolutely perfect principle of reality, labor is also *a commandment* of God. This commandment requires us to work "in the sweat of the brow" to cultivate the ground, that is, to perfect material Nature. For whose sake? In the first place, for our own and that of our neighbor. As humanity progresses, however, the scope of the word "neighbor" becomes ever broader. Originally the neighbor was only those with whom I was related by the blood-tie or personal liking; finally, it includes all humanity.

Human beings are moral beings who ought not merely to labor for all and to share in the common work of the community, but *to know that they do so* and that *they wish to do it.* Those who refuse to recognize this truth will ultimately experience its inexorable force in the impact of financial disasters and economic crises... However, the natural oneness of economic interests is not in itself sufficient to bring about the result that individuals recognize that in working for themselves they should also work for all. To accomplish this, economic conditions must be *consciously directed towards the common good.*

To accept selfishness and self-interest as the basic motive for work means that we deprive the latter of the significance of a universal commandment and transform it into something accidental. It is clear that if I work only for my own and my family's welfare, as soon as I can gain that welfare by *other* means, I automatically lose my only motive for working... Indeed, facts compel us to recognize that if we begin with private material interest as the purpose of work, we finally arrive at universal discord and destruction instead of universal happiness. If, on the other hand, the meaning and purpose of work is found in the ideal of the general welfare, understood in the true, moral sense, that is, *as the good of all and each*, and not of the majority alone, such an ideal will also include the satisfaction of every private interest, within proper limits.

Every person, whether a farmer, writer, or banker ought to work with the feeling that their labor is useful to all, and with the desire that it be so. They are to regard their work as a duty, as a fulfillment of the law of God, and as a service to the general welfare of their fellow human beings.

The duty of society is to secure to all of its members the right to enjoy unmolested *worthy* existence for both themselves and their families. Worthy existence is compatible with voluntary poverty such as St. Francis of Assisi taught and as it is practised by our wandering Russian pilgrims. However it is *not* compatible with work which reduces all the significance of the human being to a mere means of producing material wealth.

Work which is entirely and crudely mechanical or which involves too great physical strain is incompatible with human dignity. But *equally* incompatible and equally immoral is work which, though not heavy nor unduly taxing, continues all day long and consumes *all* the time and *all* the strength of the individual so that the few hours of leisure remaining simply must be devoted to physical rest, and neither time nor energy remain for thoughts and interests of a cultural-spiritual order.

From a moral point of view everyone must have the means of existence (food, clothing, shelter) and sufficient physical rest secured to them, and they must also be able to enjoy *leisure* for the sake of cultural-spiritual development. This and this alone is *absolutely essential* for the complete well-being of every farmer and workperson.

* * *

There remains the duty of humans toward material Nature itself, which they are called upon to cultivate. This duty is indicated plainly in the commandment to labor: Till the ground. The Hebrew words, *laobod ef gaadama* (Genesis 3:23), literally mean to *serve the Earth* in the sense that the angels "serve" humanity or a teacher "serves" the children. To till the ground means not to misuse, exhaust or devastate it, but to improve it, to bring to it greater strength and fullness of being.

Above all, a decisive stop must be put to the treatment of the Earth as a lifeless object for rapacious exploitation, ... an end must be put to those predatory methods of cultivation which will end in there not being enough land for one person, let alone for all. On the other hand, if the land is properly *cared for* in a moral way and *looked after* like a being one loves, the minimum amount of land sufficient for each human being may well become so small that there will be enough for all those who have none, without doing injustice to those who have.

Therefore neither our fellow human beings nor physical Nature are to be regarded as merely passive, impersonal instruments for economic production or exploitation... Nature's subordinate position in relation to the Deity and humanity does not render it rightless. *It is fully entitled to our help in transforming and uplifting it.*

In themselves objects have no rights as such, but Nature and Earth are not mere objects, but on the contrary have an objectified essence which we can and must help to become spiritualized. The goal of our work, insofar as Nature is concerned, is not to make it an instrument for obtaining goods and money, but to perfect it, to revive the lifeless, to spiritualize it... Essential in all this is the point of view, the inner attitude, and the direction of our activity resulting from it.

Without loving Nature for its own sake it is impossible to organize material life in a moral way.

Our relation to Nature is of three kinds: passive submission to it as it now exists; an active struggle with it, subjugating it and employing it merely as a means to an end; the affirmation of Nature's ideal potential state, of *what it ought to become through human activity*... Absolutely normal and final is this third relationship in which we use our efforts for the sake of uplifting Nature—and uplift ourselves along with it.

The great ideal is to cultivate the Earth, *to minister to it, to serve it* in such a way that it may be renewed and regenerated.

From the moral point of view, therefore, work is the reciprocal action taking place between people in the physical world; it must, in accordance with moral requirements, secure to each and all human beings the necessary means of worthy existence, enabling them to bring to ultimate perfection all human faculties and possibilities, and finally to transfigure and to spiritualize the life of Nature and the Earth itself.

(Italics throughout the above text follow emphasis by Soloviev in the original.)

A Short Narrative about Antichrist

VLADIMIR SOLOVIEV

EUROPE IN THE twenty-first century presented a union of more or less democratic States—the United States of Europe.

Matters of international consciousness—questions of life and death, of the last judgment, of the world and of humankind, complicated and confused by a multitude of new physiological and psychological investigations and discoveries, remained, as formerly, insoluble. Only one important negative result was made clear—the absolute fall of theoretical materialism. The representation of the universe as a system of floating atoms, and of life as the result of a mechanical agglomeration of minute alterations of matter—such a statement no longer satisfied even one thinking being. Humankind had forever outgrown the youthful capacity of a simple and unconscious belief. The idea that God created the universe out of nothing, etc., ceased to be taught even in the primary schools. A certain general and higher level of representing such matters had been worked out, below which no dogmatism could fall. And if the vast majority of thinking people remained entirely unbelievers, the few who believed became of necessity "thinkers," fulfilling the instructions of the apostle: be children at heart but not in mind.

There was at this time among the few people believing in spiritual things a remarkable man—called by many a superman—who was, however, as far from being intellectual as from being a child at heart. He was still young, but, thanks to his great talent, at thirty-three years of age was widely proclaimed as a great thinker, writer, and social worker. Being conscious within himself of great spiritual power he had been always a convinced spiritualist, and his clear understanding always showed him the truth of that in which one must believe— Good, God, the Messiah. In these he *believed*, but he *loved only himself*. He believed in God, but, in the depths of his soul, he involuntarily and unconsciously preferred himself to Him.

He believed in Good, but the All Seeing Eye of the Eternal knew that this man bowed before the power of evil when it offered him a bribe—not by the snare of the senses and lower passions, nor even by the superior attraction of power, but through his immeasurable self-love alone. Besides, this self-love was neither an unconscious instinct nor a foolish pretence. In view of his exceptional talent, his beauty, nobility of character, his supreme display of continence, his disinterestedness, and his active beneficence, it seemed that his enormous self-love was justifiable, and worthy of a great spiritualist, ascetic, and philanthropist. Was he to blame?—a man so plenteously endowed with divine gifts that he saw in them special signs of an exceptional affection from heaven for himself, and he counted himself as second to God in his origin as the only son of God. In a word, he avowed that he was, in truth, Christ. But this consciousness of his supermerit, in effect, defined itself in him not as any moral obligation of his towards God and the world, but as his right and prerogative to be before others, and, more than all, before Christ. He had no fundamental enmity towards Jesus. He recognized His Messianic significance and merit, and he really saw in Him his own august predecessor. The moral grandeur and absolute oneness of Christ were not understood by a mind clouded by self-love. He argued thus: "Christ came before me; I appeared next, but that which appears later in time is, in reality, first. I shall come last at the end of history exactly because I am the absolute and final savior. The first Christ is my forerunner. His mission was to prepare and make ready for my appearance." In this sense the great man of the twenty-first century applied to himself all that was said in the Gospel about the Second Advent, proclaiming that this advent is not a return of the same Christ but a substitution of the previous Christ which is final, that is, he himself.

On this point the coming man does not yet offer much that is characteristic or original. He regards his relation to Christ in the same way as did, for instance, Mahomet, an upright man, whom it is impossible to accuse of any evil design.

The self-loving preference of himself to Christ was justified by this man with such an argument as follows: "Christ, preaching and proclaiming moral welfare, was the *reformer* of humanity, but I am called to be *benefactor* of humanity in *part reformed*, in *part unreformed*. I shall give to everyone all that is necessary for him. Christ as a moralist divided all people into good and bad; I shall unite them by blessings which are necessary both to the good and the bad. I shall be the real representative of that God who causes the sun to shine upon the good and the bad, and the rain to fall upon the just and unjust. Christ brought a sword; I shall bring peace. He threatened the earth with a dreadful last judgment. But I shall be the final judge, and my judgment will not be a judgment of right only, but of mercy. There will be justice in my judgment; not a justice of reward, but a distributive justice. I shall make a distinction for all, and I shall give what is needful for each one."

And behold, in this beautiful frame of mind he awaits some clear, divine call for a new salvation of humanity; for some clear and striking evidence that he is the eldest and beloved firstborn Son of God. He awaits and nourishes his being with the consciousness of his superhuman beneficence and abilities—and this, as it has been said, is a man of irreproachable morality and unusual talent.

The proud and just man waits for the highest sanction in order to begin his salvation of humanity—but he waits in vain. He has passed his thirtieth year and still another three years go by. Suddenly the thought flashes into his mind and pierces to the depths of his brain with a burning shudder, "But if? if it is not I, but that other—the Galilean. If He is not my forerunner, but the real first and last? But He must be *alive*—where is He?... If He came to me now and here... What shall I say to Him? I must bend low before Him, as the very simplest Christian, and as a Russian mouzhik murmur stupidly, 'Lord Jesus Christ, have mercy upon me a sinner,' or, like an old Polish woman, prostrate myself before Him, flat on the ground. I, the brilliant genius, the superman! No, never!" And in the place of the former reasonable and cold respect for God and Christ there is born and grows up in his heart, at first a sort of horror and then a burning envy and fury which seizes and contracts all his being, a hatred which fills his soul. "It is I, and not He. He is not alive and will not be. He has not, He has not risen! He is rotting in the grave, rotting as the lost..." With foaming mouth and convulsive bounds he rushed from the house and the garden, and in the heavy, black night ran along the path on the cliffs. His fury had abated and a despair, hard and heavy as the cliff, gloomy as the night, had taken its place. He stopped near a perpendicular break in the cliff and listened to the troubled noise of the water among the stones far below him. An unbearable sorrow crushed his heart. Suddenly there was a movement within him. "Shall I call upon Him—shall I ask Him what to do?" And in the midst of the darkness appeared a gentle and sad image. "He pities me! no, never! He is not risen, He is not risen!" And he flung himself away from the brink. But something as elastic as a waterspout carried him up in the air, and he felt a vibration as from an electric current when some power hurled him back. For an instant he lost consciousness, and when he regained his senses he found himself kneeling a few steps away from the edge of the cliff. Before him was the outline of a figure, bright with a phosphorescent misty radiance, whose eyes with unbearably sharp brilliancy pierced his soul.

He saw these two piercing eyes and heard, proceeding neither from within nor from without, a strange voice, dull, as if smothered, and, at the same time, precise and entirely soulless, as if it came from a gramophone. This voice said to him: "My well-beloved son, all my affection is in thee. Why hast thou sought me? Why honour that other, the wicked One and His Father. I am god and thy father. The other—a beggar and crucified One—is a stranger to me and to thee. I have no other son but thee. Thou, my only, only begotten, equal to me. I love thee and ask nothing of thee. Thou art so beautiful, great and powerful. Act in thine own name, not in mine. I do not envy thee; I love thee. I am in need of nothing from thee. He, whom thou didst deem a god, demanded of His Son obedience and boundless subservience, even to the death of the cross, and He was unable to help thee. Receive my spirit. As, formerly, my spirit brought thee forth in beauty, so now let it beget thee in strength." At these words of the unknown the lips of the superman parted wide, two piercing eyes approached closely to his face, and he felt as if a sharp, icy current was entering into him, filling all his being. Moreover, he felt a marvellous strength, daring, lightness and ecstasy. At the same instant the shining countenance and the two piercing eyes suddenly disappeared, and something lifted the superman from earth and dropped him immediately in his garden near the door of his house.

On the following day not only the visitors of the great man, but even his servants, were amazed at his inspired appearance. But they would have been still more astonished if they had been able to see with what supernatural swiftness and easiness he, having locked himself up in his own study, wrote his remarkable work under the title of *"The Open Way to Universal Peace and Prosperity."*

The previous books and general activities of the superman had met with severe critics, although they were for the most part especially religious people, and for that reason had no authority of any kind—of course, I am speaking of the time of the coming of Antichrist—so that not many listened to them when they pointed out, in everything that the "coming man" wrote and said, the signs of an absolutely exceptional, intense self-love and conceit, with the absence of true simplicity, rectitude and zeal.

But by his new work he attracted to himself even some of his former critics and opponents. This book, written after the adventure on the cliff, showed in him an unprecedented power of genius. It was something all-embracing and calculated to reconcile all dispute. In it was united a noble reverence for ancient traditions and symbols, with a broad and daring radicalism in social-political demands and requirements; a boundless freedom of thought with the deepest understanding of all mysticism, unconditional individualism, with a burning zeal for the common good, the most exalted idealism in guiding principles, with the complete definiteness and vitality of practical solutions. And all of it was united and connected with such genius and art that it was easy for every one-sided thinker and worker to see and accept the whole, even from his personal angle of vision, in no way sacrificing truth itself, not magnifying it effectively over his "Ego," not disclaiming the practicability of his one-sidedness nor correcting the faults of his outlook and aims, nor yet completing their shortcomings. This wonderful book was at once translated into all the languages of the civilized—and some of the uncivilized—nations. A thousand newspapers in all parts of the world were filled for a whole year with editorial articles and with the raptures of the critics. Cheap editions, with portraits of the author, were sold in millions of copies, and the whole of the cultured world—which at that period comprised almost the whole earth—was filled with the fame of the incomparable great and only one! No one made any objections to this book—it seemed to each the revelation of entire truth. In it such full justice was done to all the past, all the present was estimated so dispassionately and broadly, and the best future was so clearly and realistically described, that everyone said: "Here is the very thing I need; this is the ideal which is not Utopian; this is a project which is not chimerical." And the wonderful author not only attracted everyone, but he was *welcome* to each, thus fulfilling the words of Christ: "I am come in My Father's name and ye receive Me not; if another shall come in his own name—him ye will receive." Of course, for the latter to be received he must be welcome.

It is true, some pious people, while warmly praising the book, began to ask why Christ was not once mentioned in it; but other Christians replied, "God be praised! Already, in past centuries, all holy things have been sufficiently soiled by every sort of unacknowledged zealot, and now a deeply religious writer must be very guarded. And if the contents of a book are impregnated with the truly Christian spirit of effective love and universal benevolence, what is there left to wish for?" With this all agreed. Soon after the appearance of *The Open Way*, which made its author the most popular of all the people who had lived in the world, the international constitutional assembly of the Union of European States was to meet. This Union, founded after the series of domestic and foreign wars which were connected with the throwing off of the Mongol yoke, and which considerably changed the map of Europe, was faced with the immediate danger of a collision—not between the nations, but between political and social parties. The principal directors of general European policy belonging to the powerful society of Freemasons felt the lack of a common executive authority. European unity, which had been attained with such difficulty, was ready at any moment to fall to pieces. The federated council, or universal committee (*comité permanent universel*), was not in harmony, since not all the places were occupied by real Masons devoted to the matter. Independent members of the committee entered into a separate agreement among themselves, and the matter threatened to cause a new war. Then the "devoted ones" resolved to institute a personal executive authority of one man, with full and sufficient powers. The principal candidate was a member of the Order, "the coming man."

He was the only person with a great worldwide reputation. Being by profession a clever officer of artillery, and by his possessions a large capitalist, he had friendly relations everywhere in financial and military circles. In other and less enlightened times the fact that his origin was obscured by a heavy mist of the unknown would have militated against him. His mother, a person of indulgent conduct, was well known in both hemispheres, but too many different people had good reason to believe themselves his father. These circumstances naturally could not have any significance in a century so much in the van, that even to him it appeared to be the last. The "coming man" was elected almost unanimously as life president of the United States of Europe. When he appeared in the Tribune, in all the glory of his superhuman youthful beauty and power, and in an inspired discourse of great eloquence expounded his universal programme, the assembly, enchanted and carried away, decided, in a burst of enthusiasm and without voting, to pay him the highest honour by electing him as Roman Emperor. The Congress was closed amid the greatest rejoicing, and the great man who had been chosen issued a manifesto which began thus: "Peoples of the earth, my peace I give to you," and ending with the words, "Peoples of the earth! The promises have been performed. An eternal, universal peace has been secured. Every attempt to destroy it will meet with invincible resistance. For, from henceforth, there is one central authority on earth, which is stronger than all other powers taken separately and together. This invincible, all-subduing authority, with all its power, belongs to me, as chosen autocratic Emperor of Europe. International law has, at last, a sanction hitherto unattained by it. From henceforth no power will dare to say 'War' when I say it is

'Peace.' Peoples of the earth, peace be to you!" This manifesto produced the desired effect. Everywhere outside Europe, especially in America, strong imperialistic parties were formed which forced their governments, upon various conditions, to join the United States of Europe under the supreme power of the Roman Emperor. There still remained independent tribes and smaller powers somewhere in Asia and Africa. The Emperor, with a small army, but one chosen from Russian, German, Polish, Hungarian and Turkish regiments, accomplished a march from Eastern Asia to Morocco, and without great bloodshed brought into subjection all who were disobedient. He established viceroys in all the countries of both hemispheres, men of European education and native magnates devoted to himself. The population of all pagan countries was dumbfounded, but at the same time enchanted, and proclaimed him a great god. In one year, in a real and accurate sense, he founded a universal monarchy. All tendencies to war were eradicated. The League of Universal Peace met for the last time, and having published an enthusiastic panegyric on the great peace maker, abolished itself as unnecessary. In the second year of his reign the Roman and Universal Emperor issued a new manifesto. "Peoples of the earth, I promised you peace and I have given it you. But peace is beautiful only when coupled with prosperity. He who in time of peace is threatened with the misfortune of poverty, does not find peace a joy. Now, let all who are cold and hungry come to me, so that I may warm them and feed them." Afterwards he announced a simple and all-embracing social reform which, already stated in his book, had there captivated all noble and sober minds. At present, thanks to the concentration in his hands of the world's finance and of a colossal amount of landed property, he was able to realise this reform according to the wishes of the poor, and without sensibly offending the rich. Everyone began to receive in proportion to his ability, and every ability according to its labour and merit.

The new lord of the earth was, before all things, a tender-hearted philanthropist, and not only a philanthropist but a *philosopher*. He himself was a vegetarian. He forbad vivisection, and instituted a strict watch over slaughter-houses. The society for the protection of animals was encouraged by him in every way. But more important than all these details was the solid establishment among all humankind of the most fundamental equality—*an equality of general repletion*. This was accomplished in the second year of his reign. The social-political question was definitely settled. But if repletion be the first interest of hungry people, such people, when once replete, want something more. Even animals, when replete, usually want not only to sleep, but to play. Much more than they, do human beings, who at all times, *post panem*, have demanded *circenses*.

The Emperor-superman understood what was necessary for his people. At this time a great magician from the distant Orient came to him in Rome wrapped in a thick cloud of strange happenings and curious tales. It was generally believed among the Neo-Buddhists that he was of divine origin—a son of the sun god Surga and of a water nymph.

This magician, Apollyon by name, was a man undoubtedly talented, half Asiatic, half European, a Catholic bishop *in partibus infidelium*, who, while he was to an astonishing degree in possession of the latest results of Western science and of its technical application, also united with this the knowledge of all that is really sound and significant in the traditional mysticism of the Orient and the skill to make use of it. The results of such a combination were astounding. Apollyon had attained, among other things, the skill at once, half scientific, half magical, of attracting and directing atmospheric electricity, and told the people *he brought down fire from heaven*. For the rest, while striking the imagination of the crowd by various unheard-of wonders, he had not up to now made ill use of his power for any personal aims. So this man came to the great Emperor and bowing before him as before a true son of God, declared that in the secret books of the East he had found direct prophecies about him, the Emperor, as the last savior and universal judge, and placed himself and his art at his service. The Emperor, enchanted with him, received him as a gift from heaven, and after conferring upon him the highest titles, refused henceforth to be parted from him. The peoples of the earth, loaded with the benefits of their lord, were to have, besides general peace and repletion, the possibility, moreover, of constant enjoyment of the most varied and unexpected wonders and phenomena. So ended the third year of the superman's reign.

After the happy solution of the political and social questions, the religious question arose. It was raised by the Emperor himself, particularly in its relation to Christianity. At this time Christianity found itself in the following position. In the face of a very considerable diminution in the number of its members—there were not more than 45,000,000 Christians left in all the world—morally it had pulled itself up and braced itself and had gained in quality what it had lost in quantity. There were no longer numbered among Christians any people who were not concerned with some Christian spiritual interest. The various confessions of faith diminished proportionately in numbers, and consequently they preserved approximately their former numerical relation. As to their mutual feelings, although enmity had not given place to complete reconciliation yet it was notably softened and opposition lost its sharpness. The Papacy had already for some time been driven out of Rome, and after many wanderings had found an asylum in Petersburg, on condition that it refrained from propaganda both in that town and in the country. In Russia it became noticeably simpler. While not changing the essentially necessary composition of its college and officers, it was obliged to spiritualise the character of its activities and also to reduce to a minimum its magnificent ritual and ceremonial. Many strange and enticing customs, although not formally abolished, went of themselves out of use. In all other countries, especially in North America, the Catholic Hierarchy had many representatives, firm in will, of indomitable energy and of independent position, who, more strongly than ever, insisted on the unity of the Catholic Church, and preserved for her her international and cosmopolitan importance. As to Protestantism, at the head of which Germany continued to stand—especially after the reunion of a considerable part of the Anglican Church with Catholicism—it purged itself of its extreme negative tendencies, and the supporters of those tendencies openly descended to religious indifference and unbelief. In the Evangelical churches there remained only sincere believers, at whose head stood persons who combined a wide knowledge with a deep religious consciousness, and who tried with all the more effort to revive in themselves a living image of the ancient and original Christianity. Now that political events had changed the official position of the Church, Russian Orthodoxy, although it had lost many of its former nominal members, yet experienced the joy of union with the best part of the Old Believers, and even with many sects of a definitely religious tendency. This revivified Church, though it did not grow in numbers, did grow in spiritual power, and this power it showed especially in its domestic struggle with the extreme sects which had increased amongst the people and in society, sects which were not lacking in the demoniac and satanic element.

During the first two years of the new reign the Christians, frightened and depressed by the series of revolutions and wars that had gone before, respected the new ruler and his peaceful reforms, some from a well-disposed expectation, others with absolute sympathy and burning enthusiasm. But with the appearance of the great magician in the third year, serious apprehensions and antipathies began to arise amongst many of the Orthodox, Catholics and Evangelicals. The evangelistic and apostolic texts, which spoke of the prince of this world and Antichrist, began to be read with more attention and discussed with animation. From certain indications the Emperor suspected a gathering storm and resolved to clear up the matter quickly. In the beginning of the fourth year of his reign he issued a manifesto to all his faithful Christians, without distinction of creed, inviting them to choose or designate a representative, with full powers for a general council under his presidency. His residence at this time had been changed from Rome to Jerusalem. Palestine was then an autonomous State inhabited and governed principally by Jews. Jerusalem was a free and had been made an imperial city. The Christian holy places had remained inviolate, but upon the spacious platform of Kharam-esh-Sherif, from Berket-Israin and the present barracks on one side to the mosque of El-Ak and "Solomon's Stables" on the other, was erected an enormous edifice including, besides the two ancient small mosques, a spacious "imperial" temple for the union of all cults, and two magnificent imperial palaces with libraries, museums and special apartments for magical experiments and practices. In this half-temple, half-palace, the general council was to be opened on the 14th of September. Since the Evangelical religion had no priesthood in the true sense, the Catholic and Orthodox hierarchy resolved agreeably to the wish of the Emperor, and in order to give a certain homogeneity, to allow a certain number of laymen, well-known for their piety and devoted to the interests of the Church, to have a part in the council. Once laymen were allowed it was impossible to exclude the lower clergy, both black and white. In this way the number of members of the council exceeded three thousand, and about half a million of Christian pilgrims deluged Jerusalem and Palestine. Among the members of the council there were three who especially stood out. The first was Pope Peter II, by right at the head of the Catholic part of the council. His predecessor had died on the way to the council, and a conclave having been convened at Damascus,

Cardinal Simone Barione was unanimously elected and took the name of Peter. He was of humble origin, came from the Neapolitan district, and had become known as a preacher of the Carmelite Order who rendered great service in the struggle against a Satanist sect which was growing in strength in Petersburg and the surrounding country, and which had led astray not only Orthodox but Catholics. Made Archbishop of Mogilef and then cardinal, he was early marked out for the tiara. He was a man of fifty years of age, of middle height and robust constitution, red-faced, with a hooked nose and thick eyebrows. Impetuous and full of ardour, he spoke fervently with bold gestures, and attracted his auditors more than he persuaded them. The new Pope expressed both distrust and dislike of the universal sovereign; especially was this the case as the late Pope, when leaving for the council, had yielded to the insistence of the Emperor and appointed as a cardinal the imperial chancellor and universal magician, the esoteric Bishop Apollyon, whom Peter considered a doubtful Catholic but undoubted impostor. The actual, though unofficial, leader of the Orthodox was the venerable John, very well known among the Russian people. Although he was officially considered a bishop "in retirement," he did not live in any monastery, but constantly travelled in all directions. There were various legends about him. Some believed that he was Fedor Kouzmich brought back to life, namely, the Emperor Alexander I, who had been born about three centuries before that time. Others went farther and affirmed that he was the Apostle St. John the Divine, who, never having died, now appeared openly in the latter days. He himself said nothing about his origin or youth. He was now very old, but hale and hearty, with yellowish, even greenish white curls and beard, tall, thin in body, with full, rosy cheeks and bright, sparkling eyes, sympathetic both in the expression of his face and in his conversation. He was always dressed in a white cassock and cloak. At the head of the Evangelical members of the council stood the learned German theologian Professor Ernst Pauli. He was a dried-up, little old man of medium height, with an enormous brow, sharp nose and clean-shaven chin. His eyes were distinguished by a certain ferociously kind-hearted look. He constantly rubbed his hands, shook his head, twitched his eyebrows in a strange way and stuck out his lips, while at the same time with flashing eyes he gruffly uttered broken sounds: So! nun! ja! so also! He was dressed solemnly—with a white tie and long pastor's coat, and wore the badges of certain Orders.

The opening of the council was inspiring. Two-thirds of the enormous temple consecrated to the "union of all cults" was furnished with benches and other seats for the members of the council, the remaining third was occupied by a high dais, on which behind the imperial throne and another, lower down, for the great magician—who was at the same time cardinal and imperial chancellor—there were rows of armchairs for the ministers, courtiers and secretaries of state, and on one side a still further line of armchairs, the use of which was unknown. In the choir was an orchestra and, on a neighbouring platform, two regiments of the guards were drawn up and a battery for triumphant salvos. The members of the council had already celebrated religious services in their various churches, and the opening of the council was to be entirely secular. When the Emperor entered, accompanied by the great magician and his suite, the orchestra played the "March of United Humanity," which served as the imperial international hymn, and all the members of the council arose, and waving their hats shouted three times, "Vivat! Hurrah! Hoch!" The Emperor, standing by the throne, stretching forth his hand with majestic benevolence, said in a resonant and pleasing voice: "Christians of all cults! My well-beloved subjects and brethren! From the beginning of my reign, which the Most High has blessed with such wonderful and noteworthy deeds, not once have I had cause to be displeased with you; you have always fulfilled your duty according to your belief and conscience. This concerns me but little. My sincere love for you, dear brothers, longs for some return. I desire that you, not through any feeling of duty, but through a feeling of zealous love, should recognize me as your true guide in every matter which has been undertaken for the welfare of humanity. But, besides that which I am doing for everyone, I should like to show you special favor. Christians! what can I do to make you happy? What shall I give you, not as my subjects, but as fellow-believers, as my brethren. Christians! tell me what is dearer to you than aught else in Christianity, so that I may in this matter direct your efforts." He stopped and waited. In the temple a dull echo arose. The members of the council whispered among themselves. Pope Peter, passionately gesticulating, was explaining something to those about him. Professor Pauli shook his head and smacked his lips with exasperation. The venerable John, bending over the Eastern bishops and monks, was quietly suggesting something to them. Having waited several minutes, the Emperor turned to the council and, with the same caressing tone, in which nevertheless there sounded a scarcely perceptible note of irony, said: "Dear Christians, I understand how difficult it is for you to give a direct answer. I desire to aid you in this matter. You, from time immemorial, unhappily have been so divided into various sects and parties that you have not perhaps a common object to which you are all attached. But if you are not able to agree among yourselves, then I hope to bring all parties into agreement, as I shall show to them all the same love and the same readiness to satisfy the *true* aspirations of each. Dear Christians, I know that for many, and not the meanest of you, the thing that is dearer than aught else in Christianity is that *spiritual authority* which it gives to its lawful representatives, not for their own profit, of course, but for the common good, since upon this authority is founded a regular spiritual order and moral discipline indispensable to all. Dear brother Catholics! O, how I understand your point of view, and how I should like to rest my empire on the authority of your spiritual head! In order that you should not think that this is flattery and empty phrases, we solemnly declare that it is agreeable to our autocratic will that the supreme bishop of all Catholics, the Pope of Rome, shall now ascend his throne in Rome with all the former rights and privileges of his position and chair, whensoever granted by our predecessors, beginning with the Emperor Constantine the Great. And from you, brother Catholics, I desire, in return for this, only a true and heartfelt acknowledgment of myself as your sole protector and defender. If there is anyone here who acknowledges me as such in his heart and in his conscience, let him come hither to me." And he pointed to the empty places on the dais. With joyful shouts of *"Gratias agimus Domine! Salvum fac magnum imperatorem"* almost all the princes of the Catholic Church, the cardinals and bishops, a great part of the believing laymen, and more than half of the monks ascended the dais, and, after making low bows in the direction of the Emperor, took their places. But below in the middle of the assembly, erect and immovable as a marble statue, sat in his place the Pope, Peter II. All who had surrounded him were on the dais. But the thinned ranks of monks and laymen which were left below closed around him, forming a tight ring, from whence was heard suppressed whispering: *"Non pravalebunt, non pravalebunt porta inferni."*

Glancing in amazement at the motionless Pope, the Emperor again raised his voice: "Dear brethren, I know there are among you those to whom the holy tradition of Christianity, with its old symbols, hymns and prayers, icons and divine ritual is dearer than aught else. What, indeed, can be dearer than this to the devout soul? Know, then, that today a decree has been signed by me and large sums allotted for a universal museum of Christian archaeology in our glorious imperial city of Constantinople for the purpose of collecting, studying and preserving all the monuments of ecclesiastical antiquity, preferably those of the East; and I further ask you to choose tomorrow from among yourselves a committee to consider with me those measures which it is necessary to take for the possible approximation of the traditions and institutions of the holy Orthodox Church to modern conditions, morals and customs. Brothers of the Orthodox faith, you who have my wishes at heart, who feel in your hearts that you can call me your true guide and lord, come up hither." A large part of the hierarchy of the East and North, half of the former Old Believers and more than half of the Orthodox priests, monks and laymen with joyful cries ascended the dais, glancing proudly at the Catholics who were seated there. But the venerable John did not move and gave a deep sigh. And when the crowd round him were greatly thinned, he left his bench and seated himself nearer to Pope Peter and his circle. After him followed the others who had not gone upon the dais. Again the Emperor began to speak. "I know there are some of you dear Christians to whom the personal assurance of truth and free investigation of the Scriptures is of all things the dearest in Christianity. I think there is no need to expatiate upon the matter. Possibly you know that in my early youth I wrote a long treatise on Biblical criticism, which made at the time a certain sensation and was the foundation upon which my reputation was built. Probably, in recognition of this, the university of Tubingen has sent me, at this time, a request to accept from it the honorary diploma of Doctor of Theology. I commanded an answer to be given that I accepted it with pleasure and gratitude. And today, in addition to the museum of Christian archaeology, I have allotted 1,500,000 marks from the yearly budget for the foundation of a universal institute for the free investigation of the Holy Scriptures from all possible points of view and in all possible directions and for instruction in all allied sciences. If there are any of you to whom my sincere goodwill is pleasing and who are able honestly to acknowledge me as their sovereign leader,

I ask them to come hither to the new Doctor of Theology;" and a strange smile passed lightly over the beautiful lips of the great man. More than half of the learned theologians moved, though with a certain hesitation and wavering, towards the dais. All looked round at Professor Pauli, who remained as if rooted to his seat. The learned theologians who had ascended the dais were filled with confusion, and suddenly one, waving his hand, leapt straight down past the steps and ran to Professor Pauli and the minority which remained beside him. The latter raised his head, and rising with a somewhat vague movement, went past the empty benches, accompanied by his co-believers who had resisted, and sat down with them near the venerable John and Pope Peter and their circle.

The great majority of the council, among which were included almost all the hierarchy of the East and West, found themselves on the dais. Below there remained only three groups, who were coming together and pressing about John, Pope Peter and Professor Pauli.

The Emperor turned to them and said in a sad tone: "What more can I do for you? Strange people! What do you want of me? I know not. You yourselves, who are forsaken by the majority of your brethren and leaders and are condemned by popular sentiment, tell me what is dearer to you than aught else in Christianity?" Then, like a white taper, the venerable John arose and gently answered: "For us the dearest thing of all in Christianity is Christ Himself—He alone, all is from Him, for we know that in Him dwells all the fulness of the Godhead in the flesh. From thee, sire, we are ready to accept every good thing, if only in thy generous hand we recognize the holy hand of Christ. And to thy question: 'What art thou able to do for us?'—here is our answer: 'Confess now before us, Jesus Christ, the Son of God, Who came in the flesh, Who rose from the dead, and Who will come again. Confess Him, and we, with love will receive you as the true forerunner of His glorious coming.'" He was silent and fixed his eyes on the face of the Emperor. Something untoward had happened to the latter. Within him arose a diabolical tempest, such as he had experienced on that fatal night. He completely lost all inner equilibrium, and all his thoughts were concentrated upon preventing himself from being deprived of his external self-possession or from betraying himself inopportunely. He made a superhuman effort not to throw himself with wild howls upon the speaker, and tear him to pieces with his teeth. Suddenly he heard a known but unearthly voice: "Be silent and fear not." He kept silent. Only his face, which was dark and deathlike, became all distorted, and sparks flew from his eyes. While John had been speaking the great magician, wrapped in his immense tri-coloured mantle, which covered the cardinal's crimson, seemed to be manipulating something under it; his eyes flashed in deep concentration and his lips moved. Through the open windows of the temple an enormous black cloud could be seen coming, and it soon became dark. John did not turn his astonished and frightened eyes from the face of the Emperor, till suddenly he sprang back in horror, and looking round cried out in a stifled voice: "Little children, it is Antichrist." At this moment, simultaneously with a deafening clap of thunder a great flash of lightning enveloped the old man. For an instant all were stunned, and when the dazed Christians came to themselves, the venerable John lay dead.

The Emperor, pale but composed, turned to the council: "You have witnessed the judgment of God. I desired not the death of anyone, but my heavenly Father will avenge His well-beloved Son. The matter is decided. Who will contend against the Most High? Secretaries, write: 'The General Council of All Christians, after fire from heaven destroyed the foolish opponent of divine majesty, unanimously recognize the autocratic emperor of Rome and of all the World as its supreme guide and lord.'" Suddenly a loud and distinct word is heard throughout the temple: "*Contradicitur!*" Pope Peter II arose, and with flushed face, trembling with anger, raised his staff in the direction of the Emperor. "Our only Lord is Jesus Christ, Son of the Living God. And thou hast heard who thou art. Away from us! Cain, fratricide! Away, instrument of the devil! By the power of Christ, I, the servant of the servants of God, cast thee out forever, abominable dog, from the city of God, and deliver thee up to thy father Satan. Anathema! Anathema! Anathema!" While he was speaking the great magician moved uneasily under his mantle, and louder than the last anathema the thunder rumbled, and the last Pope fell lifeless. "Thus by the hand of my Father are all my enemies destroyed," said the Emperor. *"Pereant, pereant,"* cried the trembling princes of the Church. He turned and, leaning upon the shoulder of the great magician, accompanied by all the throng, went out slowly by a door behind the dais. In the temple there remained the two dead bodies and the narrow circle of Christians, half dead with terror. The only one who was not confused was Professor Pauli. It was as if the general horror had aroused all the forces of his soul. He had changed outwardly, he had an exalted and inspired look. With a resolute step he ascended the dais, and having taken a seat vacated by one of the secretaries of state, he took a sheet of paper and began to write something on it. Having finished, he got up and read out in a loud voice: "To the glory of our only Savior, Jesus Christ. The General Council of God's Church, gathered together in Jerusalem, after our blessed brother John, representative of Eastern Christianity, had detected in the great deceiver and enemy of God the true Antichrist predicted in God's word, and after our blessed father, Peter, the representative of Western Christianity, had lawfully and rightfully consigned him to eternal separation from the Church of God; now, before these two witnesses of Christ, who have been killed for the truth, we decide to break off relations with his cursed and abominable assembly, and to go into the wilderness, there to await the imminent coming of our true Lord, Jesus Christ." Animation filled the crowd, and loud cries broke forth: "*Adveniat! adveniat cito. Komm, Herr Jesu, komm!* Come, Lord Jesus!

Professor Pauli wrote and then read out: "Having adopted this first and last act of the last general council, we sign our names"—and he made a sign of invitation to the assembly. All went up on the platform and signed. At the end, in large Gothic script, was written—"Decorum defunctorum testium locum tenens, Ernst Pauli." "Now let us go with our ark of the last covenant," he said, pointing to the two who had died. The bodies were raised on stretchers. Slowly, with Latin chants, and with German and Slavonic hymns, the Christians set forth to the entrance of Kharam-esh-Sherif. Here the procession was stopped by a secretary of state sent by the Emperor and escorted by an officer, with a platoon of guards. The soldiers stopped at the entrance, and the secretary of state read out as follows from an elevated position: "The command of his divine majesty! For the instruction of Christian people and to protect them against wickedly-disposed persons who are causing disturbances and seducing the people, we have recognized it is for the public good to exhibit publicly the bodies of the two agitators, killed by fire from heaven, in Christian Street (*Kharet-an-Nasara*), at the entrance of the great temple of that religion, named The Holy Sepulchre or The Resurrection, so that all may be persuaded of the reality of their death. Their obstinate adherents, wickedly refusing all our favours and madly closing their eyes to the obvious signs of divinity, have, by being obedient to those who were killed by fire from heaven, put themselves outside our mercy and protection in the face of the heavenly Father. They shall be given full freedom with the single prohibition, on account of the public weal, of not being allowed to live in cities or other inhabited places, so that they may not trouble or seduce innocent and simple-minded people with their evil inventions." When he had finished, eight soldiers at the command of the officer approached the stretchers bearing the bodies.

"What is written is being fulfilled," said Professor Pauli, and the Christians who bore the stretchers handed them over in silence to the soldiers, who withdrew through the northwest gates; but the Christians, issuing from the northeast gates, hurriedly set out from the city, and, passing the Mount of Olives, went towards Jericho, along a road which previously had been cleared of the mob by *gendarmes* and two cavalry regiments. On the barren hills near Jericho it was decided to wait for a few days. The following morning Christian pilgrims arrived from Jerusalem and related what had taken place in Zion. After the court dinner, all the members of the assembly were invited to the great throne room (near the supposed place of Solomon's throne), and the Emperor, turning to the representatives of the Catholic hierarchy, declared that the welfare of the Church evidently demanded from them a speedy choice of a worthy successor of the Apostle Peter; that, according to the circumstances of the time, the election would have to be summary; that the presence of himself, the Emperor, as leader and representative of the whole Christian world, abundantly made up for any omissions of ritual; and that he, in the name of all Christians, proposed that the Sacred College should elect his well-beloved friend and brother Apollyon, thus making the close bond a lasting one and the union between the Church and the empire indissoluble for their common good. The Sacred College withdrew to a special apartment for the conclave, and returned in half an hour with the new Pope Apollyon. Whilst the balloting was taking place, the Emperor gently; wisely and eloquently persuaded the Orthodox and Evangelical representatives, in view of the great new era of Christian history, to put an end to their divisions, trusting to his word that Apollyon would be able to abolish for ever all the historical abuses of the papal power. Persuaded by this speech, the representatives of Orthodoxy and Protestantism drew up an Act for the union of the Churches, and when Apollyon, accompanied by the cardinals, appeared in the throne room, amidst the joyful cries of the whole assembly, a Greek bishop and an evangelical pastor tendered him their document. *"Accipio et approbo et laetificatur cor meum,"* said Apollyon, signing the paper. "I am as truly Orthodox and Evangelical as I am Catholic," he added, and affectionately exchanged kisses with the Greek and the German. Afterwards he went to the Emperor, who embraced him and held him a long time in his arms. At this time some shining spots began to float about the palace and the temple in all directions; they grew and changed into bright forms of strange things; flowers unseen upon earth showered down from above, filling the air with an unknown perfume. From on high resounded ravishing sounds of musical instruments, unheard up to that time, which went straight to the soul and transported the heart, and the angelic voices of an invisible choir sang the praises of the new lord of heaven and earth. Meanwhile a strange subterranean rumbling was heard in the north-west corner of the middle palace under *kubet-el-aruakh*—i.e., *kupolom dush*, where, according to Mussulman tradition, was the entrance into hell. When the assembly, by invitation of the Emperor, moved in that direction, all clearly heard innumerable high and piercing voices—not childish, not devilish—which were crying out "The time has come, release us, our saviors." But when Apollyon, pressing close against the wall, cried out something three times in an unknown tongue, the voices were silent and the rumbling ceased. Meanwhile an enormous multitude of people from all quarters had surrounded Kharamesh-Sherif. At the approach of night the Emperor, together with the new Pope, went out on the eastern staircase, where his presence aroused a storm of enthusiasm. He bowed affably on all sides, and then Apollyon, from a large basket brought to him by the cardinal deacons, repeatedly took and threw into the air magnificent roman candles, rockets and fountains of fire, which had been set alight by contact with his hand, and which were sometimes pearly phosphorescent, sometimes all the colours of the rainbow. And all of them, when they reached the earth, changed into numberless particoloured leaves with full and unconditional indulgences for all sins, past, present and to come. The popular joy passed all bounds. It is true that certain people affirmed that they saw with their own eyes the indulgences change into most repulsive toads and serpents. Nevertheless, the vast majority was in ecstasies and the popular festival continued for several days, during which time the new wonder-working Pope attained to things so wonderful and improbable that to mention them would be altogether useless. Meanwhile on the deserted heights of Jericho, the Christians gave themselves up to prayer and fasting. On the evening of the fourth day as it became dark, Professor Pauli and ten companions, mounted on asses and taking with them a cart, stole into Jerusalem and through side streets past Kharam-esh-Sherif, came out on Kharet-en-Nasar and approached the entrance to the Church of the Resurrection, where on the pavement lay the bodies of Pope Peter and the venerable John. The street at this hour was empty, everybody had gone to Kharam-esh-Sherif. The soldiers on guard had fallen into a deep sleep. Those who came for the bodies found them entirely untouched by corruption, and not even stiff or heavy. Having raised them upon the stretchers and having covered them with the mantles they had brought, they returned by the same roundabout way to their own people, but scarcely had they lowered the stretchers on the ground than the spirit of life entered into the dead. They moved and attempted to throw off the cloaks in which they were wrapped. All with joyful cries began to assist them, and both having come to life, stood up on their feet, whole and sound. And the venerable John began to speak: "So, little children, we have not parted, and now I say to you, it is time to carry out Christ's last prayer about His followers, that they should be one even as He with the Father is one. So for the sake of this unity of Christ we revere, little children, our well-beloved brother, Peter. May he feed the last of Christ's sheep." And he embraced Peter. Then Professor Pauli went up to him. *"Tu est Petrus,"* he said to the Pope, *"jetzt ist es ja grundlich erwiesen und ausser jedern Zweifel gesetzt."* He seized his hand firmly with his own right hand and gave his left to the venerable John with the words: *"So also, Väterchen, nun sind wir ja Ems in Christo."* Thus was accomplished the union of the churches in the darkness of the night on a high and lonely place. But the darkness was suddenly lightened by a bright splendour and there appeared a great wonder in heaven: a woman clothed in the sun with the moon under her feet and a crown of twelve stars on her head. The apparition remained for some time in one place and then moved slowly towards the south. Pope Peter raised his staff and cried out: "there is our banner, let us follow it." And he went in the direction of the vision, accompanied by both the old men and the whole company of Christians, to the mountain of God—to Sinai.

After the spiritual leaders and representatives of Christianity withdrew to the Arabian desert, where crowds of believers jealous for the truth flocked to them from all countries, the new Pope was able, without any obstacle, to pervert by his wonders and prodigies all the superficial Christians who had not been disillusioned by Antichrist, and who remained with him. He declared that, by the power of the keys, he had opened the door between life on earth and life beyond the grave, and in fact, communication between the living and dead, and also between people and demons had been accomplished with the usual manifestations, and new unheard of scenes of mystical debauchery and demonolatry took place. But scarcely had the Emperor begun to feel himself standing upon a firm religious foundation, and scarcely had he according to the persistent inspiration of his mysterious "father's" voice, declared himself the only true incarnation of supreme and universal Divinity, than a new misfortune fell upon him from an unexpected quarter: the revolt of the Hebrews. This nation, whose numbers at that time had reached thirty million, was not entirely ignorant of the preparations for and the consolidation of the world-wide successes of the superman. When he moved to Jerusalem, secretly spreading the report in Hebrew circles that his principal problem was to establish the world-wide dominion of Israel, the Hebrews recognized him as the Messiah, and their enthusiastic devotion to him knew no bounds. But suddenly they rose in rebellion, breathing anger and vengeance. This revolution, undoubtedly predicted in the Scriptures and tradition, is set forth by Father Pansophia with, it may be, too much simplicity and realism. The trouble was, that the Hebrews, deeming the Emperor entirely Jewish by race, discovered by chance that he was not even circumcised. That very day Jerusalem, and the following day, all Palestine, was in revolt. The boundless and fervent devotion to the Savior of Israel, to the promised Messiah, was changed into equally boundless and fervent hatred of the wily deceiver and brazen impostor. All Israel rose as one, and its enemies saw with amazement that the soul of Israel, in its depths, lived not by calculations and the desires of Mammon, but by the force of a concentrated feeling—in the expectation of and passion for its eternal Messianic faith. The Emperor, who had not expected such an outbreak, at once lost his self-possession and issued an edict condemning to death all insubordinate Jews and Christians. Many thousands and tens of thousands who had not succeeded in arming themselves were slaughtered without mercy. But soon an army of a million Hebrews occupied Jerusalem, and locked up Antichrist in Kharam-esh-Sherif. He had at his disposal only a part of the guards, who were unable to overcome the masses of the enemy. By the help of the magic art of his Pope the Emperor succeeded in passing through the lines of his besiegers, and quickly appeared again in Syria with an innumerable army of pagans of different races. The Hebrews went forth to meet him with small hope of success. But hardly had the vanguard of both armies come together, when an earthquake of unprecedented violence occurred, the crater of an enormous volcano opened by the Dead Sea, about which lay the imperial army, and streams of fire flowed together in one flaming lake and swallowed up the Emperor himself and his numberless forces, together with Pope Apollyon, who always accompanied him, and for whom all his magic was of no avail. Meanwhile, the Hebrews hastened to Jerusalem in fear and trembling, calling for salvation to the God of Israel. When the holy city was already in sight, the heavens were rent by vivid lightning, from the east to the west, and they saw Christ coming towards them in royal apparel, and with the wounds from the nails in His outstretched hands. At the same time, from Sinai to Zion, went the company of Christians, led by Peter, John and Paul, and from various other parts hurried more triumphant multitudes: these consisted of all the Jews and Christians who had been killed by Antichrist. They lived and reigned with Christ for a thousand years. Thus ends the narrative, which had for its object, not a universal cataclysm of creation, but the conclusion of our historical process, which consists of the appearance, glorification and destruction of Antichrist.

Regarding Soloviev's "Conversion"

THE ACCOUNT OF Soloviev's appearance before Father Tolstoi in February 1896, his reciting the Creed and receiving Communion, described in Chapter Seven of this book cannot be regarded as clear evidence of his "conversion" to Roman Catholicism because a number of facts conflict with such a conclusion.

In the first place, among Soloviev's published letters is one in which he writes that he was ill and unable to leave his house for several days in February, 1896—among them the day on which he was reported to have received Communion from Father Tolstoi. (See Soloviev, V.S.: *Pisma*, Letters, edited by E.L. Radlov, St. Petersburg, 1908-11.)

Moreover, a number of passages in Soloviev's published letters make clear that nothing was further from his mind than a conversion to the Roman Catholic *Church*. For example, after repeated visits and a long correspondence with Bishop Strossmayer, Soloviev writes plainly in a letter to the Metropolitan Antonius (op. cit. supra, Vol. III, p. 189) that he has returned to Russia a more convinced Russian-Orthodox believer than ever before, that he is convinced that a union of the Churches on an external basis is inadmissable, and the conversion of individuals is downright harmful.

E.L. Radlov, co-editor with Sergei Soloviev of the posthumously published *Collected Writings of Vladimir Soloviev* (Moscow, 1911, 10 volumes), a friend of long standing, wrote in his *Vladimir Soloviev, Life and Teachings*, St. Petersburg,

1913, page 43: "When Vladimir Soloviev lived and died in accordance with the Greek-Orthodox Creed, was this not for the same reason which prompted Socrates to say that he was an Athenian already in his mother's womb?"

The following letter Vladimir Soloviev wrote to the editor of the *Novoya Vremia*, published in No. 3026 of that periodical, dated February 25, 1890, is of importance in relation to this subject:

With astonishment I have read in the newspapers that a lecturer in the local Theological Academy, the Hieromonk Antonius has given a public lecture on the theme: "The Advantage of Orthodox Christianity over the Papistic Teachings of Vladimir Soloviev." Therefore I regard it as my duty to make the following statements:

1. I have never changed my Creed; therefore I do not think that Father Antonius has the right to expel me from the Church.

2. I am willing to defend my convictions at any time and to prove in public debate why I am determined to conform entirely with the Orthodox Church, which is founded on the Word of God, on the laws of the seven Oecumenical Councils, and on the testimony of the Holy Fathers and Elders.

3. I refuse to accept any responsibility for ideas and points of view attributed to me because of arbitrary inferences, or based on reference to single passages in my writings which are not circulated among the Russian public, or derived from things which are not subject to public discussion.

(Signed) Vladimir Soloviev

* * *

Finally, the following letter written by a Russian Orthodox priest, N. Kosolov, published in the *Choskovskaya Viedomosti*, No. 253, for Wednesday, 3/16 November, 1910 also sheds considerable light on this question:

Concerning the Creed of Vladimir Soloviev

(A Letter to the Editor)

With reference to the statement of the *former* priest, N. Tolstoi, printed in the *Ruskii Slovo* that he gave Communion to the late philosopher Vladimir Soloviev, according to the rite of the Uniat Church (the union between the Greek Orthodox and the Roman Church under certain circumstances, abolished in Russia in 1839), I beg you to kindly publish in your paper the report of a Russian Greek-Orthodox priest, relating how he heard Vladimir Soloviev's Confession and gave him the Last Sacrament before his death. This priest, Sergei A. Belyaev, is at present stationed at the Sokolniki Hospital in Moscow. At the time Vladimir Soloviev was on his deathbed, he was the priest at the Village Uskovo in the Moscow District, near the estate of Prince Pavel Nikolayevich Troubetskoi. He can confirm the following as he related it to me:

"Prince Pavel Nikolayevich Troubetskoi was not residing on his estate near Uskovo in the summer of 1900, but his brother, the late Sergei Nikolayevich, Rector of the University of Moscow, and a close friend of Vladimir Sergeyevich Soloviev, lived there at that time. Already seriously ill, Vladimir Soloviev arrived there one evening as a guest. Soon after leaving Moscow, just after passing Kaluga, Soloviev felt unwell and intended to return to Moscow, but changed his mind and went on to Uskovo after all. Upon his arrival, however, the physician recommended that he go directly to bed, from which he was never able to rise again.

One evening a servant of the Troubetskois came to me, asked me to read the Liturgy the next morning, and afterward (at the personal wish of Vladimir Soloviev, as I afterward learned) to come with the Holy Sacrament in order to give Communion to a guest from Moscow, who was very ill.

The following morning the children's nurse of the Troubetskois came to me at the end of the early Service and asked me to hear the Confession of the guest who was mortally ill. She called him Vladimir, but I did not know his full name. Therefore I went to the Troubetskoi home and was met in the front passage by Prince Sergei Nikolayevich. After repeating the request of the sick man, he asked me if I knew who the latter was. When I replied that I did not, the Prince at once led me into the study where Vladimir Soloviev was lying on a divan, and introduced me to him. (I remember that Soloviev's hair was cut very short.)

Vladimir Sergeyevich confessed with true Christian humility (the Confession lasted at least a half hour). Among other things he said he had not been to Confession for over three years because at his last Confession—I can no longer remember whether it was in Moscow or Petersburg—he argued with the priest over a dogmatic question (he did not specify what one), and because of that, the priest refused to give him Holy Communion. 'The priest was right,' Vladimir Sergeyevich said, adding, 'for I argued with him only out of anger and arrogance; later we again argued over this question and again I refused to give in to him, even though I recognized I was wrong. Now I acknowledge my error fully, and I repent with my whole heart.'

After he had ended his Confession I asked Vladimir Sergeyevich if he could recall any other sins.

"I shall think and shall try to remember," he replied. I urged him to do so, and meanwhile prepared to go back to the church, but he detained me, asking me to give him Absolution because he feared he would lose consciousness before I returned. I gave him Absolution and went to the church to hold the Service. Afterward I again returned to Vladimir Sergeyevich with the Sacrament of the Holy Communion, and asked him if he could remember any other sins.

"No, Little Father," he replied, "I have prayed over my sins and have asked God for forgiveness, but I cannot recall anything more."

I then gave him Holy Communion. Present were Prince Sergei Nikolayevich and his wife, Praskovia Vladimirovna. Later the same day Vladimir Soloviev sank into unconsciousness and remained in that condition until his death.

(Signed) Priest N. Kolosov
October, 25, 1910

Two Recollections Concerning Vladimir Soloviev

IN HIS BOOK, *Mirosozertsaniye Vl. Solovyova* (Vladimir Soloviev's World-Conception), 2 vols., Moscow, 1913, Soloviev's intimate friend and biographer, Prince Eugene Nikolayevich Troubetskoi (1863-1920) wrote: "Anyone who saw Soloviev even a single time never forgot the experience of having seen a man who was utterly unlike ordinary human beings. His external appearance, particularly his luminous, beautiful eyes impressed one because of their unusual combination of weakness and strength, physical incapacity and profound spiritual depth. In fact, Soloviev was so nearsighted that he was unable to perceive objects everyone else could see without any difficulty. Peering out myopically beneath his heavy eyebrows, he was scarcely able to see even those things which were closest at hand. However, when he gazed into the distance it appeared as though he could see beyond the external aspect of physical objects and was able to perceive behind them the workings of spirit, which nobody else could behold. At such times his eyes were aglow with a secret light, as though he was gazing directly into the very depths of the soul itself."

* * *

The late Konstantin Vasilievich Mochuiski in his excellent biography of Soloviev (in Russian) published in Paris, 1936 reported an unusual incident recorded by Professor

A.V. Kartashev, the religious philosopher who heard it from a General Veliaminov in 1910. It seems that one summer in the mid-1890s Soloviev and General Veliaminov, at that time active as a professor in the Army Medical School in Moscow, were guests at the country house of Baroness Varvara Ivanovna Uexkuell. One day Soloviev was much pre-occupied with stories about the Antichrist and the devil, and with marked intensity related several of these to the General and their hostess.

In the twilight of a late summer evening the three of us were sitting in the garden-house talking and enjoying a leisurely tea. The conversation returned to the traditions concerning the devil, about which we had spoken earlier, and Soloviev's strange mood began to impress itself upon Varvara Ivanovna and myself as well. Suddenly, beneath our feet was something like an explosion, and from between the cracks in the rough floor-boards in the center of the garden-house appeared a column of what seemed to be dense, tawny smoke, rising nearly to the ceiling. Vladimir Sergeyevich, who had been sitting tensely in an armchair, at once sprang to his feet and, pointing toward the smoke with a long finger, shouted "There he is! That's him there!" Almost immediately the phenomenon entirely disappeared and Soloviev fell back silently into his chair as though overcome by a superhuman trial of some sort. His exhaustion also overcame Varvara Ivanovna and myself so that for several moments we were dazed and numbed with confusion.

Recovering ourselves, we tried to explain the affair, although the smoke had left behind it neither odor nor trace of burning. At first I thought I might have dropped cigar ashes through the cracks in the floor and set something afire. But if this was so, how could one account for the explosion, for the lack of smell or other evidence of burning? We called the servants and the dog, but their search under the garden-house was fruitless. I still remember that long after Vladimir Sergeyevich went to his room, Varvara Ivanovna and I sat silently in the gathering darkness, puzzling over the whole incident. And never in the years since have we found an explanation for it, nor do I draw any conclusions, but simply relate the facts as they occurred.

On Lake Saima in Winter

Vladimir Soloviev

Buried snug beneath warm furs
  I lie silent, calmly sleeping;
Free from touch of death
  Is this clear air, this tranquil stillness.

Here in this deep silence,
  My inner eye, my waking heart beholds
Your image fair, still unchanged,
  O Queen, ruler of the pines and rocks!

Pure as the snow upon far
    mountain summits,
  Wise as the thought-filled silence
    of this winter night,
Radiant as the glorious Aurora
    of the North,
  I behold you now, dark Chaos'
    happy, smiling child!

Impressions of Vladimir Soloviev

I am above all an heir of the tradition of Dostoyevski and Tolstoi, as well as of Vladimir Soloviev. From Leo Tolstoi and Vladimir Soloviev I have received an equally strong impression. I regard Soloviev's essay on *The Meaning of Love* as the best book that has ever been written on this subject.

— *Nicolas Berdyaev*
Philosopher, Author

* * *

Soloviev had the rare gift of seeing the changing scenery of life as a single process. His book about the Antichrist reads like genuine prophecy, not mere literary apocalyptic. The version impressed itself upon the seer and constrained him to describe what he had previously expounded with such zeal and conviction in his philosophy. The picture of Antichrist is so powerfully drawn, so coherent, yet so unexpected that nothing can be added or taken away. The man who was made the vessel of this powerful revelation could continue life no longer. It was not by chance, therefore, that Soloviev died from utter exhaustion after he wrote this prophetic book.

— *Nicholas Zernov*
Writer, Philosopher, Lecturer
(From a lecture given at Oxford University)

* * *

Vladimir Soloviev is Russia's greatest philosopher. In him were blended the qualities of priest, poet, prophet and philosopher. "Seer and Sage" would perhaps best characterize his essence. He holds a special place in human thought; it is small wonder that he has stimulated a broad range of minds throughout the world!

— *Egbert Munzer*
Economist, Jurist, Mathematician,
Lecturer at Fordham, Toronto and Laval Universities

* * *

Soloviev's philosophy is the most full-sounding chord in the whole history of philosophy!

— *Sergius Bulgakov*
Writer, Lecturer, Professor of Law

* * *

The present time calls for a widening of the spiritual horizon. Peoples all over the earth must come close to each other. Soloviev is a representative of the East of Europe; he can further the spiritual life of the West. To meet him means that the people of the West find something that reveals aspects of humanity which they can no longer find on the paths of knowledge of the last centuries.

— *Rudolf Steiner*
Austrian Philosopher and Educator

* * *

We must acknowledge the high value of Soloviev's philosophical ideas, not only within the history of Russian thought, but also far beyond its limits. The structure he erected is still remarkable and—what is more important—full of inspiring force and radiant with energies that have stimulated others to creative activity. He lifted Russian thought to universally human horizons, for the roots of his creative activity are not simply Russian, or Western European; they are worldwide. He was for whole generations, and remains today, the leader of a specific tendency in philosophy.

> — *Vassili V. Zenkovski*
> Professor of Psychology and Philosophy,
> Universities of Kiev and Paris

* * *

Vladimir Soloviev must be recognized as one of the greatest thinkers and spiritual leaders of the nineteenth century, a philosopher, *a perfectly original mystic*, a man of the "prophetic" type, a political thinker, a poet and literary critic. The first thing that strikes one in all of Soloviev's writings and opens out new horizons to the reader, transferring him into a different atmosphere, is the keenness and clarity with which Soloviev sees the invisible, the spiritual world. Soloviev shows the spiritual path which alone can lead humanity out of its present impasse.

> —*Simon L. Frank*
> Philosopher, Writer, Co-worker with Berdayev
> at the University of Berlin

* * *

Vladimir Soloviev, the outstanding Russian philosopher of the nineteenth century, acquired an enormous grasp of theological and mystical literature. From his ideas modern thinkers such as Bulgakov, Berdayev, and Lossky have taken their rise.

— Clarence A. Manning
Professor, Department of East-European Languages,
Columbia University, New York

* * *

The great merits of Soloviev in working out his doctrine of transfigured corporeality, his consciousness of evolution, of the meaning of the historical process, etc., are beyond doubt. He was the first to create an original Russian system of philosophy and to lay the foundations of a whole school of Russian religious and philosophical thought, which is still growing and developing.

— Nicholas O. Lossky
Professor of Philosophy in the Universities
of St. Petersburg, Prague, and Paris

* * *

Selected Bibliography

Alpatov, Mikhail: *The Russian Impact on Art*, New York, 1950.
Anon.: *The Way of a Pilgrim*, tr. by R.M. French, SPCK, London, 1954.
Baillie, John: *Revelation*, London, 1937.
Bulgakov, Sergius: *The Orthodox Church*, tr. by E.S. Cram, London, 1935.
Butler, Christopher: *Soloviev*, Donnside Review, Exeter, 1932, vol. 50.
Duddington, Natalie: *The Religious Philosophy of Soloviev*, Hibbert Journal, Boston, 1917, vol. 5.
Dunphy, William H.: *The Religious Philosophy of Soloviev*, Dissertation, University of Chicago Press, 1939.
Fedotov, George P.: *The Russian Religious Mind*, Harpers, New York, 1946.
Treasury of Russian Spirituality, New York, 1958.
Graham, Stephen: *Undiscovered Russia*, Lane, New York & London, 1912.
Gregerson, Jon: *The Transfigured Cosmos*, Ungar, New York, 1960.
Herbigny, Michel d': *Vladimir Soloviev, a Russian Newman*, tr. by A.M. Buchanan, London, 1918.
Kadloubovsky, Eugene (tr.): *Writings from the Philokalia on Prayer of the Heart*, London, 1951.
Early Fathers from the Philokalia, London, 1954.
Kluchevsky, V1.O.: *A History of Russia*, 5 vols., London, 1911-31.
Lavrin, Janko: "Vladimir Soloviev," *Slavonic & East European Review*, London, 1930-1931.
Lossky, Nicholas O.: *A History of Russian Philosophy*, New York, 1951, London, 1952.
"The Philosophy of Vladimir Soloviev," *The Slavonic Review*, vol. 2., London, 1923/24.
Macanus, Elder of Optino: *Russian Notes of Direction* (1834-1860), tr. by Julia de Beausobre, London, 1944.
Masaryk, Thomas G.: *The Spirit of Russia*, 2 vols., London, 1919.
Miliukov, P.N.: *Outlines of Russian Culture*, 3 vols., Phila., 1942.
Mirsky, Prince D.S.: *A History of Russian Literature*, London, 1927.
Munzer, Egbert: *Soloviev, Prophet of Russian-Western Unity*, London, 1956.
Pares, Sir Bernard: *A History of Russia*, London, 1937.

Plincke, Violet E.: "Vladimir Soloviev, Seeker for Sophia," in *Russia, Past, Present, Future*, ed. by John Fletcher, New Knowledge Books, London, 1968.

Rappoport, S.J.: "The Russian Philosopher, Vladimir Soloviev," *The Contemporary Review*, New York, 1913, vol. 108.

Soloviev, Alexander V.: *Holy Russia: The History of a Religious-Social Idea*, den Haag, Netherlands, 1959.

Soloviev, Vladimir: *A Soloviev Anthology*, arranged by Simon L. Frank, tr. by Natalie Duddington, SCM Press, London, 1950.

God, Man and Church: The Spiritual Foundations of Life, tr. by Donald Attwater, London, 1938.

The Justification of the Good: An Essay in Moral Philosophy, tr. by Natalie Duddington, London, 1918.

Lectures on Godmanhood, tr. with introd, by Peter P. Zouboff, New York, 1944.

The Meaning of Love, tr. by Jane Marshall, New York, 1945.

Plato, tr. by Richard Gill, London, 1935.

Russia and the Universal Church, ii. by Herbert Rees, London, 1948.

War and Christianity from the Christian Point of View — Three Conversations, London, 1915.

War, Progress and the End of History: a Short Story of the Antichrist, tr. by Alexander Bakshy, rev. ed., Hudson, New York, 1990.

Steiner, Rudolf: *The Gospel of John in Relation to the Other Gospels*; *From Jesus to Christ*; *The Inner Nature of Man*. See SteinerBooks, Great Barrington, MA.

Tavernier, Eugene: *A Great Russian Philosopher, in The Nineteenth Century*, London, 1916.

Trinick, John: *The Fire Tried Stone, History of a Symbol*, London, 1967.

Vernadsky, George: *A History of Russia*, rev. ed., New Haven, 1930.

Wesseling, Theodor: *Vladimir Soloviev*, The Eastern Churches Quarterly, London, 1937.

Zander, L.A.: *Vision and Action*, tr. by Natalie Duddington, London, 1952.

Zenkov, Stefan: *The Eastern Orthodox Church*, tr. by D.A. Lowrie, London, 1929.

Zenkovsky, Vassili V.: *A History of Russian Philosophy*, tr. by G.L. Kline, 2 vols., New York, 1953.

Zernov, Nicolas: *Moscow, the Third Rome*, London, 1942.

The Russians and their Church, London, 1954.

Three Russian Prophets: Khomiakov, Dostoyevski, Soloviev, London, 1944.

Index

About the Esalen - Lindisfarne
Library of Russian Philosophy

Though it only began to flourish in the nineteenth century, Russian philosophy has deep roots going back to the acceptance of Christianity by the Russian people in 998 and the subsequent translation into church Slavonic of the Greek Fathers. By the fourteenth century, religious writings, such as those of Dionysius the Areopagite and Maximus the Confessor, were available in monasteries. Until the seventeenth century, then, except for some heterodox Jewish and Roman Catholic tendencies, Russian thinking tended to continue the ascetical, theological, and philosophical tradition of Byzantium, but with a Russian emphasis on the world's unity, wholeness, and transfiguration. It was as if a seed were germinating in darkness, for the centuries of Tartar domination and the isolationism of the Moscow state kept Russian thought apart from the onward movement of Western European thinking.

With Peter the Great (1672-1725), in Pushkin's phrase, a window was cut into Europe. This opened the way to Voltairian freethinking, while the striving to find ever greater depths in religious life continued. Freemasonry established itself in Russia, inaugurating a spiritual stream outside the church. Masons sought a deepening of the inner life, together with ideals of moral development and active love of one's neighbor. They drew on wisdom where they found it and were ecumenical in their sources. Thomas à Kempis's *Imitation of Christ* was translated, as were works by Saint-Martin ("The Unknown Philosopher"), Jacob Boehme, and the pietist Johann Arndt. Russian thinkers, too, became known by name: among others, Grigory Skovoroda (1722-1794), whose biblical interpretation drew upon Neoplatonism, Philo, and the German mystics; N.I. Novikov (1744-1818), who edited Masonic periodicals and organized libraries; the German I.G. Schwarz (1751-1784), a Rosicrucian follower of Jacob Boehme; and A.N. Radishchev (1749-1802), author of *On Man and His Immortality*.

There followed a period of enthusiasm for German idealism and, with the reaction to this by the Slavophiles Ivan Kireevksy and Aleksei Khomaikov, independent philosophical thought in Russia was born. An important and still continuing tradition of creative thinking was initiated, giving rise to a whole galaxy of nineteenth and twentieth-century philosophers, including Pavel Yurkevitch, Nikolai Fedorov, Vladimir Soloviev, Leo Shestov, the Princes S. and E. Troubetskoi, Pavel Florensky, Sergius Bulgakov, Nikolai Berdyaev, Dmitri Merezhkovsky, Vassili Rozanov, Semon Frank, the personalists, the intuitionists, and many others.

Beginning in the 1840s, a vital tradition of philosophy entered the world stage, a tradition filled with as-yet unthought possibilities and implications not only for Russia herself but for the new multicultural, global reality humanity as a whole is now entering.

Characteristic features of this tradition are: *epistemological realism*; *integral knowledge* (knowledge as an organic, all-embracing unity that includes sensuous, intellectual, and mystical intuition); the celebration of *integral personality* (*tselnaya lichnost*), which is at once mystical, rational, and sensuous; and an emphasis upon the *resurrection* or *transformability* of the flesh. In a word, Russian philosophers sought a theory of the world as a whole, including its transformation.

Russian philosophy is simultaneously religious and psychological, ontological and cosmological. Filled with remarkably imaginative thinking about our global future, it joins speculative metaphysics, depth psychology, ethics, aesthetics, mysticism, and science with a profound appreciation of the world's movement toward a greater state. It is *bolshaya*, big, as philosophy should be. It is broad and individualistic, bearing within it many different perspectives— religious, metaphysical, erotic, social, and apocalyptic. Above all, it is universal. The principle of *sobornost* or all-togetherness (human catholicity) is of paramount importance in it. And it is future oriented, expressing a philosophy of history passing into *metahistory*, the life-of-the-world-to-come in the Kingdom of God.

At present, in both Russia and the West, there is a revival of interest in Russian philosophy, partly in response to the reductionisms implicit in materialism, atheism, analytic philosophy, deconstructionism, and so forth. On May 14, 1988, *Pravda* announced that it would publish the works of Soloviev, Troubetskoi, Semon Frank, Shestov, Florensky, Lossky, Bulgakov, Berdyaev, Alexsandr Bogdanov, Rozanov, and Fedorov. According to the announcement, thirty-five to forty volumes were to be published.

The Esalen-Lindisfarne Library of Russian Philosophy parallels this Russian effort. Since 1980 the Esalen Russian-American Exchange Center has worked to develop innovative approaches to Russian-American cooperation, sponsoring nongovernmental dialogue and citizen exchange as a complement to governmental diplomacy. As part of its program, seminars are conducted on economic, political, moral, and religious philosophy. The Exchange Center aims to stimulate philosophic renewal in both the East and West. The Esalen-Lindisfarne Library of Russian Philosophy continues this process, expanding it to a broader American audience.

It is our feeling that these Russian thinkers—and those who even now are following in their footsteps—are world thinkers. Publishing them will not only contribute to our understanding of the Russian people, but will also make a lasting contribution to the multicultural philosophical synthesis required by humanity around the globe in the twenty-first century.

ESALEN-LINDISFARNE
LIBRARY OF RUSSIAN PHILOSOPHY

The Meaning of Love, Vladimir Solovyov
War, Progress, and the End of History, Vladimir Solovyov
The Russian Idea, Nikolai Berdyaev
Sophia, The Wisdom of God, Sergei Bulgakov
Lectures on Divine Humanity, Vladimir Solovyov
The Crisis of Western Philosophy, Vladimir Solovyov
The Holy Grail and the Eucharist, Fr. Sergius Bulgakov
The Rose of the World, Daniel Andreev
On Spiritual Unity, Aleksei Khomiakov and Ivan Kireevsky

CPSIA information can be obtained
at www.ICGtesting.com
Printed in the USA
JSHW031107100323
38758JS00001B/16